ASCENDING TOGETHER

A 40-Day Journey Through the
Psalms of Ascent

Dr. John R. Sconiers II

Scripture quotations created to NIV are from the Holy Bible, New International Version. Copyright © 1973, 1978, 1984, 2011 by Biblica, Inc. Used by permission. All rights reserved.

Scripture quotations marked "NKJV" are taken from the New King James Version. Copyright © 1982, by Thomas Nelson, Inc. Used by permission. All rights reserved.

Scripture quotations from The Authorized (King James) Version. Rights in the Authorized Version in the United Kingdom are vested in the Crown. Reproduced by permission of the Crown's patentee, Cambridge University Press

Scripture quotations marked ESV are from the ESV Bible (The Holy Bible, English Standard Version), Copyright © 2001 by Crossway, a publishing ministry of Good News Publishers. Used by permission. All rights reserved.

Scripture quotations taken from the (NASB®) New American Standard Bible®, Copyright © 1960, 1971, 1977, 1995, 2020 by The Lockman Foundation. Used by permission. All rights reserved.

Scripture quotations marked (NLT) are taken from the Holy Bible, New Living Translation, copyright © 1996, 2004, 2007. Used by permission of Tyndale House Publishers Inc., Carol Stream, Illinois 60188. All rights reserved.

Printed in the United States of America

Library of Congress Control Number: 2025913089

ISBN-13: 979-8-9990504-0-3
ISBN-13: 979-8-9990504-1-0 (e-book)

Real Moments Media

1385 Wilmington Way Suite 100
Grayson, GA 30017
www.realmomentsmedia.com

REAL MOMENTS MEDIA

Dedicated in memory of my father, John R. Sconiers, Sr., my mom, Maybell, and my family. Thank You for your continued support and prayers in everything that is accomplished!

The fruit of the righteous is a tree of life, And one who is wise gains souls.
Proverbs 11:30

Table of Contents

PART I: THE DEPARTURE (Days 1-10)

PART II: THE WILDERNESS (Days 11-20)

PART III: THE VALLEY OF SHADOWS (Days 21-30)

PART IV: THE ARRIVAL (Days 31-40)

A Note from the Author

Dear Fellow Pilgrim,

The book you hold in your hands is an invitation to journey—not merely to read, but to walk a path that countless souls have traveled before us. For centuries, the fifteen Songs of Ascent (Psalms 120-134) have served as companions for those seeking God's presence. These ancient songs guided Hebrew pilgrims as they made their way to Jerusalem for annual festivals, their feet climbing the same dusty paths year after year, their voices lifting these familiar verses heavenward. I believe these songs still have much to teach us about the nature of spiritual pilgrimage.

My own encounter with the Songs of Ascent began during a particularly disorienting season of my life. Like the psalmist who opens this collection with a cry of distress from a foreign land, I found myself in unfamiliar spiritual territory—questioning assumptions I had long held, longing for a more authentic experience of God's presence, and unsure of the path forward. These fifteen psalms became my companions, teaching me that disorientation is often the beginning of a true pilgrimage.

What struck me most as I lived with these songs was their profound honesty. They don't shy away from expressing distress, longing, confusion, or even anger. Yet they consistently move toward hope, not as a naive denial of reality but as a hard-won trust in God's faithfulness. They remind us that authentic spirituality embraces the full range of human experience while maintaining unwavering confidence in divine presence.

The Songs of Ascent also revealed something I had often missed in my individualistic approach to faith—the communal nature of spiritual journey. These were songs meant to be sung together as pilgrims made their way to Jerusalem. They speak repeatedly in the first-person plural: "we," "us," "our." They envision worship not as a private experience but as a shared celebration. In our age of hyper-individualism and selfishness, these psalms call us back to the recognition that we become most fully ourselves in community with others.

This forty-day devotional is designed to honor both the personal and communal dimensions of pilgrimage. Each day's reflection invites you into deeper personal engagement with God while also creating space for shared conversation if you're journeying with others. The questions at the end of each reflection are meant not only for private contemplation but also as starting points for rich discussion.

A few suggestions as you begin:

First, embrace the daily rhythm. The number forty appears throughout Scripture as a period of preparation and transformation—forty days of rain in Noah's time, forty years in the wilderness for Israel, forty days of temptation for Jesus. There is something spiritually significant about sustaining attention over this timeframe. Try not to rush ahead or double up on days. Allow each day's reflection to have its full impact before moving to the next.

Second, consider journeying with companions. While this devotional can certainly be used for individual reflection, its impact deepens when the journey is shared. Perhaps invite a friend, family member, or small group to travel these forty days with you. Set a regular time to discuss what you're discovering—weekly over coffee, through daily text messages, or whatever works for your context. The pilgrims of old didn't journey alone, and neither should we.

Third, pay attention to resistance. On any meaningful journey, there will be days when you don't feel like continuing—when the reflections seem to demand more vulnerability than you're comfortable with, when other priorities compete for your attention, or when the path seems to lead through territory you'd rather avoid. These moments of resistance are often thresholds to deeper growth. I encourage you to notice them, honor them, and then gently persist through them.

Finally, remember that the goal is not perfect understanding or performance but faithful presence. The ancient pilgrims didn't make their journeys to Jerusalem to impress God with their piety but to place themselves in the context where encounter was possible. Similarly, this devotional isn't meant to be a spiritual achievement to complete but a context for genuine meeting with the living God. Some days, you may find yourself deeply moved; other days, you may feel little. Both experiences are valid parts of the pilgrimage.

As we begin, I invite you to adopt the posture of a pilgrim—curious, expectant, willing to be surprised, ready to notice God's presence in unexpected places, and open to the transformation that comes through sustained attention. The ancient paths await. The songs have been sung by countless voices before us. Now it's our turn to take up the journey.

May you discover, as I have, that these songs lead not only to Jerusalem but to the very heart of God.

With anticipation for the journey ahead,
Dr. John R. Sconiers II

---

*"I lift up my eyes to the mountains—where does my help come from?
My help comes from the LORD, the Maker of heaven and earth."* — *Psalm 121:1-2*

How to Use This Devotional: A Guide for Your Ascent

Beginning Your Journey

Welcome to a transformative forty-day pilgrimage through the Songs of Ascents—those fifteen remarkable psalms (120-134) that ancient pilgrims sang as they made their way up to Jerusalem for the great festivals. Just as those travelers journeyed together toward the holy city, you are about to embark on a spiritual ascent that will draw you closer to God, deepen your faith, and potentially connect you with fellow sojourners along the way. This devotional is designed to meet you wherever you are in your spiritual journey and accompany you whether you travel alone or with companions.

Each day's reading is crafted to be completed in ten to fifteen minutes, though you may find yourself lingering longer as the Holy Spirit moves in your heart. The structure remains consistent: a brief opening prayer, reflection on the day's passage from the Songs of Ascents, theological and practical insights, personal application questions, and a closing prayer. This rhythm will become familiar and comforting as you progress, creating a sacred space in your daily routine that anticipates God's presence.

Journeying Alone: The Solitary Pilgrim

If you are undertaking this devotional as a personal retreat, embrace the solitude as sacred space. Begin each morning by finding a quiet place where you can read without interruption—perhaps the same chair each day, creating a physical anchor for your spiritual practice. Keep a journal dedicated to this journey, as writing often reveals insights that remain hidden in mere thinking. When you encounter the daily reflection questions, resist the urge to rush through them. Instead, sit with them, allowing silence to speak. Some days the words will flow easily; other days you may find yourself wrestling like Jacob at the Jabbok. Both experiences are valuable.

Consider your solitary journey as preparation for community rather than isolation from it. The Songs of Ascents were always communal, and even in your private devotions, you are joining an invisible congregation of believers across time and space who have walked this same path. When particular insights strike you deeply, make note of them—they may become gifts you can share with others later. The alone time with God often prepares us to love others more fully and serve them more effectively.

Journeying with a Partner: The Sacred Friendship

Sharing this devotional with a prayer partner or spouse creates unique opportunities for spiritual intimacy and mutual encouragement. Plan to meet daily or weekly, either in person or virtually, to discuss the previous seven days' readings. This rhythm allows time for individual processing while maintaining regular connection. During your meetings, take turns sharing which passages most challenged or encouraged you, what questions arose, and how you sensed God speaking to you through the week.

Practice holy listening with your partner—this means hearing not just their words but the movement of God's Spirit in their life. When your partner shares a struggle or insight, resist the urge to immediately offer advice or share your own similar experience. Instead, ask questions that help them go deeper: "What do you think God might be inviting you into through this?" or "How did you sense God's presence in that difficulty?" Remember that your role is not to be your partner's spiritual director but their fellow traveler, equally dependent on grace.

Create simple rituals that mark your shared journey. Begin each meeting with a moment of silence and prayer, acknowledging God's presence with you. End by praying for each other based on what you've shared. Between meetings, send brief messages when something from the daily reading reminds you of your partner or when you want to ask for prayer. This creates a continuous thread of connection throughout the forty days.

Journeying with a Group: The Pilgrim Community

A small group setting—ideally four to eight people—most closely mirrors the communal experience of the original pilgrims who sang these songs together. If you are leading a group, establish clear expectations from the beginning: commit to the full forty days, maintain confidentiality about what is shared, and create space for both extroverts and introverts to participate meaningfully. Meet weekly, following a simple format: opening prayer, brief check-in (five minutes per person), discussion of the week's readings (using the provided questions as starting points), and closing prayer time.

In group settings, the diversity of perspectives becomes a gift. The same psalm that speaks of God's protection to one person may reveal themes of justice to another. Encourage this variety rather than seeking uniformity of interpretation. However, gently guide conversations back to personal application rather than abstract theological debate. The question is not primarily

"What does this text mean?" but "How is God using this text to shape us?"

Consider practical ways to support each other's journey. Perhaps group members can commit to praying for each other daily, using a simple rotation system. Or create a private online group where members can share brief insights or prayer requests throughout the week. Some groups find it meaningful to conclude their forty-day journey with a special meal or retreat day, celebrating what God has done in their midst.

Practical Considerations for All Travelers

Regardless of how you take this journey, consistency matters more than perfection. If you miss a day, simply return the next day rather than trying to catch up by rushing through multiple readings. The goal is formation, not completion. Some passages will resonate deeply while others may feel difficult or dry—both responses are normal and valuable parts of spiritual growth.

Keep realistic expectations about what forty days can accomplish. You are not trying to achieve spiritual mastery but to open yourself more fully to God's ongoing work in your life. Some days will feel transformative; others may feel routine. Trust that God is working even when you don't feel anything dramatic happening. Often the most significant changes occur gradually and are only recognized in retrospect.

Finally, approach this journey with anticipation and joy. The Songs of Ascents are ultimately about pilgrimage toward celebration, toward worship, toward the joy of God's presence. While they acknowledge the difficulties of the journey—opposition, exhaustion, longing—they are fundamentally hopeful. Allow that hope to infuse your forty days. You are not walking toward an uncertain destination but toward the God who has already proven faithful, who calls you beloved, and who delights to meet you on the way.

The path is before you. The ancient songs are ready to guide you. Whether you walk alone or with companions, the same God who met pilgrims on the road to Jerusalem awaits you now. Begin when you are ready, and trust that the One who began this good work in you will be faithful to complete it.

May this 40-day pilgrimage through the Songs of Ascent deepen your faith, strengthen your community, and draw you closer to the heart of God.

Introduction

The Sacred Journey Upward

Ancient Songs for Modern Pilgrims

Three times each year, faithful Israelites would leave their homes, fields, and familiar surroundings to make a pilgrimage to Jerusalem. From every corner of the promised land—from Dan in the north to Beersheba in the south—they would gather their families, join with neighbors, and begin the sacred journey upward to the holy city. As their feet found the ancient pathways and their eyes fixed on the distant hills where the temple stood, their voices would unite in song. These were not casual travel tunes or mindless entertainment, but carefully crafted psalms that prepared their hearts for an encounter with the living God.

The fifteen psalms that comprise the "Songs of Ascents" (Psalms 120-134) were the soundtrack of this spiritual pilgrimage. Each psalm bears the Hebrew superscription "shir hama'alot"—literally, "a song of the goings up" or "a song of ascents." These ancient hymns guided countless generations of worshipers as they made their way from the low places of ordinary life to the high places of divine encounter. More than mere geographic markers, these songs charted a spiritual topography that leads the human soul from distress to peace, from isolation to community, from doubt to trust, and from earthly concerns to heavenly perspective.

The Geography of the Soul

To understand the power of these songs, we must first grasp the profound significance of Jerusalem in Israel's spiritual imagination. Built on Mount Zion, the city sat approximately 2,500 feet above sea level, making any journey there quite literally an ascent. But the physical elevation was merely the external expression of a deeper spiritual reality. Jerusalem was not just a destination; it was the earthly dwelling place of the Most High God, the point where heaven and earth intersected most intimately.

The temple that crowned the city was more than an impressive architectural achievement—it was the beating heart of Israel's covenant relationship with Yahweh. Here the sacrifices were offered, the festivals celebrated, and the presence of God encountered in ways impossible anywhere else on earth. To journey to Jerusalem was to journey toward the source of life itself, toward the God who had chosen this people and called them into relationship with himself.

Yet the journey was never easy. Pilgrims faced dusty roads, uncertain weather, potential dangers from bandits, and the simple exhaustion that comes from walking long distances while carrying supplies for an extended stay. More challenging still were the internal obstacles: doubt, discouragement, conflict with traveling companions, and the weight of sins that felt too heavy to carry into God's presence. The Songs of Ascents acknowledge these realities honestly while providing a pathway through them.

From Fifteen Songs to Forty Days

This devotional expands upon the fifteen Songs of Ascents to create a comprehensive forty-day spiritual pilgrimage. The number forty is not arbitrary but deeply significant in biblical narrative. It represents a complete period of testing, preparation, and transformation. Moses spent forty days on Mount Sinai receiving the law. The Israelites wandered forty years in the wilderness before entering the promised land. Elijah journeyed forty days to Mount Horeb to encounter God. Jesus fasted forty days in the wilderness before beginning his public ministry. In each case, forty represents the time necessary for profound spiritual formation to occur.

By extending our journey to forty days, we create space for the deep work that authentic spiritual transformation requires. Some days we will focus intensively on a single verse from the Songs of Ascents, allowing its truth to penetrate our hearts slowly and thoroughly. Other days we will explore the broader themes that connect these ancient songs to our contemporary spiritual struggles and aspirations. Throughout, we will discover that these psalms are not museum pieces from a bygone era but living words that speak directly to our deepest needs and highest hopes.

The Songs of Ascents naturally divide into four movements, each corresponding to a distinct phase of the pilgrim's journey both geographically and spiritually. These four movements are: THE DEPARTURE, THE WILDERNESS, THE VALLEY OF SHADOWS, and THE ARRIVAL. Understanding these movements and in which movement you are in during the journey helps us successfully navigate and appreciate the careful architecture of our forty-day journey.

Your Journey Begins

This devotional invites you to become a modern pilgrim, joining the countless believers across history who have walked this path of spiritual ascent. You need not travel to Jerusalem or climb any physical mountain. The geography we will traverse is internal—the landscape of your own heart, mind, and soul. Yet the journey is no less real or transformative than that of the ancient pilgrims who sang these songs while walking dusty roads three millennia ago.

Over the next forty days, you will discover that these ancient words have remarkable power to illuminate contemporary struggles, offer hope in present difficulties, and guide you toward deeper intimacy with God. You will find yourself part of a company of travelers that spans centuries and cultures, all united by the common human longing to draw near to the divine. Whether you journey alone or with others, you will not travel unaccompanied. The God who met Moses on the mountain, who walked with Israel through the wilderness, and who sustained Jesus in the desert will be your constant companion.

Each day's reading is designed to be both manageable and meaningful—substantial enough to nourish your soul but not so lengthy as to overwhelm your schedule. You will encounter theological insights, practical applications, personal reflection questions, and prayers that help you integrate these ancient truths into your daily life. Some days will challenge you; others will comfort you. All are intended to move you forward on the path of spiritual maturity.

The Songs of Ascents begin with a cry of distress: "In my trouble I cried to the Lord, and he answered me" (Psalm 120:1). They end with an invitation to blessing: "Lift up your hands to the holy place and bless the Lord! May the Lord bless you from Zion" (Psalm 134:2-3). This arc from complaint to praise, from isolation to community, from earth to heaven, charts the trajectory of authentic spiritual growth. It is a journey that millions have taken before you and that countless others will take after you.

Your forty-day ascent begins now. The ancient songs are ready to guide you. The path stretches before you, leading upward toward the God who delights to meet his people on the way. Trust the journey, embrace the challenges, celebrate the discoveries, and prepare to be transformed by the One who calls you from glory to glory, from faith to faith, from the low places of human struggle to the high places of divine encounter.

The songs of ascent await. Your pilgrimage begins today.

PART I: THE DEPARTURE
(Days 1-10)

"I call on the LORD in my distress, and he answers me." (Psalm 120:1)

Day 1

The Call to Journey

"In my distress I called to the LORD, and he answered me. Deliver me, O LORD, from lying lips, from a deceitful tongue." — Psalm 120:1-2

HISTORICAL CONTEXT

Our forty-day pilgrimage begins where the ancient Hebrew pilgrims began their journey to Jerusalem—in a place of distress and disorientation. The Songs of Ascent (Psalms 120-134) were likely sung by worshippers as they traveled to Jerusalem for the three annual festivals: Passover, Pentecost, and Tabernacles.

Psalm 120 stands as the gateway to this collection, and strikingly, it opens not with joy or anticipation but with a cry of distress. The psalmist finds himself in "Meshech" and "Kedar" (verse 5)—foreign places far from Jerusalem. Meshech was in Asia Minor (modern Turkey) and Kedar was an Arabian tribe to the southeast. These weren't literal locations for the psalmist but metaphors expressing spiritual and emotional distance from God's presence.

Every spiritual journey begins with the recognition that we are not where we belong. We feel the dissonance between our current reality and our created purpose. This holy discontent is not a sign of failure but of spiritual awakening.

MEDITATION: DISTRESS AS INVITATION

"In my distress I called to the LORD..."

Notice how the psalm begins—not with arrival but with departure, not with answers but with questions, not with comfort but with distress. There is profound wisdom in this starting point. Spiritual journeys rarely begin when everything is perfect. More often, they commence when we recognize that something is profoundly wrong.

The Hebrew word for "distress" (הָרָצ, tsarah) literally means "narrowness" or "constriction." It describes that suffocating feeling when options seem limited, when you feel trapped by circumstances, relationships, or your own patterns of thinking and behavior. This constriction creates a pressure that forces us to look beyond ourselves.

Most of us try everything else before we turn to God. We exhaust our own resources, wisdom, and strength. We seek advice from friends, escape through entertainment, or distraction through busyness. Yet genuine spiritual journeys begin when we finally acknowledge what the psalmist discovered: our deepest distress can only find resolution in calling upon the Lord.

What causes your distress today? Perhaps it's external circumstances—financial pressure, relationship conflict, health concerns, or workplace stress. Or maybe it's internal—guilt, shame, uncertainty about your purpose, or a vague sense that life should be more meaningful than what you're experiencing. Whatever its source, your distress serves as a divine invitation.

C.S. Lewis famously observed that "pain is God's megaphone to rouse a deaf world." Distress creates a crack in our self-sufficiency through which God's light can penetrate. The psalmist's distress wasn't an obstacle to his spiritual journey; it was the catalyst.

THE NATURE OF THE CALL

"...and he answered me."

This simple declaration contains revolutionary power. The God who created galaxies and atoms, who exists outside time and space, responds to human cries. The Hebrew suggests not merely that God heard, but that God answered—a response that indicates relationship, not just acknowledgment.

The journey begins with this reciprocal movement: we call out, and God answers. This divine response doesn't always come as immediate relief from our distress. Sometimes it arrives as courage to face what we've been avoiding, clarity about the next step, or simply the strength to endure what cannot be changed. But the answer always includes the assurance that we are not alone in our distress.

Notice too that the psalmist doesn't begin by asking for directions to Jerusalem or requesting a map for the journey ahead. He simply cries out from his place of distress, and that cry itself becomes the first step on the path. Too often we delay our spiritual journey until we feel adequately prepared, until we understand theology perfectly, or until we've managed to clean up our lives. The psalmist demonstrates a different approach: start where you are, with what you have, even if all you have is distress.

THE SPECIFIC DISTRESS

"Deliver me, O LORD, from lying lips, from a deceitful tongue."

What specifically troubled this ancient pilgrim? Deception. The psalmist found himself in an environment where truth was scarce and manipulation abundant. His distress came from living amidst falsehood—perhaps being lied about, perhaps being lied to, perhaps both.

In our hyperconnected age, we face similar challenges. Social media presents carefully curated versions of reality. Advertising creates artificial needs. Political discourse often prioritizes persuasion over accuracy. Even in our closest relationships, we may hide behind masks, presenting what we think others want to see rather than our authentic selves.

This environment of deception creates profound spiritual distress because we were made for truth. Jesus identified himself as "the way, the truth, and the life" (John 14:6). When we live among lies—whether others' or our own—we experience the disorientation the psalmist describes. We lose our bearings. Our souls know we're wandering in foreign territory, far from our true home.

The psalmist's prayer acknowledges both his vulnerability to deception and his desire for deliverance from it. He doesn't pretend to have the strength to overcome this environment on his own. He calls to the One who is Truth itself to intervene.

APPLICATION: RECOGNIZING OUR DISTRESS

As we begin this 40-day journey through the Songs of Ascent, we must start where the ancient pilgrims started—by honestly acknowledging our own distress and allowing it to become our call to journey. Spiritual growth rarely happens when we're comfortable. It's in the narrow places, the constricted spaces, that we become desperate enough to cry out and receptive enough to hear the answer.

What is causing your spiritual distress today? What falsehoods have you accepted that keep you from experiencing God's presence fully? What masks are you wearing that prevent authentic relationship with God and others? What foreign territories—ways of thinking, relating, or living that don't align with your true identity—are you currently inhabiting?

Our journey toward Jerusalem—toward wholeness, restoration, and God's presence—begins with naming these realities. The psalmist teaches us that articulating our distress to God is not a sign of weak faith but the beginning of authentic spiritual pilgrimage.

As you embark on this journey, remember that the same God who answered the ancient psalmist hears your cry today. Your distress is not meaningless suffering but a holy invitation to move closer to the heart of God, one step at a time. The very fact that you recognize your need for something more indicates that God's Spirit is already at work within you, creating a divine restlessness that can only be satisfied in drawing near to Him.

Today, let your distress become the catalyst for your own song of ascent.

REFLECTION QUESTIONS

1. What forms of distress in your life might actually be God's invitation to begin a deeper spiritual journey? How have you been responding to these invitations?

_____

_____

2. The psalmist specifically mentions "lying lips" and "deceitful tongues" as sources of distress. What forms of deception (from others, from culture, or from yourself) create distress in your spiritual life?

_____

_____

3. Think about a time when you "called to the LORD" from a place of distress. How did God answer you? How did that experience shape your understanding of who God is?

_____

_____

4. The psalm suggests that spiritual journeys often begin in uncomfortable places. How comfortable are you with acknowledging your spiritual distress to God? What makes this difficult or easy for you?

_____

_____

5. What "foreign territories" (habits, relationships, thought patterns) are you currently living in that feel distant from God's presence? What might be a first step toward leaving these territories?

_____

_____

6. If you're journeying through this devotional with others, share an area of distress where you'd appreciate prayer and support. How might acknowledging our distress together strengthen your community?
'
_____

_____

PRAYER FOR TODAY

Faithful God,

I come to You today from my own place of distress. Like the ancient psalmist, I find myself surrounded by falsehood, confusion, and disorientation. I acknowledge that I have wandered into territories far from Your presence—places where Your truth is scarce and Your voice hard to hear.

Thank You that my distress is not meaningless but is Your invitation to journey deeper into relationship with You. Thank You that when I call, You answer—not always with immediate relief, but always with Your presence.

Deliver me, O Lord, from the lying lips and deceitful tongues that distort my understanding of who You are and who I am. Show me where I have believed falsehoods about myself, about others, and about You. Replace these lies with Your truth.

As I begin this journey through the Songs of Ascent, make me honest about my starting point. Give me courage to acknowledge my need, wisdom to discern Your invitation in my distress, and faith to take the first step toward Jerusalem even when I cannot see the entire path.

I trust that You not only hear my cry but that You are already at work, drawing me closer to Your heart with each step of this pilgrimage.In the name of Jesus Christ we pray, Amen.

Day 2

Leaving Deceit Behind

"What will he do to you, and what more besides, you deceitful tongue? He will punish you with a warrior's sharp arrows, with burning coals of the broom bush.

Woe to me that I dwell in Meshek, that I live among the tents of Kedar! Too long have I lived among those who hate peace. I am for peace; but when I speak, they are for war." — Psalm 120:3-7

HISTORICAL CONTEXT

As we continue our journey through the Songs of Ascent, we remain in Psalm 120—still at the starting point of our pilgrimage. While yesterday we considered the psalmist's initial cry of distress, today we examine his growing awareness that he can no longer remain where he is. Something must change.

The geographical references in this psalm are significant. Meshek was located far to the north in modern-day Turkey, while Kedar referred to nomadic tribes in the Arabian desert to the southeast. These locations represented the outer fringes of the known world to ancient Israelites—places culturally and spiritually distant from Jerusalem. By mentioning these locations, the psalmist isn't necessarily saying he physically dwells there, but rather that he feels as spiritually displaced as if he were in these foreign lands.

The image of "sharp arrows" and "burning coals of the broom bush" draws on powerful cultural metaphors. The broom bush (or "juniper" in some translations) was known for producing coal that burned exceptionally hot and long—sometimes for days. These vivid images represent the painful yet necessary process of separating from falsehood and beginning the journey toward truth.

MEDITATION: THE CONFRONTATION WITH DECEIT

"What will he do to you, and what more besides, you deceitful tongue?"

Having identified the source of his distress as deceit, the psalmist now directly confronts it. This question isn't merely rhetorical—it reflects a fundamental spiritual turning point. The psalmist is no longer passively experiencing the effects of falsehood; he's actively challenging its authority in his life.

This shift from passive victim to active participant marks an essential second step in our spiritual pilgrimage. Yesterday, we acknowledged our distress; today, we confront its source. This confrontation requires courage because deceit doesn't surrender easily. The "deceitful tongue" represents not just external lies from others but also the internal falsehoods we've embraced—the stories we tell ourselves that keep us from wholeness.

What false narratives have you accepted? Perhaps you've believed that your worth depends on your productivity, appearance, or others' approval. Maybe you've embraced the lie that God is distant, disinterested, or disappointed in you. Or possibly you've accepted society's definitions of success, happiness, or security without questioning whether they align with God's truth.

The psalmist teaches us to directly challenge these deceptions. By asking, "What will he do to you?" he acknowledges that he cannot defeat deceit through his own strength or wisdom. He appeals to God's intervention, recognizing that divine truth is the only effective weapon against entrenched falsehood.

THE NECESSARY SEPARATION

"Woe to me that I dwell in Meshek, that I live among the tents of Kedar!"

Here we find the psalmist's lament over his current spiritual location. The cry "Woe to me" expresses both regret and awakening. He sees clearly now that he has been dwelling in places incompatible with his true identity and calling. This awareness creates a holy discontent that motivates his journey.

Spiritual growth often begins with this painful recognition that we've been living in the wrong "country." Like the prodigal son who suddenly realized he was far from home feeding pigs when he belonged at his father's table (Luke 15:11-32), we experience moments of clarity that reveal the disparity between where we are and where we belong.

The reference to "dwelling" suggests this wasn't a temporary situation but a settled state. The psalmist had adapted to environments fundamentally opposed to God's presence. He had become comfortable with discomfort, accustomed to absence. His cry acknowledges both the reality of his situation and his responsibility in it.

What spiritual Mesheks and Kedars have you been dwelling in? Where have you settled for less than God's best, adapted to environments that slowly erode your faith, or made peace with patterns that separate you from authentic community? Naming these places is essential before we can leave them behind.

THE CONFLICT OF VALUES

"Too long have I lived among those who hate peace. I am for peace; but when I speak, they are for war."

The psalmist now identifies the fundamental conflict that makes his current dwelling untenable—a clash of core values. He desires peace (shalom in Hebrew, meaning wholeness, flourishing, and right relationships), while those around him are oriented toward conflict and division.

This incompatibility creates constant tension. Each time he speaks for peace, his words are met with hostility. This exhausting dynamic makes coexistence impossible; one value system must eventually yield to the other. The psalmist recognizes that he cannot simultaneously pursue God's shalom and remain immersed in environments hostile to it.

We face similar tensions in our own spiritual journeys. Jesus warned that we cannot serve two masters (Matthew 6:24), yet we often attempt precisely this impossible balancing act. We try to pursue God's kingdom while clinging to worldly security, to embrace divine truth while accommodating comfortable lies, to experience authentic community while maintaining protective masks.

The psalmist's confession—"Too long have I lived"—acknowledges that this tension has persisted longer than it should have. There comes a time when continued dwelling in Meshek or Kedar is no longer excusable as ignorance but becomes willing compromise. The recognition of this reality provides the necessary motivation to begin the journey toward Jerusalem, toward God's presence and truth.

APPLICATION: IDENTIFYING WHAT MUST BE LEFT BEHIND

Every meaningful journey involves leaving something behind. The ancient Israelites had to leave Egypt before they could enter the Promised Land. Abraham had to leave Ur before he could become the father of nations. Ruth had to leave Moab before she could be integrated into God's covenant people.

Similarly, our spiritual pilgrimage requires identifying and abandoning the deceptions that have kept us from experiencing God's presence fully. This doesn't necessarily mean geographical relocation (though sometimes it might); more often, it means leaving behind mindsets, relationship patterns, distractions, or pursuits that have become obstacles to spiritual growth.

What specifically might you need to leave behind? Consider these categories:

- **False beliefs about God** — Distorted views of God's character that portray Him as distant, harsh, indifferent, or unreliable.

- **False beliefs about yourself** — Lies about your identity, worth, purpose, or capacity for change.

- **False sources of security** — Dependence on achievements, possessions, relationships, or appearances for your sense of safety and significance.

- **False communities** — Relationships or social environments that consistently pull you away from God rather than toward Him.

- **False priorities** — Pursuits that consume your best energy while providing little eternal return.

Leaving these falsehoods behind isn't merely about rejection; it's about making space for something better. The pilgrim doesn't leave Meshek simply to wander aimlessly but to journey toward Jerusalem. So too, we abandon falsehood to embrace truth, leave deception to find authenticity, and exit conflict to discover peace.

As you continue this 40-day journey, consider what you might need to leave behind. The process may involve sharp arrows and burning coals—painful confrontations with comfortable deceptions—but this necessary separation creates space for the true peace your soul seeks. Like the psalmist, you may need to acknowledge, "Too long have I lived" in places God never intended as your dwelling. Today can mark the beginning of your departure from these foreign lands.

REFLECTION QUESTIONS

1. The psalmist identifies deceit as something that requires God's intervention through "sharp arrows" and "burning coals." What forms of deceit in your life seem most resistant to change and most in need of divine intervention?

_____

_____

2. What "Mesheks" or "Kedars" (places spiritually distant from God) have you been dwelling in? What has made these places comfortable or familiar despite their distance from God's presence?

_____

_____

3. The psalm describes a value conflict: "I am for peace; but when I speak, they are for war." Where do you experience similar conflicts between your spiritual values and the values of environments you regularly inhabit?

_____

_____

4. The phrase "Too long have I lived" suggests the psalmist had remained in an unhealthy spiritual environment longer than he should have. What situations, habits, or relationships have you remained in "too long" that may be hindering your spiritual journey?

_____

_____

5. What specific falsehoods do you need to leave behind to progress in your spiritual pilgrimage? Which of these will be most difficult to abandon, and why?

_____

_____

6. If you're journeying with others through this devotional, share one "false security" you've recognized in your life. How might your community help each other identify and leave behind these false securities?

PRAYER FOR TODAY

Faithful God,

Today I stand with the ancient psalmist, recognizing that I have dwelled too long in places far from Your presence. I have adapted to environments that oppose Your truth, accommodated falsehoods that diminish Your glory, and settled for less than the abundant life You intend for me.

Forgive me for making peace with deception—both the lies others have spoken and the ones I've told myself. With Your sharp arrows of truth, pierce the defenses I've built around comfortable falsehoods. With the burning coals of Your love, consume the false securities I've clung to instead of trusting You fully.

Show me clearly what I must leave behind as I continue this journey toward Your presence. Give me courage to name the "Mesheks" and "Kedars" where I've been dwelling—the mindsets, habits, relationships, and pursuits that keep me spiritually displaced and distant from You.
I confess that like the psalmist, I am weary of living among those who hate peace. Align my heart fully with Your shalom. When the values of Your kingdom conflict with the values I've absorbed from the world, give me wisdom to choose rightly and strength to stand firmly.

As I take these first steps away from falsehood and toward truth, steady my resolve when the journey becomes difficult. Remind me that I leave these things behind not merely to abandon them but to make room for the greater treasures You have prepared.

Thank You that You never ask me to leave anything behind without promising something infinitely better ahead. In this confidence, I continue my journey toward Jerusalem, toward Your presence, one step at a time.

In Jesus' name, who is the Way, the Truth, and the Life, Amen.

Day 3

Looking to the Hills

"I lift up my eyes to the mountains— where does my help come from? My help comes from the LORD, the Maker of heaven and earth." — Psalm 121:1-2

HISTORICAL CONTEXT

Having acknowledged our distress and being committed to leaving deception behind, we now take our first steps forward on the pilgrim journey. Today, we transition from Psalm 120 to Psalm 121—often called "The Traveler's Psalm." This psalm likely served pilgrims as they began their physical ascent toward Jerusalem, an uphill journey through challenging terrain.

Jerusalem sits atop the Judean hills at an elevation of approximately 2,500 feet. Ancient pilgrims traveling from almost any direction would experience a literal upward journey, gazing at the rising landscape before them. The hills represented both the challenge of the journey ahead and the destination itself, as Jerusalem was surrounded by mountains (Psalm 125:2).

For travelers in the ancient Near East, hills and mountains held ambiguous significance. On one hand, they represented places of worship and divine encounter; on the other hand, they harbored dangers including robbers, wild animals, and harsh conditions. A pilgrim setting out would naturally look toward these hills with a mixture of anticipation and apprehension.

This geographical reality forms the backdrop for the spiritual question that opens Psalm 121: "I lift up my eyes to the mountains—where does my help come from?" The question carries both wonder and vulnerability, acknowledging that the journey ahead requires resources beyond what the traveler possesses.

MEDITATION: THE UPWARD GAZE

"I lift up my eyes to the mountains..."

The psalm begins with a deliberate shifting of focus—from the immediate surroundings to something higher. This upward gaze represents a fundamental reorientation essential to spiritual progress. After acknowledging our distress and identifying what we must leave behind, we must now intentionally lift our eyes toward something greater.

Notice the active nature of this movement: "I lift up my eyes." This isn't a passive observation but an intentional choice. The psalmist decides where to direct his attention. In a world that constantly pulls our gaze downward—toward problems, threats, limitations, and fears—this deliberate upward orientation requires discipline and resolve.

What consumes your visual field today? Are your eyes fixed primarily on obstacles, uncertainties, or inadequacies? Are you focused on the dust of the road beneath your feet rather than the destination ahead? The pilgrim's first action teaches us that where we look shapes where we go.

The Hebrew word for "lift up" (אֶשָּׂא, nasa) carries connotations of bearing a burden. There are times when even lifting our eyes feels effortful, when hope itself seems too heavy to hold. In such seasons, the simple act of redirecting our gaze toward God becomes an act of profound faith.

THE PILGRIM'S QUESTION

"...where does my help come from?"

Having lifted his eyes, the psalmist poses a question that reveals both vulnerability and wisdom. The journey ahead requires assistance, and the pilgrim acknowledges this need openly. There is no pretense of self-sufficiency, no illusion of independent adequacy. The road to Jerusalem demands resources beyond what any traveler can provide for themselves.

This question—"Where does my help come from?"—serves as a crucial checkpoint early in our spiritual journey. Its answer determines the direction, character, and ultimate success of our pilgrimage. If we answer incorrectly, we may find ourselves climbing the wrong mountains, expending precious energy on paths that lead nowhere.

Throughout history, people have looked to many different "hills" for help:

- The hill of human achievement, believing that education, effort, or expertise will fulfill their deepest needs
- The hill of relational security, expecting other people to provide what only God can give
- The hill of material provision, trusting in financial resources to create lasting safety
- The hill of religious activity, substituting practices for presence, rituals for relationship

- The hill of personal improvement, assuming that becoming a better version of themselves will satisfy their soul's hunger

These hills may offer temporary assistance or partial solutions, but they ultimately fail to provide the comprehensive help pilgrims need. Their insufficiency isn't immediately apparent; many travelers spend years climbing these mountains before discovering they don't lead to the Jerusalem of the soul.

The psalmist's question invites honest assessment: Where are you currently looking for help? What mountains have captured your attention and energy? Which hills have promised assistance but left you stranded halfway up the slope?

THE DEFINITIVE ANSWER

"My help comes from the LORD, the Maker of heaven and earth."

Having posed the question, the psalmist doesn't leave us in suspense. He answers with a clarity and conviction that cuts through confusion: "My help comes from the LORD." Not partially, not occasionally, not as one source among many—but definitively and comprehensively.

This isn't blind religious sentiment but a reasoned conclusion based on the LORD's identity as "the Maker of heaven and earth." The Hebrew emphasizes this creative power by using the participle form of the verb "to make," suggesting ongoing creative activity. The psalmist anchors his confidence not in a historical act of creation but in God's continuing role as Creator and Sustainer of all that exists.

Consider the logic: If God created the very mountains the pilgrim gazes upon, surely He possesses resources sufficient for the journey across them. If God established the foundations of earth and stretched out the heavens, surely human challenges fall well within His capacity to address. The scale of God's creative work puts our needs into perspective without minimizing them.

This cosmic framing of God's help elevates our understanding of divine assistance. The help God offers isn't merely emotional comfort or spiritual encouragement, though it certainly includes these dimensions. Rather, the Creator of everything brings the full weight of divine resources to bear on our journey. The One who spoke light into existence illuminates our path; the One who separated waters establishes boundaries around our challenges; the One who breathed life into humanity renews our strength when it falters.

APPLICATION: DISTINGUISHING SOURCES OF HELP

As we continue our ascent, we must develop discernment about the sources of help we rely upon. Divine assistance differs from worldly solutions in several important ways:

1. Divine help addresses root causes rather than symptoms. Worldly solutions often provide temporary relief without resolving underlying issues. God's help transforms us from the inside out, beginning with our hearts and extending to our circumstances.

2. Divine help operates on a different timeline. Immediate fixes appeal to our impatience, but God's assistance often unfolds gradually, developing our character along with addressing our needs. The journey itself becomes part of the help we receive.

3. Divine help requires relationship rather than transaction. Worldly solutions can be purchased, achieved, or earned. God's help flows from covenant love, inviting us into deeper connection rather than simply solving problems from a distance.

4. Divine help integrates with divine purposes. God's assistance always aligns with His larger intentions for our lives and for creation. Unlike worldly solutions that may resolve immediate concerns while creating long-term problems, God's help coheres with His redemptive work in the world.

Divine help transforms the helper along with the situation. When we receive assistance from the LORD, we don't remain unchanged. The very act of receiving divine help shapes us into people more aware of our dependence, more grateful for grace, and more aligned with God's heart.

As you journey forward today, consciously lift your eyes above the immediate challenges before you. Look beyond the hills of human solution to the Maker of heaven and earth. Remind yourself that the distance between your need and God's provision is no greater than the distance between non-existence and creation—a gap God has already demonstrated His power to bridge.

Your help comes from the LORD. Not your cleverness, connections, credentials, or capabilities— though God may certainly work through these channels. The source remains divine even when the delivery system appears human. This fundamental orientation toward God as the ultimate helper establishes the right foundation for the entire pilgrimage ahead.

REFLECTION QUESTIONS

1. What specific "hills" (sources of help other than God) have you been looking to recently? What makes these alternate sources attractive or seemingly reliable?

_____

_____

2. The psalm begins with an intentional lifting of eyes. What practices or disciplines help you shift your focus from immediate problems to God's presence and provision?

_____

_____

3. The psalmist identifies God specifically as "the Maker of heaven and earth." How does remembering God's creative power change your perspective on the challenges you currently face?

_____

_____

4. Consider a recent situation where you needed help. How did you determine where to look for assistance? What might have changed if you had more intentionally sought help from God first?

_____

_____

5. Divine help often differs from worldly solutions in its timing, approach, and ultimate effects. Share an experience where God's help came in a form different from what you expected or requested.

_____

_____

6. If you're journeying with others through this devotional, discuss how your community might help each other remember to "look to the hills" rather than settling for easier but less reliable sources of help.

PRAYER FOR TODAY

Creator God,

Today I deliberately lift my eyes to You, acknowledging that my journey requires assistance beyond what I can provide for myself. Like the ancient pilgrim gazing at the hills surrounding Jerusalem, I look up from my immediate circumstances toward Your transcendent presence.

Forgive me for the many times I've sought help from sources that cannot ultimately satisfy or sustain. I've looked to my own strength and found it insufficient, to human wisdom and discovered its limitations, to material resources and experienced their temporary nature. Redirect my gaze when it drifts toward these lesser hills.

I declare with the psalmist that my help comes from You, the Maker of heaven and earth. The One who formed mountains can surely guide me over them; the One who placed stars in their courses can certainly direct my steps. Nothing about my journey exceeds Your creative power or falls outside Your loving concern.

As I continue this pilgrimage toward deeper intimacy with You, teach me to distinguish between worldly solutions and divine assistance. Give me patience when Your help unfolds differently than I expect, wisdom to recognize Your provision when it appears, and humility to receive from Your hand rather than grasping for control.

Thank You that I never journey alone. With every upward step, You are both my companion on the path and my destination beyond it. When the mountains seem too high or the valley too deep, remind me again where my help comes from.

In the name of Jesus, who taught us to look to You for our daily bread, Amen.

Day 4

The Watchful Guardian

"He will not let your foot slip— he who watches over you will not slumber; indeed, he who watches over Israel will neither slumber nor sleep.

The LORD watches over you— the LORD is your shade at your right hand; the sun will n ot harm you by day, nor the moon by night.

The LORD will keep you from all harm— he will watch over your life; the LORD will watch over your coming and going both now and forevermore." — Psalm 121:3-8

HISTORICAL CONTEXT

Yesterday, we focused on the opening verses of Psalm 121, where the pilgrim identified the true source of help for the journey. Today, we explore the rich promises that flow from that foundational truth. As we continue in this second Song of Ascent, we see a subtle but significant shift in voice. The psalm begins with "I" (the pilgrim's perspective) but transitions to "you" (verses 3-8), suggesting that these words might have been spoken by priests or fellow travelers as encouragement along the way.

For ancient pilgrims traveling to Jerusalem, the journey presented numerous physical dangers. The roads through Judean hills were notorious for bandits and wild animals. Travelers faced harsh conditions including intense daytime heat and dangerous nighttime cold. A misstep on rocky terrain could result in a serious or even fatal injury. Without modern amenities like accurate maps, weather forecasts, or communication devices, travelers were acutely aware of their vulnerability.

In this precarious context, the promise of divine watchcare took on profound significance. The image of God as a vigilant guardian who "neither slumbers nor sleeps" offered tangible comfort to weary travelers making their way through uncertain territory. The assurance that the LORD would protect from both "sun" and "moon" covered the entire journey—day and night, without interruption.

MEDITATION: THE GOD WHO NEVER SLEEPS

"He will not let your foot slip—he who watches over you will not slumber..."

The psalm begins its promises with attention to the pilgrim's feet—the most vulnerable and essential part of the traveler's body. On rugged mountain paths, a single misplaced step could lead to injury or worse. The promise that God "will not let your foot slip" speaks directly to this primal fear of falling, of losing one's footing on the journey.

Notice the active language: God will not "let" your foot slip. This suggests not merely passive observation but active intervention—a divine grip that steadies the wavering step, a supportive hand that catches the stumbling traveler. The Hebrew word for "slip" (טוֹמ, mot) implies tottering or shaking, suggesting that God's care extends not just to catastrophic falls but to moments of unsteadiness and uncertainty.

This promise connects to the deeper fears we face on our spiritual journeys. We worry about making wrong turns, missing important signposts, or finding ourselves on dangerous paths. The assurance that God actively prevents our slipping reminds us that divine guidance isn't merely informational (showing the right path) but relational (supporting us along that path).

The psalm then moves to the extraordinary claim that this divine guardian "will not slumber." In ancient cultures where gods were often depicted as capricious and unreliable, the image of a deity who never falls asleep—who maintains constant, unwavering attention—was revolutionary. The repetition in verse 4 ("will neither slumber nor sleep") employs two different Hebrew terms to emphasize complete wakefulness. There is no moment of reduced alertness, no period of diminished awareness.

Consider the contrast with human guardians, who inevitably require rest. The most vigilant human protector must eventually sleep, creating periods of vulnerability for those under their care. But the psalmist declares that Israel's God transcends this limitation. Divine watchcare knows no interruption, no shift change, no momentary lapse of attention.

This sleepless vigilance offers profound comfort for times when we feel forgotten or overlooked. In seasons of apparent divine silence, when prayers seem to echo unanswered and God's presence feels distant, the psalm reminds us that God's attention never wavers. The absence of visible intervention doesn't indicate absence of divine awareness.

THE COMPREHENSIVE NATURE OF GOD'S PROTECTION

"The LORD watches over you—the LORD is your shade at your right hand; the sun will not harm you by day, nor the moon by night."

Having established the constancy of God's watchcare, the psalm now expands on its comprehensive nature. The repetition of "watches over" (רָמַשׁ, shamar) emphasizes attentive guardianship. This Hebrew word carries connotations of keeping, preserving, and protecting—the kind of care a shepherd provides for vulnerable sheep or a gardener gives to delicate plants.

The image of God as "shade" speaks directly to travelers in the Near Eastern climate, where sun exposure presented a serious threat. The specific mention of shade "at your right hand" reflects the sun's position in the southern sky (for those in the northern hemisphere), casting shadows to the north. The right side would typically receive the most direct sunlight during the journey, making shade particularly valuable there. This precise detail reminds us that God's care isn't generic but precisely calibrated to our specific vulnerabilities.

The protection extends from sun to moon—covering the complete cycle of day and night. In ancient understanding, the moon was believed to cause various maladies (reflected in words like "lunacy"). Whether these dangers were real or perceived, the psalm assures travelers that God's protection encompasses all potential threats, both the obvious ones (sunstroke) and the mysterious ones (moon-related ailments).

For modern pilgrims, this comprehensive care speaks to God's protection across all dimensions of our experience—the bright, exposed places where dangers are obvious and the shadowy, uncertain territories where threats are harder to identify. Divine watchcare extends to our public journeys and our private struggles, our daylight decisions and our midnight doubts.

THE SCOPE OF DIVINE WATCHCARE

"The LORD will keep you from all harm—he will watch over your life; the LORD will watch over your coming and going both now and forevermore."

The psalm concludes with expansive promises that stretch the boundaries of our understanding. The declaration that "The LORD will keep you from all harm" (literally "all evil" in Hebrew) seems to collide with our lived experience of suffering and pain. How do we reconcile this sweeping assurance with the reality that faithful people do experience injury, illness, loss, and death?

This tension invites us to look deeper at what constitutes true "harm" from an eternal perspective. The promise isn't that we'll never experience difficulty or suffering, but that nothing can ultimately destroy what matters most—our connection to God and our eternal destiny. Even death itself, from this perspective, is not final "harm" but a transition within God's continued care.

The psalm extends this protection temporally as well as circumstantially. God watches over our "coming and going," covering all movements and transitions. This care extends "now and forevermore," transcending the limitations of time. This eternal dimension reminds us that God's guardianship doesn't end with physical death but continues through and beyond it.

The sixfold repetition of "watches over" or "keep" (רָמַשׁ, shamar) throughout these verses creates a rhythmic reinforcement of the central message. Like waves repeatedly washing against shore, this repetition gradually reshapes our understanding of divine care, eroding doubt and building confidence in God's vigilant presence.

APPLICATION: TRUSTING THE WATCHFUL GUARDIAN

As we continue our ascent, this portion of Psalm 121 invites us to internalize the reality of God's comprehensive care. This isn't merely intellectual assent to divine protection but the cultivation of moment-by-moment trust that transforms how we navigate uncertainty.

This trust doesn't eliminate the objective challenges of the journey. The mountains remain steep, the paths narrow, the weather unpredictable. Trusting God's watchcare doesn't mean pretending these difficulties don't exist or expecting miraculous removal of every obstacle. Rather, it means journeying through these realities with the confidence that we never face them alone or unprotected.

What does this trusting journey look like practically?

1. **We travel lighter.** When we trust God's watchcare, we can release the heavy burden of excessive worry and contingency planning. We prepare responsibly but without the exhausting weight of trying to anticipate and prevent every possible negative outcome.

2. **We see differently.** Through the lens of trust, we interpret our experiences—even difficult ones—as occurring within the context of divine oversight rather than outside it. Challenges become opportunities to experience God's shade rather than evidence of divine absence.

3. **We recover faster.** When we do stumble or face harm (as we all will), trust in God's watchcare accelerates our recovery. We view setbacks as temporary rather than terminal, as occurring within God's larger purposes rather than defeating them.

4. **We extend our vision.** Believing that God watches over our "coming and going both now and forevermore" expands our perspective beyond immediate circumstances to eternal realities. This extended timescale helps us evaluate our present difficulties more accurately.

In the uncertain segments of your journey—where the path seems unclear, the dangers numerous, or your strength inadequate—remember the watchful Guardian who neither slumbers nor sleeps. Your steps are not casual to God. Your journey occurs under constant divine supervision. The same care that guided ancient pilgrims to Jerusalem accompanies your spiritual ascent today.

REFLECTION QUESTIONS

1. The psalm promises "He will not let your foot slip." What areas of your life currently feel most unstable or uncertain? How might trusting God's active stabilizing presence change your approach to these situations?

_____

_____

2. The image of God as one who "will not slumber" addresses the human fear of being forgotten or overlooked. When have you felt most "unseen" by God? How does the promise of constant divine attention speak to that experience?

_____

_____

3. The psalm presents God as "shade at your right hand," suggesting protection precisely where we're most vulnerable. What are your particular vulnerabilities in this season of life, and how might God's customized protection be manifesting there?

_____

_____

4. The promise of protection from both "sun" and "moon" covers the entire cycle of day and night. In what "nighttime" experiences (times of darkness, confusion, or obscurity) do you most need to remember God's watchcare?

_____

_____

5. The statement that "The LORD will keep you from all harm" creates tension with our experience of suffering. How do you understand this promise in light of the very real pains and losses we face? What might "harm" mean from an eternal perspective?

_____

_____

6. If you're journeying with others through this devotional, share a story about a time when you experienced God's watchcare in a way that strengthened your trust. How might your community better remind each other of God's constant protection?

_____

_____

PRAYER FOR TODAY

Watchful Guardian,

I marvel today at Your constant, comprehensive care. You who created mountains and seas, stars and atoms, somehow maintain perfect attention to every detail of my journey. You neither slumber nor sleep; Your vigilance never wavers; Your protection never pauses.

In the places where my foot feels most likely to slip—where uncertainty makes the path treacherous or fear makes my steps unsteady—I claim Your promise of divine stability. Hold me firm when I cannot hold myself, and guide my feet when the way ahead seems unclear.

Thank You for being my shade in scorching times, for standing at my right hand where I'm most exposed and vulnerable. In situations that drain my strength and threaten to overwhelm me, I rest in the cool relief of Your presence.

I confess that I've often doubted Your watchcare, interpreting difficulty as abandonment or suffering as evidence of Your indifference. Forgive this shortsightedness. Help me see the wider perspective—that Your protection encompasses not just momentary comfort but eternal wellbeing, not just physical safety but spiritual flourishing.

As I continue this pilgrimage, teach me what it means to trust You with each step. Free me from the exhausting burden of trying to be my own guardian. Let me travel lighter, see differently, recover faster, and extend my vision beyond immediate circumstances to eternal realities.

I rest in the magnificent promise that You watch over my coming and going both now and forevermore. In life, in death, and beyond death, I remain within Your unwavering gaze and unfailing care.

In the name of Jesus, who taught us to call You "Father," Amen.

Day 5

The Joy of Fellowship

"I rejoiced with those who said to me, 'Let us go to the house of the LORD.' Our feet are standing in your gates, Jerusalem." — Psalm 122:1-2

HISTORICAL CONTEXT

Today we begin our journey through the third Song of Ascent, Psalm 122. After acknowledging our distress, leaving deception behind, identifying our true source of help, and embracing God's watchful care, we now encounter a significant shift in tone and focus. While the previous psalms largely addressed individual spiritual experience, Psalm 122 introduces a communal dimension that will characterize much of the remaining journey.

For ancient Israelites, the pilgrimages to Jerusalem for the three annual festivals—Passover, Pentecost, and Tabernacles—were fundamentally communal events. Families, neighbors, and entire villages would travel together along the roads leading to the holy city. As they neared Jerusalem, different pilgrimage groups would converge, creating a growing stream of worshippers approaching the city gates.

These festivals were not mere religious obligations but joyful celebrations. Imagine the scene: dusty roads filled with travelers singing, children running ahead with excitement, elders sharing stories of previous pilgrimages, the distant view of Jerusalem growing clearer with each step. The anticipation of worship mingled with the pleasure of shared journey created a unique spiritual atmosphere.

The architectural setting matters as well. Jerusalem's gates were not simply entry points but gathering places where public affairs were conducted, judgments rendered, and community life centered. To stand within these gates meant to have arrived not just at a physical destination but at the heart of Israel's communal identity. For a people whose relationship with God was mediated through corporate worship and covenant community, this arrival represented the fulfillment of both religious obligation and social belonging.

MEDITATION: THE INVITATION TO JOY

"I rejoiced with those who said to me, 'Let us go to the house of the LORD.'"

The psalm begins with a striking emotion: joy. Not duty, not obligation, not even reverence—but simple, unrestrained delight. The Hebrew word translated "rejoiced" (שָׂמַח, samach) conveys a sense of gladness and celebration. This isn't the solemn, subdued religious sentiment we sometimes associate with worship but an effervescent response that wells up unbidden.

What triggers this joy? An invitation: "Let us go to the house of the LORD." Note the plural form—"let us go." This is not a solitary suggestion but a communal call. Someone (or perhaps several people) invited the psalmist to join them in journey and worship. The joy emerges not just from the destination but from the shared nature of the pilgrimage, the companionship of fellow travelers.

There's something powerful about receiving spiritual invitation from others. When someone says, "Let's pray together" or "Let's study Scripture" or "Let's worship," they offer more than a religious activity; they extend relationship. They communicate: "I want to experience God's presence with you. I value your companionship on this journey." Such invitations honor both the vertical relationship (with God) and the horizontal one (with each other).

Have you experienced the joy of spiritual invitation? Have you felt that spark of anticipation when someone suggests shared worship or prayer? Or have religious obligations become so routinized that they evoke obligation rather than delight? The psalmist reminds us that the journey toward God's presence should stir anticipation and pleasure, especially when undertaken in company.

The invitation specifically mentions "the house of the LORD"—the temple in Jerusalem. For ancient Israelites, this represented the dwelling place of God's presence, the meeting point between heaven and earth. While we no longer require a physical temple to access God's presence (John 4:21-24), we still benefit from designated spaces and times for communal encounter with the divine. The "house of the LORD" for us might be a church building, a home group, a prayer gathering, or any context where believers collectively seek God's face.

THE ARRIVAL IN COMMUNITY

"Our feet are standing in your gates, Jerusalem."

The second verse signals a transition—from anticipation to arrival, from journey to destination. Note the shift from singular ("I rejoiced") to plural ("our feet"). The psalmist doesn't say "my feet" but "our feet," emphasizing the shared nature of the experience. The pilgrim has arrived not as an isolated individual but as part of a community of worshippers.

Jerusalem's gates were more than entry points; they represented thresholds between ordinary life and sacred space, between the secular and the holy. To stand within these gates meant entering the story of God's covenant people, joining one's individual narrative with the larger story of divine redemption. The plural "our" reminds us that faith is never merely personal; it always connects us to a community that extends both horizontally (across the present world) and vertically (through historical tradition).

The present tense—"are standing"—creates an immediacy that invites readers to place themselves within the scene. The psalmist isn't simply recounting a past experience or anticipating a future one; he's savoring the present moment of arrival. This mindfulness, this awareness of threshold moments, enhances spiritual experience. Too often we rush through significant spiritual transitions without pausing to recognize where we stand and what it means.

For contemporary pilgrims, "standing in the gates" might represent those threshold moments when we consciously enter spaces of corporate worship or fellowship. It asks us to be present to these transitions, to notice when we cross from individual spiritual practice into communal experience. Each time we gather with others in God's name—whether in formal worship, small groups, service projects, or informal fellowship—we too can say, "Our feet are standing in your gates."

APPLICATION: THE TRANSFORMATIVE POWER OF FELLOWSHIP

As we continue our ascent through the Songs of Ascent, Psalm 122:1-2 invites us to embrace the joy and transformative power of spiritual fellowship. While individual devotion forms an essential foundation (as we've seen in the previous psalms), our journey reaches new dimensions when shared with others.

How does communal worship and fellowship transform our spiritual experience?

1. **It expands our perspective.** When we worship alongside others—particularly those from different backgrounds, generations, or life experiences—we encounter aspects of God's character that we might miss on our own. Each believer reflects a facet of divine truth; together, we see a more complete picture.

2. **It reinforces our commitments.** Human beings naturally tend toward what psychologists call "social conformity"—we adopt the behaviors and values of our community. When we

surround ourselves with others pursuing God, their example strengthens our resolve and helps maintain our focus.

3. **It amplifies our joy.** Positive emotions intensify when shared. The delight of divine encounter multiplies when experienced alongside others who recognize and celebrate what we're witnessing. As C.S. Lewis observed, shared joy is doubled joy.

4. **It supports our weakness.** The journey toward God's presence includes difficult stretches where our individual strength fails. In these moments, community carries us forward. When we cannot pray, others pray for us; when our faith wavers, others believe on our behalf; when we lose sight of the path, others guide us back.

5. **It authenticates our witness.** Jesus indicated that unity among believers would testify to the truth of the gospel (John 17:23). When we journey together despite differences—when we demonstrate love that transcends natural affinities—we offer the world a compelling picture of God's kingdom.

6. **This psalm challenges** the individualistic approach to spirituality prevalent in many contemporary contexts. While personal devotion remains essential, isolation diminishes our spiritual experience. The fullness of joy comes through shared journey and destination.

Consider your own spiritual practices: How much of your journey occurs in isolation, and how much in company? Do you regularly experience the joy of invitation—either extending it to others or receiving it yourself? Have you felt the unique delight of standing with fellow believers in the "gates" of worship and fellowship?

If your spiritual life has become solitary, today's psalm beckons you back into community. This doesn't necessarily require dramatic changes—it might mean simply inviting one trusted friend to pray with you, joining a small study group, or participating more fully in corporate worship. The goal isn't busy religious activity but genuine spiritual companionship.

For those already embedded in community, the psalm invites deeper appreciation for this gift. Notice the joy that emerges when you gather with others in God's name. Pay attention to the unique contributions different companions bring to your journey. Express gratitude for those who have invited you into shared spiritual experience.

As we continue our ascent through the Songs of Ascent, let us embrace the paradox that our most profound individual encounters with God often occur in the context of community. Let us rejoice when fellow travelers invite us to join them, and let us savor the moment when our collective feet stand in the gates of worship.

REFLECTION QUESTIONS

1. Recall a time when someone invited you to participate in a spiritual activity or practice. How did you respond, and what emotions did their invitation evoke? How might Psalm 122:1 reshape your response to similar invitations in the future?

_____

_____

2. The psalmist shifts from "I" to "our" between verses 1 and 2. How do you experience the transition between individual and communal aspects of faith in your own spiritual journey? Which comes more naturally to you?

_____

_____

3. Jerusalem's gates represented a threshold between ordinary life and sacred space. What "gates" or thresholds help you transition into awareness of God's presence? How might you become more mindful of these transition moments?

_____

_____

4. The psalm begins with rejoicing at the mere invitation to worship. Have religious activities become more duty than delight in your experience? What practices or perspectives might help recapture the joy of worship?

_____

_____

5. Consider the five ways communal worship transforms spiritual experience (expands perspective, reinforces commitment, amplifies joy, supports weakness, authenticates witness). Which of these have you personally experienced, and which might you need to explore more fully?

_____

_____

6. If you're journeying with others through this devotional, discuss how your shared experience has affected your individual spiritual growth. How has reading, reflecting, and praying together deepened your connection both with God and with each other?

PRAYER FOR TODAY

Gathering God,

Thank You for the gift of community on this spiritual journey. Like the ancient psalmist, I want to rejoice when invited into Your presence alongside others who seek Your face. Forgive me for the times I've approached corporate worship as obligation rather than opportunity, when I've missed the joy of standing with fellow believers in the gates of fellowship.

I celebrate today the companions You've placed in my life—those who invite me closer to You, who journey alongside me when the path grows difficult, who help me see aspects of Your character I might miss on my own. Thank You for each person who has said to me, "Let us go to the house of the LORD," drawing me out of isolation into shared worship.

As I continue this pilgrimage, help me to value both individual devotion and communal experience. Show me where I've leaned too heavily toward solitary spirituality or, conversely, where I've substituted busy religious activity for genuine communion with You and others.

Make me attentive to threshold moments—those transitions into sacred spaces and gatherings where I can truly say, "Our feet are standing in your gates." In a fragmented, individualistic world, let me experience the unique joy that comes from shared pursuit of Your presence.

Where appropriate, use me to extend the invitation of fellowship to others who journey alone. Give me courage to say, "Let us go" to those who need companionship, and wisdom to create spaces where authentic spiritual community can flourish.

I rejoice today that You have designed us not as isolated seekers but as a covenant community, a body with many members, a family bound by love. As I stand with others in the gates of worship, let me glimpse more fully the joy that awaits when all Your children gather in Your eternal presence.

In Jesus' name, who prayed that we might be one as He and the Father are one, Amen.

Day 6

City of Peace

"Jerusalem is built like a city that is closely compacted together. That is where the tribes go up— the tribes of the LORD— to praise the name of the LORD according to the statute given to Israel. There stand the thrones for judgment, the thrones of the house of David." — Psalm 122:3-5

HISTORICAL CONTEXT

Yesterday, we focused on the joy of fellowship as we joined the pilgrim standing at Jerusalem's gates. Today, we step further into Psalm 122, moving from the threshold into the city itself. The psalm shifts from the pilgrim's personal response to a meditation on Jerusalem's nature and purpose.

Jerusalem occupies a unique place in biblical history and theology. Originally a Jebusite stronghold captured by David (2 Samuel 5:6-10), the city became Israel's capital and, more significantly, the location of the temple—God's dwelling place among His people. Its very name carries meaning: most scholars connect "Jerusalem" (יְרוּשָׁלַיִם, yerushalayim) with "salem" or "shalom," suggesting "foundation of peace" or "city of peace."

The physical layout of ancient Jerusalem was distinctive. Built on hills and surrounded by valleys, the city featured tightly packed buildings constructed close together within strong walls. Unlike sprawling cities built on plains, Jerusalem's topography necessitated efficient use of limited space. This compact design created a dense urban environment where buildings literally supported one another, sharing walls and foundations.

During Israel's three annual pilgrimage festivals, Jerusalem's population would swell dramatically as worshippers from throughout the land converged on the city. The tribes mentioned in verse 4 refer to the twelve tribes of Israel, emphasizing the unity of the nation despite its tribal divisions. These pilgrimages fulfilled the command in Deuteronomy 16:16 that all Israelite men should "appear before the LORD" at the appointed festivals.

The reference to "thrones for judgment" in verse 5 reflects Jerusalem's role as not only a religious center but also the seat of civil authority. King David established his dynasty there, and his descendants administered justice from Jerusalem. This integration of spiritual and civic life was characteristic of ancient Israel's theocratic structure, where religious and governmental authorities operated in close relationship.

MEDITATION: THE CITY CLOSELY COMPACTED

"Jerusalem is built like a city that is closely compacted together."

The psalmist begins with an architectural observation that carries profound spiritual implications. The Hebrew term translated "closely compacted" (חֻבְּרָה, chubbar) literally means "joined" or "coupled"—suggesting buildings so interconnected that they function as a unified whole rather than independent structures. This physical reality creates a powerful metaphor for community, unity, and mutual support.

Consider the significance of this image: in Jerusalem, no building stood entirely alone. Each structure shared walls with others, provided support to adjacent buildings, and received stability from those around it. This interdependence wasn't a design flaw but an intentional feature that maximized limited space and created a stronger overall city.

The New Testament develops this architectural metaphor, describing God's people as "living stones... being built into a spiritual house" (1 Peter 2:5) and as a temple "joined together and rising to become a holy temple in the Lord... built together to become a dwelling in which God lives by his Spirit" (Ephesians 2:21-22). The image of interconnected stones creating a greater structure perfectly captures the communal nature of authentic faith.

This concept challenges our individualistic tendencies. Western culture particularly celebrates self-sufficiency and independence, often viewing reliance on others as weakness. But the "closely compacted" city reminds us that we were designed for interconnection. Spiritual maturity doesn't mean achieving perfect autonomy but rather finding our proper place in the larger structure, both supporting others and allowing ourselves to be supported.

What would it mean for your faith community to be "closely compacted together"? Not merely occupying the same space on Sunday mornings, but genuinely sharing burdens, pooling resources, resolving conflicts, celebrating joys, and creating such unity that an observer might say, "See how they are joined together!"

THE GATHERING OF DIVERSE TRIBES

"That is where the tribes go up—the tribes of the LORD—to praise the name of the LORD according to the statute given to Israel."

Jerusalem served as the gathering point for Israel's twelve tribes—groups with distinct territories, histories, and even rivalries. Despite these differences, the tribes converged in Jerusalem for a common purpose: to praise the LORD's name. The city created space where tribal identities remained intact but became secondary to shared worship.

Notice the repeated "tribes of the LORD"—a reminder that diversity exists within a more fundamental unity. Each tribe brought its unique character and contribution, but all acknowledged the same divine authority. Their differences enriched rather than threatened their common identity as God's covenant people.

This tribal gathering foreshadows the expansive vision of Revelation 7:9, where John sees "a great multitude that no one could count, from every nation, tribe, people and language, standing before the throne and before the Lamb." The heavenly Jerusalem will gather not just Israel's twelve tribes but representatives from all human diversity, united in worship while maintaining their distinctive identities.

For contemporary faith communities, this image offers both challenge and encouragement. We need not erase cultural, theological, or personal differences to experience genuine unity. True community accommodates diversity within a framework of shared allegiance to Christ. The question is not whether we can eliminate all differences but whether we can subordinate those differences to our primary commitment to "praise the name of the LORD."

The phrase "according to the statute given to Israel" reminds us that this gathering wasn't spontaneous or self-designed but responsive to divine instruction. God commanded these pilgrimages, recognizing humanity's need for regular communal worship experiences. Even today, the practice of gathering regularly with other believers isn't optional but essential to spiritual formation. As the writer of Hebrews admonishes, we must not "give up meeting together, as some are in the habit of doing" (Hebrews 10:25).

THE CENTER OF JUSTICE

"There stand the thrones for judgment, the thrones of the house of David."

The psalm concludes this section by highlighting Jerusalem's role as a center for justice. The "thrones for judgment" were where kings and officials heard cases, resolved disputes, and administered the law. These weren't separate from the city's spiritual function but complementary to it. The "house of David" ruled by divine appointment, theoretically implementing God's justice rather than merely human preference.

This integration of worship and justice appears throughout Scripture. The prophets frequently condemned religious rituals divorced from ethical practice, insisting that true worship must express itself in just relationships and social structures (Isaiah 1:10-17; Amos 5:21-24). Jesus similarly critiqued those who meticulously observed religious regulations while "neglecting justice and the love of God" (Luke 11:42).

For ancient pilgrims, seeing the "thrones for judgment" served as a reminder that encountering God's presence should transform how they treated others. The same journey that brought them to worship also brought them to the center of justice—a powerful symbol that these two dimensions of life belong together.

Our own spiritual journeys must maintain this connection. Authentic spirituality never remains private but inevitably affects our social ethics, economic choices, and treatment of others. As James writes, "Religion that God our Father accepts as pure and faultless is this: to look after orphans and widows in their distress and to keep oneself from being polluted by the world" (James 1:27).

APPLICATION: BUILT TOGETHER AS GOD'S PEOPLE

As we continue our ascent through the Songs of Ascent, Psalm 122:3-5 invites us to move beyond individual spiritual experience to embrace our place in the "closely compacted" community of faith. Like Jerusalem's buildings that gained stability by connecting with others, we find our greatest strength not in isolation but in proper relationship with fellow believers.

This doesn't mean uncritically accepting every expression of religious community. Jerusalem represented an ideal—a city built according to divine design, where diverse tribes gathered for authentic worship, and where justice reigned through divinely appointed leadership. Many religious communities fall short of this vision, just as the historical Jerusalem often failed to embody its ideal identity as the "city of peace."

Yet we need not wait for perfect community before engaging with the body of Christ. Even with its flaws, the gathered community offers something essential to our spiritual formation. The accountability, perspective, support, and collective wisdom available through genuine fellowship cannot be replicated through individual spirituality alone.

Consider how these aspects of Jerusalem might translate into your experience of spiritual community:

1. **Closely compacted structure** — Are you connected to others in ways that provide mutual support and accountability? Have you allowed yourself to be "joined" to fellow believers, or do you maintain careful distance that limits both what you receive and what you contribute?

2. **Gathering of diverse tribes** — Does your faith community embrace meaningful diversity while maintaining unity around essential beliefs? How might you better appreciate the distinct contributions of those who differ from you in background, perspective, or spiritual gifting?

3. **Center of worship** — Do you participate regularly in corporate worship, recognizing its unique value beyond what you can experience individually? How might you engage more fully in these gatherings, contributing your presence and participation rather than remaining a passive observer?

4. **Seat of justice** — Does your spiritual journey connect seamlessly with how you treat others and engage with social issues? How might your community better embody God's justice in practical, tangible ways?

For many contemporary believers, genuine spiritual community represents both our greatest need and our greatest challenge. Individualism, hurried schedules, digital distractions, past church wounds, and fear of vulnerability all create barriers to the "closely compacted" fellowship depicted in this psalm. Yet the journey toward God's presence necessarily includes reconnecting with God's people.

Today, consider what steps you might take toward deeper integration with the community of faith. This might mean committing more consistently to a local congregation, joining a small group, serving alongside others, or simply being more vulnerable about your needs and struggles. Whatever form it takes, movement toward authentic community represents movement toward the Jerusalem of God's design—the city of peace where diverse people find unity in worship and justice.

REFLECTION QUESTIONS

The psalm describes Jerusalem as "closely compacted together," with buildings interconnected and mutually supportive. Where in your life do you experience this kind of interdependence with other believers? What makes this kind of connection difficult in contemporary culture?

_____

_____

Jerusalem gathered diverse tribes for a common purpose. How does your faith community handle diversity? Where have you seen differences either enrich or threaten unity, and what factors determine which outcome occurs?

_____

_____

The pilgrims went to Jerusalem "according to the statute given to Israel"—following divine instruction rather than personal preference. How do you decide when and how to engage with community? What role do obligation, habit, and desire play in your decisions about gathering with other believers?

_____

_____

Jerusalem housed both the temple and "thrones for judgment," integrating worship and justice. Where do you see this integration in your own spiritual journey? In what ways might your worship be disconnected from how you treat others or engage with social issues?

_____

_____

The psalm presents an idealized vision of Jerusalem, though the historical city often fell short of this ideal. How do you maintain commitment to community despite the inevitable disappointments and failures of real churches? What helps you persist when community proves difficult?

_____

_____

If you're journeying with others through this devotional, discuss how your group embodies (or could better embody) the "closely compacted" nature of Jerusalem. What practical steps might you take to strengthen your connections and support for one another?

PRAYER FOR TODAY

Builder of Jerusalem,

I marvel today at Your vision for community—a city closely compacted together, where diverse tribes gather in unity, where worship and justice intertwine. Thank You for designing us not as isolated individuals but as living stones meant to be built together into a dwelling place for Your Spirit.

Forgive me for the ways I've resisted this divine architecture. I confess my tendencies toward self-sufficiency, my reluctance to be truly known by others, my preference for comfortable distance over vulnerable connection. Help me recognize these patterns not as strength but as limitation—walls that prevent me from experiencing the full measure of Your presence among Your people.

As I continue this pilgrimage, grant me courage to find my place in the closely compacted city. Show me where I might offer support to those around me and where I need the stability that others provide. Help me value the distinct gifts and perspectives of fellow travelers, seeing our differences not as threats but as reflections of Your multifaceted wisdom.

I pray for the communities where You've placed me—my local congregation, small group, family, and friends. Transform these relationships into something that echoes Jerusalem's beauty and purpose. Where conflict exists, establish Your peace; where superficiality prevails, create depth; where injustice persists, establish righteousness; where worship has grown routine, restore authentic praise.

Thank You that even our imperfect attempts at community provide glimpses of the greater Jerusalem toward which we journey—that city with foundations, whose architect and builder is You. Until we reach that perfect dwelling place, help us create outposts of Your kingdom wherever we gather in Your name.

In Jesus' name, the cornerstone on whom the whole building is joined together, Amen.

Day 7

Praying for Peace

"Pray for the peace of Jerusalem: 'May those who love you be secure. May there be peace within your walls and security within your citadels.' For the sake of my family and friends, I will say, 'Peace be within you.' For the sake of the house of the LORD our God, I will seek your prosperity." — Psalm 122:6-9

HISTORICAL CONTEXT

As we complete our journey through Psalm 122, we turn to its concluding verses, which shift from description to imperative. After celebrating the joy of fellowship and meditating on Jerusalem's significance, the psalmist now calls for active engagement through prayer for the city's welfare.

For ancient Israelites, Jerusalem's peace was never guaranteed. Throughout its history, the city faced numerous threats—from foreign powers like Egypt, Assyria, and Babylon, from internal divisions between the northern and southern kingdoms, and from the consequences of spiritual unfaithfulness. The command to "pray for the peace of Jerusalem" emerged from this context of fragility and vulnerability.

The Hebrew word for "peace" here—שָׁלוֹם (shalom)—carries much richer meaning than merely the absence of conflict. Shalom encompasses wholeness, well-being, prosperity, and right relationships at every level. It describes the integrated flourishing of a community in its spiritual, social, economic, and physical dimensions.

Jerusalem's significance extended beyond its political importance. As the location of the temple—God's dwelling place among His people—the city's welfare affected Israel's religious life profoundly. Disruption in Jerusalem meant disruption in the sacrificial system, the priestly ministry, and the corporate worship gatherings that sustained Israel's covenant relationship with God.

The mention of "walls" and "citadels" (or "palaces" in some translations) in verse 7 references Jerusalem's physical defenses and the residences of its leaders. In ancient Near Eastern cities, these structures represented both protection from external threats and the governance systems that maintained internal order. Praying for peace "within your walls" meant seeking both security from invasion and harmony among the city's inhabitants.

MEDITATION: THE COMMAND TO PRAY

"Pray for the peace of Jerusalem..."

The psalm transitions from description to directive with a straightforward command: pray. This isn't presented as optional or supplementary but as an essential response to Jerusalem's significance. Having recognized the city's importance as the center of worship and justice, the pilgrim is now called to actively participate in its welfare through intercession.

This command challenges passive spirituality. The pilgrim isn't merely a tourist admiring Jerusalem's beauty or significance; nor is he simply a recipient of the blessings that flow from the city's religious institutions. Rather, he bears responsibility for Jerusalem's shalom through his prayers. Privilege brings obligation; blessing creates responsibility.

Notice that this prayer isn't primarily for individual benefit but for communal flourishing. While the pilgrim would certainly derive personal advantages from Jerusalem's peace, the focus remains outward—on the collective welfare of God's people and the institutions that sustained their covenant life.

What might it mean for contemporary believers to "pray for the peace of Jerusalem"? While this question inevitably intersects with complex geopolitical realities surrounding modern Jerusalem, the psalm's principle extends beyond any single physical location. We are called to pray for the peace, wholeness, and flourishing of the communities that nurture our faith—our local congregations, denominational structures, and the global church in all its diversity.

This kind of prayer doesn't come naturally to many of us. Our petitions often focus narrowly on personal concerns—health, finances, relationships, and individual spiritual growth. While these matters deserve prayer, the psalmist reminds us to expand our vision, recognizing how our welfare connects with the larger community's flourishing.

THE CONTENT OF PEACE PRAYERS

"May those who love you be secure. May there be peace within your walls and security within your citadels."

The psalm doesn't just command prayer but provides its content—a model of what praying for communal peace involves. This prayer encompasses several dimensions:

First, it seeks security for "those who love you"—the community of faithful worshippers committed to Jerusalem and what it represents. This recognizes that a community's strength lies primarily in the welfare of its devoted members. Before buildings, programs, or institutions, the church consists of people who "love" its mission and identity.

Second, it requests "peace within your walls"—internal harmony and cohesion. Jerusalem's greatest threats sometimes came not from external enemies but from division, conflict, and strife among its inhabitants. Similarly, faith communities often suffer more damage from internal discord than from outside opposition. Praying for "peace within" means seeking unity, reconciliation, and healthy relationships within our spiritual family.

Third, it asks for "security within your citadels"—protection for leadership and governance structures. Leaders often bear disproportionate burdens and face unique spiritual attacks. Their decisions affect the entire community, making their wisdom, integrity, and stability crucial to collective flourishing. Praying for our spiritual leaders represents an essential dimension of seeking communal peace.

This model prayer demonstrates remarkable balance—concern for individual members, community relationships, and leadership structures. It recognizes that true shalom requires attention to each of these dimensions, as weakness in any area compromises the whole.

THE MOTIVATION FOR PEACE PRAYERS

"For the sake of my family and friends, I will say, 'Peace be within you.' For the sake of the house of the LORD our God, I will seek your prosperity."

The psalm concludes by articulating two primary motivations for seeking Jerusalem's peace: relational connections ("family and friends") and spiritual devotion ("the house of the LORD our God"). These motivations balance human bonds with divine covenant, personal attachments with transcendent commitment.

The mention of "family and friends" reminds us that communities consist of people we love—not abstract entities but individuals with names, stories, and connections to our lives. When we pray for our faith communities, we're not merely supporting an institution but seeking the welfare of specific people with whom we share life's journey.

Yet the psalm doesn't stop with human connections. The ultimate motivation extends to "the house of the LORD our God"—recognizing that Jerusalem's significance derived primarily from God's presence there. The pilgrim seeks the city's prosperity not merely for human benefit but for divine glory, not just for earthly flourishing but for covenant faithfulness.

The phrase "I will seek" in the final verse indicates active engagement beyond prayer alone. While intercession forms an essential foundation, seeking peace also involves practical action, tangible service, and concrete commitment to community welfare. Prayer and action work together—neither replacing nor negating the other but forming an integrated response to God's call.

APPLICATION: EXPANDING OUR PRAYER HORIZONS

As we continue our ascent through the Songs of Ascent, Psalm 122:6-9 challenges us to expand our prayer horizons beyond individual concerns to embrace communal flourishing. This expansion transforms not only our prayers but our entire relationship with faith community—shifting our posture from consumer to contributor, from critic to intercessor, from observer to participant.

Consider how your own prayers might grow through this psalm's guidance:

1. **Broaden your prayer scope.** Do your prayers typically focus primarily on personal concerns, or do they regularly include your faith community's welfare? Practice intentionally praying for your local congregation, denomination, and the global church—not as brief additions to your "real" prayers but as central concerns.

2. **Pray for all dimensions of community.** Following the psalm's model, include prayers for individual members, internal relationships, and leadership structures. Recognize that true shalom requires flourishing in each of these areas, as weakness in one dimension affects all others.

3. **Connect prayer with action.** As the psalmist moved from "I will say" to "I will seek," allow your intercession to inform your participation. Let your prayers for community shape your service, giving, reconciliation work, and commitment to congregational life.

4. **Balance your motivations.** Like the pilgrim who prayed both for "family and friends" and for "the house of the LORD," examine what drives your concern for community. Healthy engagement combines genuine love for people with devoted commitment to God's purposes and presence.

5. **Expand your definition of "peace."** Remember that biblical shalom extends far beyond conflict resolution to encompass wholeness, justice, prosperity, and right relationships. Pray not just for the absence of problems but for the presence of flourishing in all its dimensions.

For those journeying through significant church pain or disappointment, this psalm offers both challenge and comfort. It acknowledges Jerusalem's importance without idealizing its reality; it commands prayer without denying difficulty. Even when our faith communities fall short of their calling, they remain worthy of our intercession and engagement—not because they're perfect but because they're purposed for God's presence.

As we complete our reflection on Psalm 122, we've traced a progression from individual joy at the invitation to worship (verses 1-2), through meditation on community's nature (verses 3-5), to active participation in its welfare through prayer (verses 6-9). This movement from personal to communal, from receiving to contributing, characterizes the ascending spiritual journey. The path toward God's presence necessarily includes growing concern for God's people.

REFLECTION QUESTIONS

1. Examine your recent prayers. What percentage focuses on personal concerns versus community welfare? How might the command to "pray for the peace of Jerusalem" reshape your prayer priorities?

_____

_____

2. The psalm provides specific content for prayers about community—security for faithful members, peace within walls, and protection for leadership. Which of these dimensions do you find easiest to pray for? Which seems most overlooked in your intercession?

_____

_____

3. Consider the dual motivations for seeking community peace: "family and friends" and "the house of the LORD." Which of these resonates more strongly with you? How might balancing these motivations enrich your connection to faith community?

_____

_____

4. The Hebrew concept of shalom encompasses wholeness, well-being, prosperity, and right relationships. What aspects of "peace" does your faith community most need right now? How specifically might you pray for these dimensions?

_____

_____

5. The command to pray for Jerusalem acknowledges that the city's welfare wasn't guaranteed but required active intercession. What threats or challenges to your faith community's flourishing seem most pressing? How might focused prayer address these concerns?

_____

_____

6. If you're journeying with others through this devotional, consider establishing a regular practice of praying together for your shared faith communities. What specific aspects of communal life will you commit to holding before God in intercession?

_____

_____

PRAYER FOR TODAY

God of Shalom,

Today I hear afresh the call to pray for peace—not just personal tranquility but the comprehensive flourishing of the communities where You've placed me. Forgive me for prayers too small, too self-focused, too disconnected from Your heart for collective welfare and wholeness.

I pray for the peace of Your church: May those who love her be secure. Strengthen the faith, hope, and love of committed believers who form the core of our congregations. Protect them from discouragement, division, and spiritual attack. Renew their joy in service and deepen their roots in Your truth.

May there be peace within her walls—harmony in relationships, unity amid diversity, reconciliation where conflict has created barriers. Heal broken trust between members, bridge divides across generations and backgrounds, and create genuine community that witnesses to Your transforming presence.

Grant security within her citadels. I lift before You the leaders of my local congregation, denomination, and the global church. Shield them from unique pressures and temptations that accompany their calling. Grant them wisdom, integrity, courage, and deep dependence on Your Spirit. Protect their families from the particular stresses of ministry life.

For the sake of my family and friends—those I know and love within the community of faith—I say, "Peace be within you." I recognize that my welfare is inseparably connected with theirs, that we journey together rather than alone.

For the sake of Your dwelling place—the glory of Your presence among Your people—I will seek the church's prosperity. Beyond mere sentiment or words, help me contribute tangibly to communal flourishing through my presence, service, resources, and reconciling love.

As I continue this pilgrimage through the Songs of Ascent, transform me from passive recipient to active participant in the welfare of Your people. Let my prayers expand beyond my personal concerns to embrace Your vision for the community that bears Your name.

In Jesus' name, who prayed for unity among all believers, Amen.

Day 8

Eyes of Dependence

"I lift up my eyes to you, to you who sit enthroned in heaven. As the eyes of slaves look to the hand of their master, as the eyes of a female slave look to the hand of her mistress, so our eyes look to the LORD our God, till he shows us his mercy." — Psalm 123:1-2

HISTORICAL CONTEXT

Today we begin our journey through Psalm 123, the fourth Song of Ascent. After exploring the joy of community and the call to pray for communal peace in Psalm 122, we now encounter a shift in tone. Psalm 123 opens with an expression of profound dependence and longing for divine mercy.

The image of servants watching their masters' hands would have resonated deeply with the original audience. In ancient Near Eastern households, servants carefully observed their masters' hand gestures, which communicated instructions without words. A slight movement might indicate approval or disapproval, permission or prohibition, reward or correction. Attentiveness to these subtle signals determined a servant's effectiveness and, potentially, their well-being.

This master-servant dynamic permeated ancient societies, where hierarchical relationships provided the primary framework for social organization. Unlike modern employment arrangements based on contracts and mutual agreement, ancient servant-master relationships were characterized by significant power imbalance, with servants deeply dependent on their masters' goodwill.

The psalmist lived in a culture familiar with foreign domination. Whether composed during Babylonian exile, Persian rule, or another period of subjugation, this psalm emerged from a context where Israel experienced political subordination to foreign powers. The nation's dependence on God for mercy paralleled their historical situation of vulnerability and powerlessness.

The phrase "enthroned in heaven" (literally "sitting in the heavens") uses royal imagery that would have contrasted with earthly thrones occupied by human rulers. While Israel might be subject to earthly powers, the psalmist affirms that ultimate authority belongs to God, whose throne transcends all temporal governments.

MEDITATION: THE UPWARD GAZE

"I lift up my eyes to you, to you who sit enthroned in heaven."

The psalm begins with a deliberate redirection of attention—from horizontal to vertical, from earthly circumstances to divine sovereignty. This upward gaze represents a fundamental spiritual orientation that recognizes where true power and help originate.

Notice the contrast with contemporary tendencies. When faced with challenges, we typically look horizontally—to experts, technologies, methodologies, or strategies that promise solutions. Or we look inward—to our own resources, resilience, creativity, or determination. The psalmist models a different response: looking upward to the One "enthroned in heaven."

This upward orientation doesn't deny the value of human solutions or personal resources but places them in proper perspective. It acknowledges a transcendent reality beyond our immediate circumstances—a sovereign God who remains enthroned regardless of earthly conditions.

The vertical gaze requires intentionality. The phrase "I lift up" indicates active choice rather than passive observation. Like physical muscles that strengthen with regular exercise, this spiritual muscle of upward attention develops through deliberate practice. In a world filled with horizontal distractions and internal preoccupations, the decision to lift our eyes heavenward requires conscious effort and regular recommitment.

Where are your eyes focused today? Have temporal concerns, relational challenges, or inner turmoil captured your attention so completely that you've lost sight of the enthroned One? The psalmist invites us to redirect our gaze—not denying earthly realities but viewing them within the larger context of divine sovereignty.

THE SERVANT'S ATTENTIVENESS

"As the eyes of slaves look to the hand of their master, as the eyes of a female slave look to the hand of her mistress..."

Having established the upward direction of his gaze, the psalmist now describes its quality using a powerful domestic image. Servants watching their masters' hands exemplified heightened awareness, complete attention, and readiness to respond. This wasn't casual observation but focused vigilance that anticipated direction and prepared for immediate obedience.

The repetition—male servants watching masters, female servants watching mistresses—emphasizes that this attentiveness transcended individual relationships. It represented a universal posture within that cultural context, an expected orientation within the social order. Similarly, dependence on God isn't just for certain personality types or spiritual temperaments but constitutes the appropriate stance for all humanity before their Creator.

This servant metaphor challenges our cultural ideal of independence. Modern Western societies particularly celebrate autonomy, self-reliance, and personal freedom. We often measure maturity by decreasing dependence on others. The psalmist presents a radically different paradigm—one where attentive dependence represents spiritual maturity rather than developmental failure.

Though the master-servant analogy may initially seem outdated or even troubling to contemporary readers, its essential truth transcends cultural frameworks. Created beings necessarily depend on their Creator; finite minds require infinite wisdom; temporal creatures need eternal perspective. Rather than diminishing human dignity, acknowledging this dependence aligns us with fundamental reality.

Notice that the servants watch their masters' hands—the instruments of action, provision, guidance, and authority. In Scripture, God's "hand" frequently symbolizes His active engagement with creation and human affairs. The psalmist isn't watching abstract theological concepts but looking for concrete divine activity in real-world circumstances.

THE COMMUNAL DIMENSION

"...so our eyes look to the LORD our God, till he shows us his mercy."

After beginning with singular pronouns ("I lift up"), the psalm shifts to plural ("our eyes"), suggesting that this dependence isn't merely individual but communal. The entire pilgrim community—and by extension, the whole covenant people—adopts this posture of attentive waiting before God.

This communal dimension reminds us that authentic spirituality, while deeply personal, is never purely individual. We learn dependence together, support one another in maintaining upward focus, and collectively experience divine mercy. The vertical relationship with God necessarily shapes horizontal relationships with others sharing the same posture.

The psalmist specifically awaits mercy (חָנַן, chanan)—favor or grace undeserved by the recipient. This isn't contractual expectation based on performance but humble recognition of need beyond what justice might dictate. The servant watches the master's hand not demanding rights but seeking gracious provision.

The phrase "till he shows us his mercy" indicates persistent watching despite delayed response. Unlike modern servants who might give two weeks' notice if dissatisfied, ancient servants remained attentive through extended periods of waiting. Their dependence wasn't conditional on immediate gratification but endured through uncertain timing.

This patient persistence challenges our demand for instant spiritual results. Contemporary culture conditions us to expect immediate outcomes—one-click shopping, on-demand entertainment, instant communication. When transferred to our relationship with God, this impatience becomes spiritually corrosive, causing us to abandon the upward gaze when divine timing doesn't match our preferred schedule.

APPLICATION: CULTIVATING DEPENDENCE

As we continue our ascent through the Songs of Ascent, Psalm 123:1-2 invites us to develop a spiritual posture that runs counter to many cultural messages: humble, attentive dependence on God. This posture doesn't come naturally in societies that celebrate self-sufficiency, but it represents an essential quality for spiritual maturity.

How might we cultivate this dependence in practical terms?

1. Practice regular reorientation. Like the psalmist who deliberately lifted his eyes, we need disciplines that redirect our attention from horizontal preoccupations to vertical awareness. Regular prayer, worship, Scripture reading, and creation appreciation can serve as reorientation practices that lift our gaze toward the enthroned One.

2. Embrace your limitations. Dependence begins with honest acknowledgment of our finite nature. Rather than pretending to possess unlimited capacity, wisdom, or strength, spiritual maturity recognizes and accepts the boundaries of human experience. This isn't self-deprecation but realistic assessment that opens us to divine resources beyond our own.

3. Study the Master's hand. Servants became experts at reading subtle hand movements because they studied their masters carefully over time. Similarly, we learn to recognize God's activity by immersing ourselves in Scripture (where God's "hand" is revealed in historical acts), by reviewing our own experiences of divine guidance, and by sharing stories of God's work within community.

4. Develop patient persistence. The servant's watching wasn't momentary but continuous—"till he shows us his mercy." Cultivate spiritual staying power that maintains attention through seasons of apparent divine silence or delayed response. Recognize that steadfast watching itself forms Christlike character beyond whatever specific mercy you await.

5. Join with others in watching. Notice how the psalm moves from "I" to "our," suggesting that dependence flourishes in community. Share your watching with fellow believers—speaking honestly about your needs, listening to others' experiences of divine activity, and maintaining collective attention on God's movement even when individual focus wavers.

This humble dependence doesn't diminish human dignity but fulfills our created purpose. Jesus himself modeled this posture perfectly, maintaining constant attention to the Father's will and working only as he saw the Father working (John 5:19). Far from being demeaning, this dependence connected him to the source of all wisdom, power, and love.

In a world that measures worth by independence and self-determination, the practice of humble dependence offers countercultural witness. It demonstrates an alternative way of being human—not grasping for control but receiving life as gift, not striving for autonomy but finding freedom in submission to divine authority.

As you journey forward today, consider what might change if you approached your circumstances with the attentive dependence of a servant watching their master's hand. How might your anxieties, decisions, relationships, and work be transformed by this deliberate upward gaze? What mercy might you receive when you acknowledge your need rather than asserting your self-sufficiency?

REFLECTION QUESTIONS

1. The psalm begins with "I lift up my eyes to you," suggesting intentional redirection of attention. What tends to capture your gaze instead of God? What practices help you most effectively lift your eyes toward divine reality?

_____

_____

2. The image of servants watching their masters' hands implies minute attention to subtle signals. How carefully do you watch for God's guidance in your life? What might help you become more attuned to divine direction?

_____

_____

3. Western culture highly values independence and self-reliance. How has this cultural emphasis shaped your spiritual journey, for better or worse? Where do you find it most difficult to embrace dependence on God?

    _____

    _____

4. The psalm shifts from singular ("I lift up") to plural ("our eyes"), suggesting both personal and communal dimensions of dependence. How does your faith community support or hinder your practice of humble dependence on God?

5. The servants watch "till he shows us his mercy," indicating persistent attention despite delayed response. Where in your life are you currently waiting for God's mercy? What helps you maintain spiritual focus during extended periods of waiting?

    _____

    _____

6. If you're journeying with others through this devotional, share an experience where you learned deeper dependence on God through challenging circumstances. How did that experience change your understanding of the servant-master relationship with God?

PRAYER FOR TODAY

Sovereign Lord,

Today I deliberately lift my eyes to You, enthroned in heaven yet intimately present in my life. Forgive my horizontal preoccupation with circumstances, solutions, and limitations that has kept my gaze earth-bound rather than heaven-directed.

I confess the subtle pride that resists dependence—the false belief that maturity means requiring less of You rather than acknowledging my need more honestly. In a culture that celebrates self-sufficiency, train my spiritual reflexes to turn first toward Your provision rather than my own resources.

Like an attentive servant watching their master's hand, help me develop heightened awareness of Your movement in my life. Sharpen my spiritual perception to recognize Your guidance in Scripture, circumstances, wise counsel, and the inner promptings of Your Spirit. When Your direction comes through subtle indicators rather than dramatic signs, give me discernment to understand and courage to follow.

I join with others in fixing our collective gaze upon You, acknowledging that we watch not as isolated individuals but as a community of dependence. Thank You for fellow servants who help me maintain focus when my attention wanders and who remind me of Your faithfulness when my vision grows dim.

Grant me patient persistence to watch "till You show me Your mercy." When answers delay and guidance seems unclear, strengthen my resolve to maintain an upward orientation rather than returning to self-reliance or horizontal solutions. In waiting, form in me the character of Christ, who perfectly modeled the attentive dependence You desire.

I celebrate that true freedom comes not through independence but through proper dependence on You—the Creator who designed me, the Redeemer who saved me, the Sustainer who holds all things together. In this dependence, may I discover the purpose and dignity for which I was created.

In Jesus' name, who lived in perfect dependence on the Father, Amen.

Day 9

When Contempt Surrounds

"Have mercy on us, LORD, have mercy on us, for we have endured no end of contempt. We have endured no end of ridicule from the arrogant, of contempt from the proud." — Psalm 123:3-4

HISTORICAL CONTEXT

Yesterday, we explored the first half of Psalm 123, which established a posture of humble dependence with eyes lifted toward God. Today, we examine the second half, which reveals the difficult circumstances prompting this upward gaze—relentless contempt and ridicule from others.

The historical setting for this psalm likely reflects a period when God's people faced mockery and derision from surrounding nations or ruling powers. This could have occurred during the Babylonian exile (586-538 BC) when displaced Israelites endured scorn from their captors. Alternatively, it might reflect the post-exilic period when returning exiles rebuilding Jerusalem faced opposition and ridicule from neighboring peoples (Nehemiah 2:19, 4:1-3).

The Hebrew word for "contempt" (בּוּז, buz) conveys a sense of being belittled, despised, or treated as insignificant. Similarly, "ridicule" suggests active mockery rather than mere disapproval. The psalmist describes this contempt as coming from "the arrogant" and "the proud"—those who position themselves above others and look down with disdain.

For ancient Israelites, such mockery struck at core identity issues. As God's covenant people, their distinctive practices and beliefs set them apart from surrounding cultures. When these differences became targets for ridicule, it challenged not just their social standing but their understanding of themselves as God's chosen community.

MEDITATION: THE REALITY OF CONTEMPT

"Have mercy on us, LORD, have mercy on us, for we have endured no end of contempt."

The psalm shifts abruptly from the serene image of servants watching their master's hand to an urgent plea for divine mercy. This transition reflects life's actual texture—how quickly circumstances can move from quiet dependence to desperate need, from peaceful watching to painful endurance.

Notice the repetition: "Have mercy on us, LORD, have mercy on us." This doubling communicates urgency, like someone knocking repeatedly on a door during emergency. The psalmist doesn't mask his desperation with formal religious language but allows raw need to shape his prayer. There's no pretense of having everything under control, no spiritual posturing to appear stronger than he feels.

The cause of this urgent plea follows immediately: "for we have endured no end of contempt." The phrase "no end" (literally "we are greatly filled with" in Hebrew) suggests prolonged exposure rather than isolated incidents. This isn't about occasional criticism but sustained disdain that has filled the community's experience to overflowing.

Contempt represents a particularly painful form of opposition. Unlike mere disagreement (which engages with ideas) or even anger (which acknowledges significance), contempt dismisses the other as beneath serious consideration. It communicates "You don't matter" and "Your perspective isn't worth my time"—attacking dignity rather than just disputing viewpoints.

Have you experienced contempt for your faith? Perhaps from family members who treat your beliefs as childish superstition, colleagues who roll their eyes at your moral convictions, or a broader culture that portrays religious people as intellectually deficient or dangerously fanatical. Such experiences connect you with the ancient psalmist and countless believers throughout history who have faced similar disdain.

The psalm gives us permission to acknowledge this pain rather than pretending it doesn't hurt. Spiritual maturity doesn't mean developing immunity to contempt but rather learning to process it honestly before God. The psalmist doesn't deny the sting of ridicule but brings it directly to the One whose opinion ultimately matters.

THE SOURCES OF CONTEMPT

"We have endured no end of ridicule from the arrogant, of contempt from the proud."

The psalm identifies the source of this ridicule: "the arrogant" and "the proud." These terms describe not just confident people but those who position themselves above others, who derive identity from perceived superiority. Their contempt doesn't emerge from thoughtful evaluation but from pre-existing arrogance that needs targets to maintain its elevated self-perception.

Throughout history, faith communities have faced contempt from various sources:

- Intellectual elites who dismiss religious belief as unsophisticated or anti-rational
- Political authorities who view faith commitments as competing allegiances threatening their power
- Majority cultures that treat religious minorities as backward or dangerous
- Secular paradigms that relegate faith to private sentiment without public relevance
- Even religious insiders who look down on expressions of faith different from their own

While these sources change across time and cultural contexts, the experience of contempt remains remarkably consistent—the feeling of being looked down upon, dismissed, or treated as inherently inferior because of one's faith commitments.

Understanding contempt's source provides important perspective. When we recognize that ridicule often says more about the mocker than the mocked, we can avoid internalizing false messages about our worth or the validity of our faith. The problem lies not in the believer's devotion but in the critic's pride that needs to elevate itself by diminishing others.

APPLICATION: FINDING DIGNITY AMID DERISION

As we continue our ascent through the Songs of Ascent, Psalm 123:3-4 speaks powerfully to anyone facing opposition or ridicule for their spiritual journey. It offers wisdom for maintaining dignity and worth when others treat faith with contempt.]

The psalm's structure provides our first insight into handling contempt: it begins with upward focus before addressing horizontal opposition. Verses 1-2 establish the foundation—eyes lifted toward God in dependent trust—before verses 3-4 confront the reality of human ridicule. This ordering isn't accidental but instructional. Before facing contempt from others, we must secure our identity in relationship with God.

The positioning of our passage within the larger pilgrim collection also matters. These verses appear early in the journey (the fourth of fifteen Songs of Ascent), suggesting that opposition should be expected rather than surprising. The path toward deeper spiritual experience often triggers resistance, both external and internal. Preparedness for such opposition prevents disillusionment when it inevitably comes.

How do we maintain dignity and worth when facing contempt? The psalm suggests several approaches:

1. Bring contempt directly to God. Rather than simply enduring ridicule or responding in kind, the psalm models bringing the pain of contempt directly to the divine throne. "Have mercy on us, LORD" acknowledges both the hurt and our need for supernatural perspective beyond human opinions.

2. Recognize contempt's commonality. The plural pronouns throughout these verses ("we," "us") remind us that contempt for faith is a shared experience, not an individual targeting. Knowing that others—both contemporaries and those throughout history—have faced similar opposition creates solidarity in suffering.

3. Name the true source. By identifying contempt as coming from "the arrogant" and "the proud," the psalm helps us see ridicule in proper context. The problem often lies not in the validity of our faith but in others' need to elevate themselves through dismissing what matters to us.

4. Balance honesty with hope. The psalm doesn't minimize suffering ("no end of contempt") but places it within the context of dependence on God established in the opening verses. This balance allows us to acknowledge pain without being defined by it, to recognize opposition without losing sight of divine presence.

5. Seek mercy rather than vengeance. Notably, the psalmist asks for mercy rather than for enemies' destruction. Unlike some imprecatory psalms, this prayer focuses on divine relief for the sufferers rather than punishment for the mockers. This orientation preserves our hearts from the corrosive effects of bitterness and retribution.

Contemporary believers facing ridicule for their faith can draw strength from this ancient prayer. Whether enduring subtle dismissal in academic settings, workplace marginalization for ethical convictions, family tensions over religious commitments, or broader cultural contempt for traditional beliefs, the psalm reminds us to lift our eyes above horizontal opposition to the One whose gaze defines our true worth.

This upward orientation doesn't magically remove the sting of contempt. The psalmist doesn't pretend that divine focus immediately erases human pain. But it does provide crucial perspective that prevents contempt from becoming identity-defining. We may be looked down upon by the proud, but we are looked upon with love by the One enthroned in heaven. This divine gaze, not human assessment, ultimately determines our worth and dignity.

As you continue your spiritual journey, expect that meaningful faith will sometimes attract ridicule. Rather than being surprised by opposition, prepare your heart through establishing the upward gaze of dependence described in the psalm's opening verses. When contempt comes, bring it honestly before God, recognize its source in human pride rather than your inadequacy, and remember that you belong to a long tradition of believers who have endured similar scorn while continuing to fix their eyes on the enthroned One.

REFLECTION QUESTIONS

1. The psalm describes "no end of contempt" from others. Have you experienced ridicule or dismissal because of your faith? How did this affect your spiritual journey, and what helped you continue despite opposition?

_____

_____

2. Consider how the psalm shifts from focusing upward (verses 1-2) to addressing horizontal opposition (verses 3-4). How does your relationship with God influence how you process criticism or contempt from others?

_____

_____

3. The contempt described comes specifically from "the arrogant" and "the proud." How does recognizing the source of ridicule in others' pride (rather than your inadequacy) change how you might respond to mockery of your faith?

_____

_____

4. Notice that the psalm uses plural pronouns ("we," "us") throughout. How might connecting with others who face similar opposition strengthen your ability to endure contempt? Who in your life shares your experiences of faith-based ridicule?

_____

_____

5. The psalmist specifically asks for mercy rather than for vengeance against mockers. Where do you find yourself tempted toward bitterness or retribution when your faith is ridiculed? How might focusing on receiving God's mercy change these responses?

_____

_____

6. If you're journeying with others through this devotional, discuss how your community might better support members facing contempt for their faith. What practices or perspectives could help create a sanctuary of dignity when the outside world offers ridicule?

_____

_____

PRAYER FOR TODAY

Merciful Lord,

Today I join my voice with the ancient psalmist and countless believers throughout history who have lifted their eyes to You while enduring contempt. Have mercy on me, LORD, have mercy on me, for I too have faced ridicule for following You in a world that often treats faith with disdain.

I bring before You those specific moments and relationships where I've experienced contempt for my beliefs, values, or practices aligned with Your ways. [Take a moment to silently name these experiences.] Rather than pretending these encounters don't hurt, I acknowledge their sting and ask for Your healing presence in these wounded places.

Help me recognize that contempt often says more about its source than its target. When "the arrogant" and "the proud" look down on faith, remind me that their ridicule springs from their own insecurity rather than my inadequacy. Guard my heart from internalizing false assessments of my worth based on others' dismissal.

Thank You that I don't face this opposition alone. Connect me more deeply with the community of believers—both those present in my life and the great cloud of witnesses throughout history—who have endured similar contempt while keeping their eyes fixed on You. In their companionship, strengthen my resolve to continue the journey despite ridicule.

When contempt tempts me toward bitterness or desires for revenge, redirect my heart toward seeking Your mercy instead. Transform my pain into compassion, remembering that pride damages the proud themselves most deeply. Where appropriate, help me extend to mockers the same mercy I seek from You.

Above all, fix my gaze so firmly on Your face that human opinion—whether approval or contempt—loses its power to define me. Like a servant watching the master's hand, let me become so attuned to Your perspective that the dismissal of others neither crushes my spirit nor diverts my path.

Have mercy on us, LORD, have mercy on us, for we have endured no end of contempt. Yet in Your mercy, we find dignity that no human ridicule can diminish and worth that no contempt can erase.

In the name of Jesus, who endured the ultimate contempt of the cross yet continued in perfect obedience, Amen.

Day 10

Divine Deliverance

If it had not been the LORD who was on our side—let Israel now say—if it had not been the LORD who was on our side when people rose up against us, then they would have swallowed us up alive, when their anger was kindled against us; then the flood would have swept us away, the torrent would have gone over us; then over us would have gone the raging waters. Blessed be the LORD, who has not given us as prey to their teeth! We have escaped like a bird from the snare of the fowlers; the snare is broken, and we have escaped! Our help is in the name of the LORD, who made heaven and earth." — Psalm 124:1-8

HISTORICAL CONTEXT

As our pilgrimage continues through the Songs of Ascent, we encounter in Psalm 124 a powerful communal testimony of divine rescue. This psalm is attributed to David, though it reflects the collective experience of Israel rather than just one individual's story.

The imagery used—floods, torrents, raging waters, predators with teeth, and bird snares— suggests real historical dangers that threatened Israel's existence. Throughout their history, the Israelites faced numerous existential threats: Egyptian slavery, wilderness wanderings, Canaanite opposition, Philistine aggression, and later, Assyrian and Babylonian empires. Any of these historical moments could have been the background for this psalm of thanksgiving.

The psalm was particularly meaningful for pilgrims making their way to Jerusalem. The journey itself was perilous, with natural hazards and the threat of bandits. As travelers joined together on the road to the Holy City, they would recall God's faithfulness not just to them individually but to the entire community throughout their national history. This collective memory strengthened their identity and resolve as they ascended to worship.

For us today, this psalm invites us to participate in both individual and communal remembrance of divine deliverance, acknowledging that our personal stories are woven into God's larger redemptive narrative.

MEDITATION: THE POWER OF COMMUNAL REMEMBRANCE

"If it had not been the LORD who was on our side—let Israel now say—"

Notice how the psalm begins with an invitation to communal testimony. The psalmist doesn't simply declare God's deliverance as a personal truth but calls the entire community to affirm it together: "let Israel now say." There is something profoundly powerful about declaring God's faithfulness in community.

When we share our stories of divine intervention with others, several things happen. First, our own faith is strengthened as we articulate what God has done. Second, those who hear our testimony are encouraged that the same God might work similarly in their lives. Third, a communal identity forms around these shared experiences of grace, creating bonds that transcend superficial connections.

The repetition in verses 1-2 ("If it had not been the LORD who was on our side") serves to emphasize the absolute dependence of the community on divine intervention. This is not a casual acknowledgment but an existential recognition—without God's action, they simply would not have survived.

THE NATURE OF THE DELIVERANCE

The psalm employs three powerful metaphors to describe the threats from which God delivered Israel:

First, we see the imagery of being "swallowed up alive" by enemies whose anger was "kindled" against them (verses 2-3). This suggests not merely opposition but active hostility—enemies intent on complete destruction. The vivid image reminds us that some threats we face are personal and intentional, coming from those who actively seek our harm.

Second, the psalm shifts to natural disasters: "the flood would have swept us away, the torrent would have gone over us; then over us would have gone the raging waters" (verses 4-5). Water, especially flooding water in the arid Middle East, represented chaotic, overwhelming force that no human could control. These verses acknowledge that sometimes our greatest threats are impersonal circumstances that threaten to overwhelm us by their sheer magnitude.

Third, the psalmist employs hunting imagery: "prey to their teeth" and "a bird from the snare of the fowlers" (verses 6-7). This represents calculated threats—traps set with patience and planning. Some dangers in our lives come not as sudden attacks or overwhelming circumstances but as subtle entanglements that gradually restrict our freedom until we are caught.

What's remarkable is that the psalm declares God's deliverance from all these types of threats—from active enemies, overwhelming circumstances, and subtle entrapments. No danger lies outside God's saving power.

THE RESPONSE TO DELIVERANCE

The appropriate response to such comprehensive deliverance is twofold:

First, blessing: "Blessed be the LORD" (verse 6). The Hebrew word for "blessed" (דּוּרְבָ, baruch) carries the sense of acknowledging worth and expressing gratitude. It recognizes that God deserves praise not just for what He does but for who He is. In blessing God, we realign our perspective, recognizing that even our ability to acknowledge God's goodness is itself a gift. Second, declaration of dependence: "Our help is in the name of the LORD, who made heaven and earth" (verse 8). This final verse serves as both conclusion and foundation. Having recounted specific deliverances, the psalm returns to the fundamental truth that grounds all others—our help comes from the Creator of heaven and earth. The One who established the cosmos is the same One who watches over us with personal care.

This concluding statement links divine transcendence (creating heaven and earth) with divine immanence (being "on our side"). The vastness of God's power does not make Him distant from our concerns but rather makes His intimate involvement in our lives all the more remarkable.

APPLICATION: SEEING OUR STORIES THROUGH THE LENS OF DIVINE DELIVERANCE

As we continue our pilgrimage, Psalm 124 invites us to reexamine our personal histories—to look back and identify the moments when, "If it had not been the LORD who was on our side," our stories would have ended differently. This practice of spiritual remembrance does not deny human agency or natural causality but perceives God's presence working within and through these realities.

Consider the various threats mentioned in the psalm and how they might manifest in your own experience:

Have there been times when others rose up against you—when relationships turned hostile, when you faced opposition at work, when your integrity or faith was challenged? How did God preserve you through these conflicts? Have you faced overwhelming circumstances—financial crises, health emergencies, grief, or periods of profound uncertainty—that threatened to sweep you away? How did God keep your head above the raging waters?

What about subtle entrapments—patterns of thinking or behavior, unhealthy relationships, or cultural pressures that threatened to snare you? How has God broken these snares and set you free?

The practice of remembering God's deliverances serves multiple purposes. It cultivates gratitude, countering our tendency toward entitlement. It builds faith for present challenges, reminding us that the God who delivered in the past remains on our side today. And it provides testimony that can strengthen others who face similar threats.

As you reflect today, consider not only your own stories of divine deliverance but also the larger story of God's faithfulness to His people throughout history. Your personal experiences are threads in this grand tapestry of redemption, and recognizing this connection can provide both perspective and purpose in your current circumstances.

Like the ancient pilgrims, we journey not alone but in community, strengthened by shared testimonies of God's faithfulness. Today, let your awareness of divine deliverance become a song of gratitude as you continue your ascent.

REFLECTION QUESTIONS

1. What specific moment in your life prompts you to say, "If it had not been the LORD who was on my side…" What might have happened without divine intervention?

_____

_____

2. The psalm uses vivid imagery of floods, predators, and snares. Which of these metaphors best describes the most significant threat you've faced? How does naming the nature of your threat help you better appreciate God's specific deliverance?

_____

_____

3. Verse 1 emphasizes communal remembrance: "let Israel now say." How has hearing others' testimonies of God's deliverance strengthened your own faith? Whose story might benefit from hearing yours?

_____

_____

4. The psalm concludes by connecting God's role as Creator with His role as Deliverer. How does recognizing God's cosmic power affect your trust in His care for your personal circumstances?

_____

_____

5. What "snares" in your current life might need divine breaking? Where do you feel entangled or trapped, and how might remembering past deliverances give you hope for freedom?

_____

_____

6. The pilgrims sang this psalm while physically journeying toward Jerusalem. How does remembering God's past deliverances equip you for the journey ahead? What specific challenge are you facing that needs the perspective this psalm provides?

_____

_____

PRAYER FOR TODAY

Creator and Deliverer,

Today I pause on this journey to remember Your faithfulness. If it had not been You who was on my side, I would not be here. The waters would have overwhelmed me, the snares would have held me, the enemies would have prevailed.

Thank You for specific deliverances in my life: [pause to name them]. When I faced opposition that threatened to swallow me alive, You stood with me. When circumstances rose like flood waters, You kept me from drowning. When subtle traps were set for my feet, You broke the snare and set me free.

Forgive me for the times I've attributed these deliverances to luck, coincidence, or my own strength. Open my eyes to see Your hand at work even in circumstances where I missed Your presence at the time.

Lord, I join my voice with the community of faith throughout history who declare: "Our help is in the name of the LORD, who made heaven and earth." Help me to live today in the confidence that the same power that created galaxies is actively engaged in my life.

For those in my community currently facing overwhelming opposition, raging waters, or hidden snares, be their Deliverer as You have been mine. Use my testimony to strengthen their faith, and when my own faith falters, remind me of these moments of divine intervention.

As I continue this pilgrimage, let gratitude for past deliverances fuel hope for the journey ahead. May my life become a living testimony that the Lord is indeed on our side.

In the name of Jesus Christ, our ultimate Deliverer, Amen.

PART II: THE WILDERNESS (Days 11-20)

Day 11

Unshakable Trust

"Those who trust in the LORD are like Mount Zion, which cannot be moved, but abides forever. As the mountains surround Jerusalem, so the LORD surrounds his people, from this time forth and forevermore." — *Psalm 125:1-2*

HISTORICAL CONTEXT

As our pilgrimage through the Songs of Ascent continues, we encounter in Psalm 125 a powerful metaphor drawn from the physical geography of Jerusalem itself. For the ancient pilgrims making their way to the Holy City, this psalm would have taken on vivid meaning as they approached Jerusalem and witnessed its unique topography.

Jerusalem sits on a plateau surrounded by hills and mountains. To the east lies the Mount of Olives, to the south is the Hill of Evil Counsel, to the west rise the hills of Judah, and to the north stands Mount Scopus. This geographic reality created not only natural protection for the city but also a striking visual metaphor that the psalmist employs to describe God's relationship with His people.

For pilgrims who had traveled great distances—crossing valleys, climbing ridges, and navigating difficult terrain—the sight of Jerusalem nestled among protective mountains would have been both physically reassuring and spiritually significant. The city's geographical stability amid the surrounding hills became a perfect picture of the spiritual stability available to those who place their trust in the Lord.

This psalm likely dates from the post-exilic period, when Israel had experienced the traumatic destruction of Jerusalem and the temple, followed by exile in Babylon and eventual return to rebuild. The imagery of unmovable mountains and divine protection would have resonated deeply with a community seeking to reestablish their identity and security after profound displacement and loss.

MEDITATION: THE NATURE OF UNSHAKABLE TRUST

"Those who trust in the LORD are like Mount Zion, which cannot be moved, but abides forever."

The psalm begins with a striking comparison between believers and Mount Zion itself. The Hebrew word for "trust" (חָטַב, batach) conveys not casual optimism but complete reliance—placing the full weight of one's being upon something. This trust is not mere intellectual assent but whole-life commitment.

Notice that the psalmist doesn't say that those who trust in the Lord receive stability as a reward but that they themselves become like Mount Zion—immovable and enduring. Trust transforms the very nature of the believer, imparting qualities that echo the character of God Himself: permanence, steadfastness, reliability.

The image of Mount Zion "which cannot be moved" would have been particularly meaningful in an ancient Near Eastern context where earthquakes were common and buildings could be destroyed in moments. In a world of physical instability, the mountains represented the most permanent features of the landscape. By comparing believers to Mount Zion, the psalmist is making an extraordinary claim about the spiritual stability available through relationship with God.

This stability is not portrayed as temporary or contingent but as eternal—Zion "abides forever." The Hebrew word for "forever" (בָלֹעֵל, le'olam) literally means "for the age" or "for eternity." The psalmist is describing a quality of steadfastness that transcends circumstantial changes and continues beyond our limited human timeframe.

THE SURROUNDING PRESENCE

"As the mountains surround Jerusalem, so the LORD surrounds his people, from this time forth and forevermore."

In the second verse, the metaphor shifts from comparing believers to Mount Zion to comparing God Himself to the mountains surrounding Jerusalem. This creates a beautiful reciprocal image:

those who trust in the Lord become like the central mountain, while the Lord Himself becomes like the encircling mountains—creating a picture of mutual indwelling and protection.

The Hebrew word for "surround" (בִיבָס, sabib) suggests encirclement on all sides. There is no direction from which Jerusalem is not protected by mountains, and similarly, there is no dimension of the believer's life that exists outside of God's encompassing presence. This total surround speaks to the comprehensiveness of divine protection.

Note that the psalmist specifies the timeframe of this divine surrounding: "from this time forth and forevermore." God's protective presence is not just a historical reality but a present and eternal one. It begins now—"from this time forth"—regardless of the believer's past experiences or failures, and continues without interruption into eternity—"forevermore."

This promise would have been particularly poignant for post-exilic pilgrims who had witnessed the apparent failure of divine protection when Jerusalem fell to the Babylonians. The psalm reasserts God's protecting presence despite historical evidence that might suggest otherwise, calling believers to a trust that transcends circumstantial interpretation.

APPLICATION: CULTIVATING UNSHAKABLE TRUST

In our own spiritual journey, this psalm invites us to examine the nature and object of our trust. We often place our confidence in things far less stable than mountains—financial security, professional achievements, relationships, health, political systems, or our own capabilities. All of these, while valuable, are subject to change and failure. They are more like sand than stone, shifting under pressure rather than standing firm.

True stability comes not from favorable circumstances but from trust placed in the unchanging character of God. This trust is not naive optimism that denies difficulty but profound confidence that acknowledges challenges while remaining anchored to eternal realities.

How do we cultivate such unshakable trust? Like most spiritual qualities, it develops gradually through practice and experience:

First, we must honestly assess where our trust actually lies. Our calendars, bank statements, and anxiety patterns often reveal the true objects of our confidence more accurately than our stated beliefs. Where do you turn first in times of crisis? Whose approval do you seek most earnestly? What loss would devastate you most completely? Your answers reveal what mountains you're trusting to support and surround you.

Second, we must intentionally remember God's faithfulness, both in Scripture and in our own experience. Trust grows through relationship, and relationship deepens through shared history. The practice of regularly recounting specific instances of God's provision, protection, and presence builds our capacity to trust Him with current and future challenges.

Third, we must reinterpret our circumstances through the lens of God's encompassing presence. The mountains surrounding Jerusalem didn't prevent all attacks or difficulties, but they provided context for interpreting those experiences. Similarly, God's surrounding presence doesn't eliminate life's challenges but reframes them within the larger reality of divine purpose and protection.

Finally, we must practice community trust through the church. The psalmist's imagery applies not just to individual believers but to God's people collectively—"the LORD surrounds his people." Our individual trust is strengthened when we witness others standing firm amid difficulties and when we share our own stories of God's faithfulness within community.

As you continue your pilgrimage today, consider the areas where trust comes easily for you and where it proves more difficult. Invite God to transform you into Mount Zion—unmovable, abiding, characterized by steadfast confidence in His goodness regardless of circumstances. And take comfort in the mountains of His presence that surround you on every side, not just in moments of devotional clarity but in every dimension of your daily experience.

Like the ancient pilgrims who looked up at Jerusalem's surrounding mountains and saw in them a picture of divine protection, may you develop eyes to see the evidence of God's encompassing presence in your own life. The same Lord who established the mountains continues to surround His people—including you—from this time forth and forevermore.

REFLECTION QUESTIONS

1. The psalm compares those who trust in the Lord to Mount Zion, "which cannot be moved." What circumstances or challenges most easily shake your trust in God? What would it look like for you to remain unmoved in those situations?

2. Jerusalem is surrounded by mountains on all sides. In what areas of your life do you most clearly sense God's surrounding presence? Where do you struggle to recognize His encompassing protection?

_____

_____

3. Our trust often reveals itself in times of crisis. Recall a recent difficult situation—where did you turn first for help or comfort? What does this reveal about where your deepest trust lies?

_____

_____

4. The phrase "from this time forth and forevermore" suggests that God's surrounding presence is both immediate and eternal. How might your daily decisions change if you lived with constant awareness of being divinely surrounded?

_____

_____

5. Mountains in Scripture often represent permanence and stability. What "mountains" have you trusted that proved less stable than you expected? How has this affected your willingness to place ultimate trust in God?

_____

_____

6. This psalm speaks of God surrounding "his people" collectively, not just individuals. How has being part of a faith community strengthened your trust in God? How might you contribute to building unshakable trust within your community?

_____

_____

PRAYER FOR TODAY

Unchanging God,

Today I stand in awe of Your steadfast presence. Like the mountains that have surrounded Jerusalem for millennia, You encircle my life with Your protection, wisdom, and love. Forgive me for the times I've placed my trust in lesser things—temporary securities that shift and change with circumstance.

Transform me, Lord, into Mount Zion—unmovable, firmly established, characterized by unwavering trust in Your goodness. When doubts arise like tremors beneath my feet, anchor me to the bedrock of Your character and promises. When fears threaten to overwhelm me, remind me of Your encompassing presence on every side.

I confess the specific areas where my trust wavers: [pause to name them]. Pour Your strength into these places of weakness. Help me recognize when I'm building my security on sand rather than stone, and guide me back to the solid foundation of relationship with You.

Thank You that Your surrounding presence begins now—"from this time forth"—regardless of my past failures or current struggles. And thank You that it continues "forevermore," beyond my limited perspective and into eternity. Today, I choose to live in the security of being divinely encompassed.

For those in my community whose trust has been shaken by disappointment, tragedy, or unanswered questions, be their surrounding mountains. Use me as a reminder of Your faithfulness when others struggle to see it. And when my own vision grows dim, send others to help me recognize the mountains of Your presence that haven't moved, even when I have.

As I continue this pilgrimage, may each step be taken in growing confidence that the God who established the mountains holds me secure in the hollow of His hand.

In the name of Jesus, my Rock and my Redeemer, Amen.

Day 12

Standing Against Evil

"For the scepter of wickedness shall not rest on the land allotted to the righteous, lest the righteous stretch out their hands to do wrong. Do good, O LORD, to those who are good, and to those who are upright in their hearts! But those who turn aside to their crooked ways the LORD will lead away with evildoers! Peace be upon Israel!" — Psalm 125:3-5

HISTORICAL CONTEXT

As we continue our pilgrimage through the Songs of Ascent, we move from the comforting imagery of God's protective presence in the first two verses of Psalm 125 to the sobering reality of moral struggle in verses 3-5. This shift reflects the full experience of God's people throughout history—divine protection does not exempt believers from confronting evil, both within and around them.

The historical setting for this psalm is likely the post-exilic period when the returned Jewish community faced both external opposition and internal corruption. After returning from Babylonian exile, the people discovered that rebuilding their society involved more than reconstructing the temple and city walls—it required moral reconstruction as well. Leaders like Ezra and Nehemiah confronted issues of intermarriage with idol-worshipping nations, economic exploitation of the poor, and compromise with surrounding cultures.

In this context, the psalmist's concern about "the scepter of wickedness" resting on "the land allotted to the righteous" reflects real political and social pressures. The returned exiles lived under Persian authority and later under Greek rule. These foreign powers (symbolized by the "scepter") often appointed local officials who abused their positions, creating systems that tempted even the righteous to compromise their integrity to survive.

For pilgrims making their way to Jerusalem, this psalm reminded them that their journey was not merely geographical but moral—a commitment to stand against evil and maintain integrity even when surrounded by corrupt systems. As they entered the holy city, they were called to remember that true worship included both trust in God's protection (verses 1-2) and commitment to righteousness in community (verses 3-5).

MEDITATION: THE DANGER OF UNCHECKED WICKEDNESS

"For the scepter of wickedness shall not rest on the land allotted to the righteous, lest the righteous stretch out their hands to do wrong."

The psalmist begins with a profound insight into human moral psychology—prolonged exposure to corrupt systems eventually corrupts even the righteous. The "scepter" symbolizes authority and governance. When that authority becomes characterized by wickedness, its influence gradually reshapes the moral landscape, normalizing what should be unacceptable.

The danger identified here is not primarily external oppression but internal compromise. The deepest threat is not that the righteous will suffer under wicked rule (though they certainly might), but that they will "stretch out their hands to do wrong"—that they will begin to participate in the very systems they should oppose.

This insight remains startlingly relevant. We often recognize external threats while remaining blind to the subtle ways corrupt systems reshape our own moral thinking and behavior. We may begin with clear convictions about justice and righteousness, only to find ourselves gradually accommodating to patterns we once recognized as wrong. The path to compromise is rarely dramatic; it happens through small adjustments, practical concessions, and the slow erosion of moral clarity.

The psalmist's prayer—that the scepter of wickedness "shall not rest" on the righteous—acknowledges both divine sovereignty and human responsibility. It recognizes that God will not permit wickedness to have unlimited dominion while also calling believers to remain vigilant against its influence.

THE MORAL ARCHITECTURE OF COMMUNITY

"Do good, O LORD, to those who are good, and to those who are upright in their hearts!"

This verse establishes a foundational principle for community life—alignment between character and consequence. The psalmist prays for a moral order where goodness leads to blessing and uprightness to prosperity. This is not a simplistic prosperity gospel promising material wealth to the virtuous, but rather a recognition that communities thrive when virtue is rewarded and integrity is valued.

Notice the distinction between external behavior ("those who are good") and internal character ("those who are upright in their hearts"). The psalmist recognizes that true righteousness begins with heart orientation before manifesting in visible actions. Moral communities require both—behaviors that contribute to common flourishing and heart commitments that sustain those behaviors even when they become costly.

In praying for God to "do good" to the righteous, the psalmist is not merely seeking personal blessing but advocating for a community where moral choices lead to positive outcomes. This creates an environment where righteousness becomes sustainable rather than leading to exploitation or martyrdom.

THE CONSEQUENCES OF MORAL COMPROMISE

"But those who turn aside to their crooked ways the LORD will lead away with evildoers!"

The stark language of this verse may make modern readers uncomfortable, but it reflects the psalmist's understanding that moral choices have consequences that cannot be evaded indefinitely. The image of being "led away" evokes both the historical experience of exile and the personal experience of moral deterioration.

The phrase "turn aside to their crooked ways" suggests deliberate deviation from a known path of righteousness. The Hebrew word for "crooked" (תוֹלְקַלְקָע, 'aqalqallot) literally means "twisting" or "winding," conveying the idea of moral complexity that obscures clear ethical sight. Crooked paths make it difficult to see far ahead or to discern where seemingly small deviations might ultimately lead.

Significantly, the psalmist doesn't distinguish between those who initiate evil and those who merely "turn aside" to join it. Both are ultimately "led away" together, suggesting that moral compromise eventually leads to the same destination as outright wickedness, even if the path appears less direct.

THE VISION OF PEACE

"Peace be upon Israel!"

The psalm concludes with this blessing that encompasses the community's deepest aspiration. The Hebrew word for "peace" (םֹולְשׁ, shalom) signifies not merely the absence of conflict but the presence of wholeness, harmony, and flourishing. This comprehensive well-being can only exist where justice prevails and where moral integrity shapes both individual lives and communal structures.

By placing this blessing at the conclusion, the psalmist reminds us that standing against evil is not an end in itself but a means to creating communities characterized by shalom. Resistance to wickedness is ultimately in service of a positive vision—a society where peace (in its fullest sense) becomes the defining reality.

APPLICATION: STANDING AGAINST EVIL TODAY

As we continue our spiritual pilgrimage, this portion of Psalm 125 challenges us to examine how we respond to the "scepters of wickedness" in our own context. These may take various forms—cultural pressures that normalize greed or exploitation, institutional systems that perpetuate injustice, or personal temptations that compromise our integrity.

Standing against evil requires both discernment and courage. Discernment to recognize corrupting influences that others might accept as normal, and courage to maintain integrity even when compromise seems expedient or universal.

This stand begins with honest self-examination. Where have we begun to "stretch out our hands to do wrong" by participating in systems we know to be unjust? Where have we turned aside to "crooked ways" through moral reasoning that justifies what our conscience once clearly recognized as wrong? The psalmist calls us back to moral clarity and straight paths.

Beyond personal integrity, this psalm calls us to consider our role in shaping communities that reward goodness rather than exploitation. This may involve advocating for just policies, creating organizational cultures that value integrity, or simply being voices that name injustice rather than normalizing it. When we pray for God to "do good to those who are good," we commit ourselves to being part of the answer to that prayer by creating structures where righteousness leads to flourishing rather than disadvantage.

Finally, this psalm reminds us that standing against evil is fundamentally an act of hope. When we resist corruption and maintain integrity despite pressure to compromise, we express confidence in God's ultimate establishment of justice. Our stand is not merely protest against what is wrong but testimony to what we believe will ultimately prevail—a community characterized by the comprehensive shalom with which the psalm concludes.

Today, as you continue your journey, consider where God may be calling you to stand against evil—not in self-righteous judgment of others but in humble commitment to integrity and justice that reflects His character. Like the ancient pilgrims who sang this psalm on their way to Jerusalem, may your worship be expressed not just in songs and prayers but in a life that resists the scepter of wickedness and contributes to communities of righteousness and peace.

REFLECTION QUESTIONS

1. The psalm warns that "the scepter of wickedness" can eventually lead even the righteous to "stretch out their hands to do wrong." What cultural influences or systemic pressures most threaten your moral clarity and integrity today?

_____

_____

2. Consider a time when you compromised your values because "everyone was doing it" or because standing firm seemed too costly. What might have helped you maintain integrity in that situation?

_____

_____

3. The psalmist prays for God to "do good to those who are good." Where do you see a disconnect between goodness and positive outcomes in your context? How might you help create systems where integrity is rewarded rather than exploited?

_____

_____

4. Verse 5 refers to those who "turn aside to their crooked ways." What are some seemingly minor moral compromises that could potentially lead you down a path you would not want to follow to its conclusion?

_____

_____

5. The psalm concludes with "Peace be upon Israel!" How might your stand against specific forms of evil contribute to greater shalom (wholeness, harmony, flourishing) in your family, workplace, or community?

_____

_____

6. This psalm suggests that righteousness shapes community. Think about a community you belong to—how has the integrity (or lack thereof) of its members affected the health and character of the whole group?

PRAYER FOR TODAY

Righteous God,

In a world where evil often seems to hold the scepter of power, I thank You for the assurance that wickedness will not have the final word. Thank You for Your commitment to justice and for inviting me to participate in Your work of creating communities characterized by righteousness and peace.

Examine my heart today, Lord. Show me where I have begun to stretch out my hands to do wrong—where I have accommodated myself to systems or practices that contradict Your character. Forgive me for the times I have turned aside to crooked paths because they seemed easier or more advantageous. Restore my moral clarity and strengthen my commitment to integrity, even when it proves costly.

I pray for discernment to recognize the subtle ways wickedness seeks influence in my life and community. Help me distinguish between compromise that enables greater good and compromise that simply normalizes wrong. Give me courage to stand firm where standing is required, wisdom to work for change where change is possible, and grace toward others who may see these matters differently.

Do good, O Lord, to those who are good. Create communities—in my workplace, neighborhood, church, and family—where righteousness leads to flourishing and where integrity is valued rather than exploited. Use me as an instrument of this transformation, not through self-righteous judgment but through humble commitment to Your ways.

For those in positions of authority—in government, business, education, and religious institutions—I pray for hearts upright before You. May they wield their influence not as scepters of wickedness but as instruments of justice and catalysts for shalom.

And as I continue this pilgrimage, keep my feet on the straight path that leads to life. When others turn aside, give me conviction to remain faithful. When I stumble, restore me quickly through Your grace. May my life contribute, however modestly, to that final vision with which this psalm concludes: "Peace be upon Israel!"—comprehensive well-being for all Your people.

In the name of Jesus Christ, who perfectly embodied righteousness in a corrupt world, Amen.

Day 13

Streams in the Desert

"When the LORD restored the fortunes of Zion, we were like those who dream. Then our mouth was filled with laughter, and our tongue with shouts of joy; then they said among the nations, 'The LORD has done great things for them.' The LORD has done great things for us; we are glad." — *Psalm 126:1-3*

HISTORICAL CONTEXT

As our pilgrimage through the Songs of Ascent continues, we encounter in Psalm 126 one of the most poignant expressions of restoration in Scripture. This psalm almost certainly refers to Israel's return from Babylonian exile—a pivotal moment in their national history when what seemed impossible suddenly became reality.

In 586 BC, Jerusalem fell to the Babylonian empire. The temple was destroyed, the city walls demolished, and many of the people forcibly relocated to Babylon. For seventy years, the exiles lived in a foreign land, their hopes of return growing dimmer with each passing decade. Prophets like Jeremiah had foretold their eventual restoration, but as generations passed, such promises may have seemed increasingly remote.

Then, in 538 BC, the Persian king Cyrus conquered Babylon and issued a decree allowing the Jewish exiles to return home and rebuild their temple. This unexpected reversal of fortune was so extraordinary that the first returnees described themselves as people caught in a dream—unable to fully process the reality of their deliverance.

For the pilgrims singing this psalm generations later, the memory of that restoration remained foundational to their identity. As they journeyed toward Jerusalem, they recalled their ancestors' experience of captivity and release, finding in that story both gratitude for past deliverances and hope for present challenges.

The psalm's placement among the Songs of Ascent is significant. It comes after psalms that speak of trusting God amid threat (Psalms 123-125) and before a psalm about building with God (Psalm 127). This suggests that remembering God's past restorations strengthens us to face present difficulties and empowers us to participate in future rebuilding.

MEDITATION: THE DREAMLIKE QUALITY OF DIVINE RESTORATION

"When the LORD restored the fortunes of Zion, we were like those who dream."

The Hebrew phrase translated "restored the fortunes" (שׁוּב שְׁבוּת, shuv shevut) literally means "brought back the captivity" or "returned the returning ones." This wordplay emphasizes both the physical return from exile and the spiritual restoration that accompanied it. God not only brought His people back geographically but restored their identity, purpose, and relationship with Him.

The comparison to dreamers captures the surreal quality of unexpected deliverance. Dreams exist in that liminal space between imagination and reality, where the impossible becomes momentarily possible. When captives suddenly find themselves free, when the long-desired but seemingly unattainable suddenly materializes, the mind struggles to process this new reality. There's a suspended moment where joy feels almost disorienting because it contrasts so sharply with what came before.

This dreamlike state isn't skepticism or doubt but rather the mind and heart adjusting to a new reality too wonderful to immediately comprehend. It's the experience of Sarah who laughed in disbelief when told she would bear a child in her old age, or the disciples who "disbelieved for joy" (Luke 24:41) when they saw the resurrected Jesus. Some miracles require time to fully absorb because they so radically redefine what we believed possible.

Consider your own experiences of unexpected restoration. Perhaps a relationship you thought permanently broken was surprisingly healed. Maybe a dream you had abandoned suddenly became viable again. Or perhaps you experienced spiritual renewal after a season of alienation from God. These moments of "dreaming while awake" are sacred spaces where we encounter the God who specializes in doing "immeasurably more than all we ask or imagine" (Ephesians 3:20).

THE VISIBLE MANIFESTATIONS OF RESTORATION

"Then our mouth was filled with laughter, and our tongue with shouts of joy..."

Profound restoration produces visible effects. The psalmist describes two specific manifestations: laughter and shouts of joy. Both expressions are spontaneous, unfiltered, and physically expressive.

This isn't polite appreciation but overwhelming gratitude that must find bodily expression.

The Hebrew word for "filled" (אָלְמ, male) suggests completeness or overflowing. This isn't a quiet chuckle but consuming laughter that fills the mouth and overflows in shouted joy. Divine restoration doesn't produce measured responses but overwhelming expressions that sometimes defy social conventions or personal comfort zones.

This visible joy serves an important purpose beyond personal expression. It becomes testimony. The text continues: "then they said among the nations, 'The LORD has done great things for them.'" Restoration witnessed becomes restoration proclaimed, not merely through formal testimony but through the unmistakable evidence of transformed lives. The nations (םיוג, goyim)—those outside the community of faith—observe and acknowledge that something extraordinary has happened, something that can only be attributed to divine action.

This dynamic remains true today. When God brings unexpected restoration—whether personal, communal, or societal—the resulting joy becomes a powerful witness. A marriage healed beyond reasonable expectation. A community revitalized after devastating loss. An addiction broken when all treatment had failed. These restorations, and our visible responses to them, communicate God's character and power more eloquently than any theological argument could.

FROM OBSERVATION TO CONFESSION

"The LORD has done great things for us; we are glad."

Notice the progression in these verses: what begins as the observation of outsiders ("they said among the nations, 'The LORD has done great things for them'") becomes the personal confession of the community ("The LORD has done great things for us; we are glad"). External testimony becomes internal acknowledgment. What others observe about God's work among us, we must personally affirm and embrace
.

The Hebrew word for "glad" (חָמְשׂ, sameach) expresses a settled state of joy rather than merely the initial outburst of emotion. While restoration may begin with overwhelming, dreamlike joy, it matures into steady gladness—a continuing recognition of divine goodness that sustains us long after the initial euphoria has passed.

This progression from others' observation to personal confession reminds us that lasting restoration requires our participation. We must own the story of what God has done, integrating divine intervention into our understanding of ourselves and our community. When we declare, "The LORD has done great things for us," we both acknowledge God's action and accept our identity as recipients of His grace.

APPLICATION: RECOGNIZING STREAMS IN OUR DESERTS

As we continue our pilgrimage today, Psalm 126:1-3 invites us to look for the "streams in the desert" that God has placed in our own lives—those unexpected moments of joy and restoration that come in difficult seasons. Like the returning exiles, we may initially struggle to fully perceive or believe these gifts, seeing them as "dreams" rather than reality. Yet acknowledging and celebrating these moments of grace strengthens us for the journey ahead.

Begin by reflecting on your own "captivities"—not just external constraints but internal bondages. Where do you feel stuck, limited, or held captive? Perhaps you're constrained by fear, resentment, unhealthy relationships, or destructive patterns of thinking. Maybe circumstances beyond your control—health challenges, financial limitations, or systemic injustices—have created a sense of exile from the life you believe God intends for you.

Now consider where you've already experienced unexpected restoration. The stream in your desert might be a small joy that arrived in a dark time—a friendship that sustained you, a creative outlet that provided expression, or a moment of clarity that offered direction. Or it might be a more dramatic deliverance—freedom from addiction, healing from trauma, or reconciliation of a broken relationship. Whatever its form, pause to recognize and name this restoration.

Allow yourself to fully experience the emotions that accompany remembering God's restorative work. The psalmist doesn't describe intellectualizing God's goodness but physically expressing it through laughter and shouts. While your expression might take different forms, genuine gratitude engages both mind and body. Consider how you might physically express thanksgiving for specific restorations—perhaps through song, dance, art, tears, or simply sharing your story with others.

Finally, let the memory of past restoration shape your expectations for present challenges. The God who brought Israel back from exile, who filled their mouths with laughter when all seemed lost, remains active in your life today. Your current desert may not disappear immediately, but the streams God provides along the way remind you that captivity will not have the final word.

Like the ancient pilgrims who sang this psalm as they journeyed toward Jerusalem, we travel toward our ultimate restoration with both memories of God's faithfulness behind us and promises of His continuing work before us. Today, may you recognize the streams in your desert—those gracious provisions that sustain you in difficult seasons and point toward the complete restoration that awaits.

REFLECTION QUESTIONS

1. The psalmist compares divine restoration to dreaming—a state where the mind struggles to process unexpected joy. When have you experienced something so good that it seemed dreamlike or unreal? How did that experience shape your understanding of God?

_____

_____

2. Verse 2 describes visible manifestations of joy—laughter and shouts. How comfortable are you with expressing gratitude and joy physically? What might be preventing you from fuller expression of thanksgiving for God's work in your life?

_____

_____

3. The nations observed Israel's restoration and acknowledged God's work before the Israelites themselves declared it. Has someone else ever recognized God's restorative work in your life before you fully acknowledged it yourself? What did they see that you didn't initially perceive?

_____

_____

4. The psalmist moves from "the LORD has done great things for them" (others' observation) to "the LORD has done great things for us" (personal confession). Which statement more closely reflects your current perspective on God's work? What would help you move toward greater personal ownership of God's restorative acts?

_____

_____

5. This psalm celebrates the restoration of a community, not just individuals. How have you experienced God's restoration within a community context—family, church, or other group? How might communal restoration differ from individual healing?

_____

_____

6. What "captivity" in your life most needs divine restoration right now? What would it look like to hold both honest acknowledgment of this captivity and hopeful expectation of God's restorative work?

_____

_____

PRAYER FOR TODAY

Creator of Streams in the Desert,

Today I come before You with the words of the psalmist echoing in my heart: "The LORD has done great things for us; we are glad." Thank You for the moments of unexpected joy and restoration You have already placed along my journey—those times when, like the returning exiles, I found myself living a dream I had almost stopped believing could come true.

I remember specific streams You have provided in my desert places: [pause to name them]. For each of these restorations, whether dramatic or subtle, I offer my gratitude. Forgive me for the times I've failed to recognize Your hand at work, or when I've received Your gifts without proper acknowledgment. Open my eyes to see the breadth and depth of Your restorative work in my life.

Lord, I confess the areas where I still feel captive—circumstances, relationships, or internal struggles that seem to hold me in exile from the life You intend: [pause to name them]. For these situations that remain unresolved, I ask not just for deliverance but for the streams that sustain me in the desert—those graces that make captivity bearable while I await complete restoration.

Fill my mouth with laughter and my tongue with shouts of joy for what You have done and what You will yet do. Help me to express gratitude in ways that honor the magnitude of Your gifts. May my visible joy become testimony that causes others to recognize Your work, just as the nations observed Israel's restoration and acknowledged Your power.

For those journeying alongside me who remain in various captivities—those struggling with illness, grief, injustice, or internal bondage—provide streams in their deserts today. Use me, if You will, as a channel of that refreshment. And help us as a community to celebrate each other's restorations, knowing that each dream fulfilled points toward the ultimate restoration when all creation will be made new.

As I continue this pilgrimage, keep me ever mindful that the same God who restored the fortunes of Zion continues to work unexpected deliverances today. Give me eyes to see the streams in the desert, ears to hear the laughter of the restored, and a heart that dares to dream of what You might yet do.

In the name of Jesus Christ, through whom all restoration flows, Amen.

Day 14

Sowing Tears, Reaping Joy

"Restore our fortunes, O LORD, like streams in the Negeb! Those who sow in tears shall reap with shouts of joy! He who goes out weeping, bearing the seed for sowing, shall come home with shouts of joy, bringing his sheaves with him." — Psalm 126:4-6

HISTORICAL CONTEXT

As we continue our pilgrimage through the Songs of Ascent, we now encounter the second half of Psalm 126, which shifts from celebrating past restoration to petitioning for present renewal. This movement from remembrance to request reflects the lived reality of faith—we draw on God's past faithfulness to fuel hope for current challenges.

The historical setting remains the post-exilic period, when Jewish exiles had returned from Babylon to rebuild Jerusalem. While the first three verses celebrated the initial return as a dream-like experience of joy, these final verses acknowledge that complete restoration remained unfinished. The returnees faced significant hardships: opposition from neighboring peoples, economic struggles, disappointing harvests, and the enormous task of rebuilding both physical structures and communal identity.

The agricultural metaphor that dominates these verses would have resonated deeply with the original audience. The Negeb (or Negev) mentioned in verse 4 is the arid southern region of Israel, characterized by dry streambeds (wadis) that remain empty most of the year. However, during the rainy season, these channels can suddenly fill with rushing water, bringing dramatic transformation to the parched landscape. This vivid image of desert streams represents the kind of dramatic reversal the community seeks—abundant life surging into desolate circumstances.

For the pilgrims singing this psalm as they journeyed to Jerusalem for festivals, these verses connected their individual struggles to both communal experience and agricultural rhythms. Their tears and toil were not meaningless but part of a larger pattern of sowing and reaping that promised eventual harvest. The journey to Jerusalem itself embodied this truth—the difficulty of the pilgrimage would culminate in the joy of arrival and celebration.

MEDITATION: THE PARADOX OF PAINFUL SOWING

"Those who sow in tears shall reap with shouts of joy!"

This verse establishes one of Scripture's most profound spiritual principles—the paradoxical relationship between suffering and joy, between sacrifice and reward. The Hebrew syntax emphasizes the certainty of this relationship through parallel statements that progress from sowing to reaping, from tears to joy.

The image of sowing in tears speaks to the reality that meaningful investment often involves sacrifice. For the returned exiles, this included the physical labor of rebuilding with limited resources, the emotional toll of starting over, and the spiritual discipline of reestablishing covenant faithfulness. For farmers in ancient Israel, sowing literally meant taking precious grain that could immediately feed their hungry families and instead burying it in the ground, trusting the seemingly wasteful act would eventually yield greater provision.

This agricultural metaphor illuminates several spiritual truths. First, there is an intrinsic connection between what we sow and what we reap—the harvest corresponds to the seed. Second, a significant time gap typically exists between sowing and reaping—the farmer must wait through seasons of dormancy before seeing results. Third, the quantity harvested vastly exceeds what was sown—a single seed can produce thirty, sixty, or a hundredfold return.

Most powerfully, this metaphor reveals how tears themselves become productive. The Hebrew doesn't merely say that those who sow while crying will later reap with joy; it suggests that the tears themselves are part of what is sown. Our suffering, our sacrifice, our loss—these are not merely contexts for sowing but can themselves become seeds that, when surrendered to God, produce unanticipated harvest.

THE JOURNEY FROM WEEPING TO REJOICING

"He who goes out weeping, bearing the seed for sowing, shall come home with shouts of joy, bringing his sheaves with him."

This verse expands the metaphor through a more detailed narrative. We see the farmer departing with two things: tears and precious seed. The "seed for sowing" (עֶרְזַה הֶשֶׁמ, meshek hazzara) literally means "the drawing out of seed"—the careful allocation of limited resources for future growth rather than immediate consumption. This represents the costliness of true investment, whether material, emotional, or spiritual.

The Hebrew word for "goes out" (הָלֹךְ יֵלֵךְ, halok yelek) suggests continuous action—"going forth he goes." This repetition emphasizes the deliberate, persistent nature of the journey. Sowing is not a one-time act but a sustained commitment through difficulty. Similarly, the weeping is not momentary emotion but ongoing experience that accompanies the entire sowing process.

The transformation comes in the return journey. The one who "goes out" weeping "comes home" rejoicing. The Hebrew word for "come home" (בֹּא יָבֹא, bo yabo) carries connotations of arrival, completion, and fulfillment. What began in sorrow concludes in celebration, with overflowing joy expressed in shouts and with tangible evidence of harvest—"his sheaves"—clutched in arms once heavy with nothing but seed.

This movement from departure to return, from scarcity to abundance, from solitary labor to communal celebration reflects the larger spiritual journey. Our present difficulties are not permanent states but passages on the way to divinely appointed fulfillment.

APPLICATION: EMBRACING SACRIFICIAL INVESTMENT

As we continue our forty-day pilgrimage, these verses invite us to reframe our understanding of suffering and sacrifice. Rather than viewing tears as merely reactive responses to pain, we can recognize them as potentially productive investments into future joy. This perspective doesn't diminish the reality of suffering but infuses it with meaning and expectation.

Consider the various "seeds" you may be called to sow in tears:

The seed of forgiveness, where you relinquish your right to resentment and plant seeds of reconciliation, even when the soil of relationship seems unpromising.

The seed of costly obedience, where following God's direction requires sacrificing comfort, security, or approval, with no immediate evidence of benefit.

The seed of perseverance through suffering, where illness, loss, or disappointment becomes the context for demonstrating faith that transcends circumstances.

The seed of service to others, where pouring out your limited energy and resources for another's benefit depletes you even as it nourishes them.

The seed of spiritual disciplines, where time devoted to prayer, study, or solitude seems unproductive by worldly standards yet cultivates unseen growth.

In each case, the immediate experience may involve tears—the grief of letting go, the pain of self-denial, the weariness of continuing without visible results. Yet the psalm assures us that this tearful sowing will not prove fruitless. The one who "goes out weeping, bearing seed for sowing" will ultimately "come home with shouts of joy."

This principle finds its fullest expression in Jesus Christ, who "for the joy set before him endured the cross" (Hebrews 12:2). His sacrificial death—the ultimate sowing in tears—produced the abundant harvest of redemption. As his followers, we participate in this pattern of death and resurrection, of sacrifice and multiplication, whenever we willingly embrace the cost of love.

Importantly, the psalm's promise is not that tears will immediately or magically transform into joy, but that they become the prelude to joy when offered as faithful investment. Between sowing and reaping lies waiting—seasons of dormancy where growth occurs underground, invisible to the sower. This requires patience and trust in the God who oversees both seedtime and harvest. Today, consider what tears you are currently sowing. Perhaps you're investing in a relationship that shows little immediate return. Maybe you're persevering through illness or loss without clear resolution. Or perhaps you're pouring yourself into work, ministry, or creative endeavors without visible fruit. Whatever your particular field of labor, this psalm assures you that tears shed in faithful service are not wasted but planted—becoming seeds that, in God's perfect timing, will produce a harvest of joy disproportionate to your investment.

Like the pilgrims who sang this psalm on their arduous journey to Jerusalem, we travel toward God's presence carrying both our tears and our hope. We acknowledge the reality of present difficulty while simultaneously affirming the certainty of future joy. In this tension between current sorrow and anticipated celebration, we find the courage to continue sowing, even through our tears.

REFLECTION QUESTIONS

Think about a time when your "tears" (sacrifice, suffering, or difficult obedience) eventually led to a harvest of joy. What did you learn about God and yourself through that process?

_____

_____

The psalm uses the image of "streams in the Negeb"—sudden water in desert places. Where do you most need God's reviving presence to flow in the "desert" areas of your life or community?

_____

_____

Sowing requires giving up something valuable (seed that could be immediately eaten) for the promise of future increase. What is God asking you to sacrifice or surrender right now that might lead to greater fruitfulness later?

_____

_____

There is typically a waiting period between sowing and reaping, a time when the seed seems dormant. How do you maintain hope and faith during seasons when you see no visible evidence of growth from your sacrificial investments?

_____

_____

The imagery in verse 6 shows a solitary figure going out to sow but implies a community celebrating the harvest. How might your current individual struggles or sacrifices ultimately benefit others beyond yourself?

_____

_____

Jesus said, "Unless a grain of wheat falls into the earth and dies, it remains alone; but if it dies, it bears much fruit" (John 12:24). How does this gospel principle relate to the psalm's promise that "those who sow in tears shall reap with shouts of joy"?

_____

_____

PRAYER FOR TODAY

Divine Gardener,

Today I come before You with the paradoxical truth of Psalm 126 resonating in my heart: those who sow in tears shall reap with joy. Thank You for this promise that infuses meaning into my suffering and purpose into my sacrifice.

Lord, I acknowledge the tears I am currently shedding: [pause to name specific struggles, losses, or difficult investments]. Rather than merely asking for these tears to stop, I offer them to You as seeds. Transform my suffering through Your redemptive power. Help me to see my tears not just as expressions of pain but as plantings that, in Your hands, can produce a harvest beyond my imagination.

I confess the times I've resisted sacrificial sowing—when I've held tightly to what You asked me to surrender, when I've chosen immediate comfort over costly obedience, when I've withdrawn my investment because the soil seemed too hard or the season too long. Forgive my shortsightedness and strengthen my faith to persist in faithful sowing, even when the ground receives my seeds and tears with apparent indifference.

Restore our fortunes, O Lord, like streams in the Negeb! Pour Your reviving presence into the desert places of my life, my relationships, my community, and Your church. Where staleness and stagnation have settled, bring the rushing waters of Your Spirit. Where hope has withered, bring unexpected renewal.

In seasons of waiting between sowing and harvest, grant me patience and discernment. Help me recognize the subtle signs of growth beneath the surface. Protect the seeds I've sown from the birds of doubt, the scorching sun of disillusionment, and the thorns of competing concerns.

For those journeying alongside me who feel only the weight of the seed bag and the wetness of tears, with no evidence of coming harvest, renew their strength and vision. May we encourage one another with testimonies of Your faithfulness, supporting each other until we all return with shouts of joy, bringing our sheaves with us.

I offer this prayer in the name of Jesus Christ, who sowed His very life in tears and reaped the harvest of our redemption with joy, Amen.

Day 15

Unless the Lord Builds

"Unless the LORD builds the house, those who build it labor in vain. Unless the LORD watches over the city, the watchman stays awake in vain. It is in vain that you rise up early and go late to rest, eating the bread of anxious toil; for he gives to his beloved sleep." — Psalm 127:1-2

HISTORICAL CONTEXT

As our pilgrimage through the Songs of Ascent continues, we encounter in Psalm 127 a profound meditation on human effort and divine empowerment. This psalm is one of only two in the Songs of Ascent attributed to Solomon (the other being Psalm 72). This attribution is significant, as Solomon was known as both a great builder and a wisdom teacher.

During Solomon's reign, Israel reached the height of its architectural achievements. He constructed the magnificent first temple, an elaborate royal palace, and numerous cities throughout the kingdom (1 Kings 7-9). As the supervisor of massive building projects requiring thousands of laborers, Solomon understood well the relationship between human effort and divine blessing. His wisdom literature consistently emphasizes that human success ultimately depends on divine favor: "The blessing of the LORD makes rich, and he adds no sorrow with it" (Proverbs 10:22). For the pilgrims journeying to Jerusalem, this psalm would have taken on special significance as they approached the city and beheld its impressive structures—particularly the temple that stood as the physical center of worship. The temple represented both human craftsmanship and divine presence. Though rebuilt after the exile on a smaller scale than Solomon's original, it still stood as a testament to the principle that meaningful construction requires both human hands and divine blessing.

The historical setting also includes the reality of ancient city security. Jerusalem's walls and watchtowers were essential for protection against enemies. Watchmen would stand guard through the night, scanning the horizon for approaching threats. This critical role represented another arena where human vigilance intersected with divine protection.

MEDITATION: THE VANITY OF SELF-RELIANT LABOR

"Unless the LORD builds the house, those who build it labor in vain."

The psalm opens with a conditional statement that establishes its central premise: human labor disconnected from divine purpose and power ultimately proves futile. The Hebrew word for "in vain" (אָוְשׁ, shav') appears three times in these two verses, emphasizing the emptiness, meaninglessness, and ineffectiveness that characterize self-sufficient striving.

This is not a dismissal of human effort but a clarification of its proper context. The psalm doesn't say, "Don't build houses" or "Watchmen are unnecessary." Rather, it reframes human activity within a theology of divine partnership. True productivity emerges when our work aligns with and relies upon God's purposes and power.

The house-building metaphor operates on multiple levels. In its most literal sense, it refers to physical construction—the architecture of homes, temples, and cities. But in Hebrew thought, "house" (תַּיב, bayit) also referred to family lineage and legacy. This connection becomes explicit in the second half of the psalm (verses 3-5) where children are described as a heritage from the Lord. Thus, the futility of building without the Lord applies not just to physical structures but to family formation, career development, community building, and all forms of human enterprise. What does it mean for the Lord to "build the house"? It suggests divine authorization (building what God has called us to build), divine wisdom (building according to God's design), divine provision (building with resources God supplies), and divine empowerment (building with strength God provides). When these elements are missing, even impressive achievements prove ultimately hollow.

THE ILLUSION OF SECURITY THROUGH VIGILANCE

"Unless the LORD watches over the city, the watchman stays awake in vain."

The psalm's second metaphor shifts from construction to protection. Ancient cities employed watchmen who would scan the horizon from towers built into the city walls, providing early warning of approaching threats. Their vigilance represented the human responsibility for security and safety.

Yet the psalmist asserts that even the most alert watchman proves ineffective without divine oversight. The Hebrew presents a wordplay between "watches" (רָמָשׁ, shamar) and "watchman" (רְמוֹשׁ, shomer), emphasizing the parallel between human and divine watching. Human vigilance finds its proper place within the larger reality of God's vigilance.

This principle extends beyond literal city defense to all forms of protection we attempt to establish—financial security, health maintenance, relationship boundaries, or organizational safeguards. These measures have their place, but when divorced from recognition of divine oversight, they create an illusion of control rather than genuine security.

Jesus echoed this teaching when he asked, "And which of you by being anxious can add a single hour to his span of life?" (Matthew 6:27). Anxiety-driven hypervigilance reflects the false belief that security depends primarily on our capacity to anticipate and prevent all potential threats—a burden too heavy for any human to bear.

THE PROBLEM WITH ANXIOUS TOIL

"It is in vain that you rise up early and go late to rest, eating the bread of anxious toil; for he gives to his beloved sleep."

The psalm now addresses the personal cost of self-reliant striving: exhaustion, anxiety, and the sacrifice of rest. The Hebrew phrase "anxious toil" (סיבְצָעָה מֶחֶל, lechem ha'atsavim) literally means "bread of sorrows" or "bread of pains," suggesting that such labor produces sustenance tainted by the distress involved in obtaining it.

This verse describes a familiar pattern: extending working hours (rising early, going to bed late), pushing physical limits, and carrying the psychological burden of believing results depend entirely on one's efforts. Such patterns characterize many contemporary workplaces and personal lives, where worth becomes tied to productivity and rest is viewed as an impediment to success rather than a divine gift.

The contrast comes in the psalm's final phrase: "for he gives to his beloved sleep." The Hebrew term for "beloved" (דִּיד, yedid) conveys the idea of one deeply cherished. Those who recognize their dependence on God receive not only the fruit of their labor but also the gift of rest— physical sleep and the deeper spiritual rest that comes from surrendering outcomes to divine care.

This doesn't mean believers are exempt from hard work. Rather, it suggests a qualitative difference in how work is experienced. When we labor with awareness of divine partnership, we can work diligently without the crushing weight of believing everything depends on us. We can rest without anxiety because we trust God continues working even when we don't.

APPLICATION: FROM SELF-RELIANCE TO GOD-DEPENDENCE

As we journey toward deeper intimacy with God, Psalm 127:1-2 invites us to examine the subtle ways self-reliance infiltrates our approach to work, relationships, ministry, and personal development. This examination requires honest assessment of our motivations, methods, and measures of success.

Begin by considering what "houses" you're currently building—projects, relationships, career paths, ministries, or family cultures. What would it look like for the Lord to be the primary builder of these structures? This might involve seeking divine guidance before initiating projects, acknowledging God's provision of resources and abilities, inviting God's wisdom to shape your plans, and recognizing divine timing that might differ from your preferred schedule.

Next, examine your approach to security and protection. Where do you function as a "watchman" in your life—monitoring finances, safeguarding relationships, protecting your health, or maintaining organizational integrity? How might acknowledging God's ultimate oversight reshape your vigilance? This doesn't mean abandoning responsibility but contextualizing it within trust in divine care.

Then reflect on your relationship with rest. Do you view sleep and sabbath as divine gifts or as obstacles to productivity? Consider how anxiety about outcomes might be driving you to "rise early and go late to rest." Practice receiving rest as an expression of God's love for you rather than as a reluctant concession to physical limitation.

Finally, evaluate your metrics for success. Self-reliant striving often measures value by visible results, social recognition, or comparative advantage over others. God-dependent labor finds satisfaction in faithfulness to divine calling, alignment with divine values, and participation in divine purposes—even when outward results appear modest by worldly standards.

The invitation of this psalm is not to cease striving but to strive differently—to work diligently while holding outcomes loosely, to exercise responsibility while practicing trust, to employ your gifts while acknowledging their Source. This paradoxical approach allows you to invest fully in your labor while remaining free from the crushing burden of self-reliance.

Like the pilgrims who sang this psalm as they approached Jerusalem and beheld the temple— that magnificent structure representing both human craftsmanship and divine dwelling—may you discover the joy of partnering with God in building something more significant than you could ever construct alone.

REFLECTION QUESTIONS

1. Consider a current project, relationship, or goal in your life. What would it practically look like for "the Lord to build the house" in this specific situation? What might need to change in your approach?

_____

_____

2. The psalm mentions "anxious toil"—work characterized by worry and strain. Where do you experience this kind of anxiety-driven labor in your life? What beliefs about God and yourself might be contributing to this pattern?

_____

_____

3. The text says God "gives to his beloved sleep." How do you view rest—as a divine gift or as a necessary evil that limits productivity? What might help you receive rest as an expression of God's love rather than as a concession to human limitation?

_____

_____

4. This psalm doesn't discourage building or watching but reframes these activities within divine partnership. Think of a time when you experienced the difference between self-reliant striving and God-dependent labor. What distinguished these experiences?

_____

_____

5. Solomon, the attributed author, was known for grand building projects. Yet this psalm warns against labor disconnected from divine purpose. Where might you be pursuing impressive achievements that lack deeper meaning or alignment with God's purposes for your life?

_____

_____

6. The repetition of "in vain" (three times in two verses) emphasizes the futility of self-reliant effort. What specific area of your life feels most futile or frustrating right now? How might surrendering this area to God transform your experience of it?

PRAYER FOR TODAY

Master Builder and Faithful Guardian,

Today I come before You with the humbling truth of Psalm 127 echoing in my heart: Unless You build the house, I labor in vain. Unless You watch over my life, my vigilance accomplishes nothing lasting. Free me from the exhaustion of self-reliant striving and the anxiety of believing everything depends on my efforts.

Examine my heart, Lord, and reveal the places where I've been building without consulting Your blueprint—pursuing goals, relationships, or achievements driven more by ego, fear, or cultural expectations than by Your purpose. Show me where I've been staying awake in anxious hypervigilance rather than resting in Your protective care.

I confess the specific areas where I've relied primarily on my own wisdom, strength, and control: [pause to name them]. Forgive my prideful self-sufficiency and my failure to acknowledge You as the source of every good gift.

Teach me the art of God-dependent labor—working diligently while trusting You with outcomes, exercising responsibility while practicing faith, employing my gifts while acknowledging their Source. Help me distinguish between faithful stewardship of what You've entrusted to me and the anxious striving that reveals my lack of trust.

Thank You for the gift of rest—both physical sleep and the deeper spiritual rest that comes from surrendering my work and worries into Your capable hands. When I'm tempted to "rise early and go late to rest, eating the bread of anxious toil," remind me that I am Your beloved, to whom You freely give sleep. Help me receive this gift without guilt or fear of falling behind.

For those journeying alongside me who carry the heavy burden of believing everything depends on them—in their families, workplaces, ministries, or communities—grant the liberating revelation that You are the ultimate builder and watchman. May we encourage one another toward faithful labor that acknowledges its dependence on Your grace.

As I continue this pilgrimage, may each step be taken in the freedom of knowing I walk with the God who builds what truly lasts and watches over what truly matters.

In the name of Jesus Christ, who perfectly modeled God-dependent living, Amen.

Day 16

The Heritage of Children

"Behold, children are a heritage from the LORD, the fruit of the womb a reward. Like arrows in the hand of a warrior are the children of one's youth. Blessed is the man who fills his quiver with them! He shall not be put to shame when he speaks with his enemies in the gate." — *Psalm 127:3-5*

HISTORICAL CONTEXT

As our pilgrimage through the Songs of Ascent continues, we encounter the second half of Psalm 127, which shifts focus from the vanity of self-reliant labor to the blessing of children. This transition is not abrupt but organic, as both sections address what constitutes true security, legacy, and divine blessing.

In ancient Israel, children were viewed not merely as personal blessings but as essential components of community survival and covenant continuity. The promise to Abraham included numerous descendants (Genesis 15:5), and the cultural understanding was that one lived on through one's children. In a society without retirement plans or social security, children provided economic security for aging parents and ensured the family name and inheritance continued.

The imagery of arrows and warriors reflects the reality of ancient city life, where security depended on having enough defenders. The "gate" mentioned in verse 5 was where legal proceedings occurred and where elders would gather to resolve disputes and conduct business. Having adult sons present at the gate provided both physical protection and social standing when confronting accusers or opponents.

This psalm is attributed to Solomon, who would have understood the significance of being a son (of David) and having sons to continue the dynastic line. The future of the Davidic covenant depended on generational continuity. For pilgrims journeying to Jerusalem, this psalm would have reinforced the communal and generational nature of their faith—they traveled not merely as individuals but as families, connecting their children to the covenant community and its practices.

MEDITATION: CHILDREN AS DIVINE HERITAGE

"Behold, children are a heritage from the LORD, the fruit of the womb a reward."

The psalm begins with "behold" (הִנֵּה, hinneh), a call to attention that signals something significant follows. What merits this special attention? The recognition that children are a "heritage" or "inheritance" (נַחֲלָה, nachalah) from the Lord. This term typically referred to land allotments given to Israelite tribes and families—property that provided sustenance and remained within the family across generations.

By applying this term to children, the psalmist establishes several important truths. First, children are gifts, not achievements. The language of "heritage" and "reward" places the emphasis on divine giving rather than human producing. Second, like land inheritances, children represent a trust to be stewarded rather than a possession to be controlled. Third, children connect us to both past and future—they are living links in the chain of covenant continuity.

The psalm describes children as both "heritage" and "reward" (שָׂכָר, sakar), a term often used for wages earned through labor. This creates an interesting tension with the first half of the psalm, which warned against anxious toil and self-reliant work. Perhaps the suggestion is that while such striving cannot secure what truly matters, faithful living within covenant relationship does bring divine blessing—including the blessing of children.

CHILDREN AS ARROWS: DIRECTION, DISTANCE, AND IMPACT

"Like arrows in the hand of a warrior are the children of one's youth."

This striking metaphor compares children to weapons of war, which may seem jarring to modern sensibilities. However, the comparison illuminates several aspects of the parent-child relationship that transcend cultural contexts.

Arrows require careful crafting to fly true. Similarly, children require intentional formation—not to become what parents demand but to fulfill their divine design. The image suggests both the responsibility of parents to shape their children's character and the ultimate purpose of launching them toward targets beyond parental reach.

Arrows are designed to travel far beyond the archer, affecting distant places the archer cannot personally go. Children likewise extend our influence beyond our physical presence and temporal lifespan. They carry our values, faith, and legacy into contexts and generations we will never directly experience.

Arrows are also instruments of protection for the warrior. In ancient contexts where security often depended on family strength, adult children provided defense against both physical threats and social vulnerabilities. Even in contexts where physical protection is less relevant, children often serve as advocates and caregivers for aging parents.

Finally, arrows require release to fulfill their purpose. The most beautifully crafted arrow brings no benefit if kept permanently in the quiver. This aspect of the metaphor speaks to the necessary transition from protecting and directing children to releasing them to fulfill their unique calling. The parent who cannot release the "arrows" ultimately limits both their flight and function.

THE BLESSING OF A FULL QUIVER

"Blessed is the man who fills his quiver with them! He shall not be put to shame when he speaks with his enemies in the gate."

The psalm concludes by describing the man with many children as "blessed" (יַאְשֵׁ, ashrei)—a term that suggests deep contentment and divine favor. In ancient Israel, having many children represented both divine blessing and practical advantage. The image of the "full quiver" would have resonated in a society where large families contributed to agricultural productivity, community influence, and physical security.

The reference to "not being put to shame" when confronting enemies "in the gate" speaks to the social standing conferred by having numerous children, particularly sons who could stand with their father in legal proceedings or conflicts. The city gate was where justice was administered and where disputes were settled. Having sons present in these proceedings provided both moral support and tangible backing when facing accusations or opposition.

APPLICATION: EXPANDING OUR VISION OF LEGACY

As we continue our spiritual pilgrimage, these verses invite us to expand our understanding of legacy beyond individual accomplishment to embrace our responsibility toward future generations. While the psalm's primary reference is to biological children, its principles apply to all forms of generational influence—mentoring, teaching, creating institutional structures, or investing in young lives through various forms of spiritual parenthood.

Begin by recognizing all children—biological, adopted, or those within your sphere of influence—as divine gifts rather than personal projects or extensions of your ego. This perspective transforms both the joy and challenges of nurturing young lives. When children succeed, this view promotes gratitude rather than pride. When they struggle, it encourages prayerful dependence rather than shame or controlling behavior.

Consider how you are "crafting arrows" through your influence on younger generations. What values, skills, perspectives, and faith elements are you intentionally forming in those who will outlive you? This craft requires both purposeful instruction and consistent modeling. More is caught than taught, and children often absorb our actual priorities rather than our stated values.

Reflect on your willingness to "release arrows" toward divinely appointed targets that may differ from your preferences or expectations. Many parents and mentors struggle with allowing young people to pursue paths that feel unfamiliar or risky. Yet the metaphor reminds us that arrows kept permanently in the quiver never fulfill their purpose. True legacy requires the courage to release those we've nurtured toward their unique calling.

Expand your conception of "filling your quiver" beyond biological family to embrace spiritual parenthood in its many forms. In a culture that often isolates generations from each other, intentional cross-generational investment becomes increasingly countercultural and valuable. Whether through formal mentoring, teaching, organizational leadership, or simply being present in the lives of young people in your community, you can participate in shaping the future beyond your lifespan.

Finally, consider how this psalm's perspective might reshape your community's approach to children and young people. Do your faith community's priorities, budget, and attention reflect the view that children are a "heritage from the LORD"? Are younger generations genuinely welcomed as full participants in community life, or merely tolerated as distractions from "real" spiritual activity? The psalm challenges us to see investment in children not as secondary but as central to covenant faithfulness.

Like the pilgrims who journeyed to Jerusalem with their children, transmitting faith practices across generations, may we recognize that our spiritual pilgrimage is not merely individual but connected to both those who preceded us and those who will follow. Our journey toward deeper intimacy with God includes embracing our role in nurturing the faith of others who will continue the journey long after our steps have ceased.

REFLECTION QUESTIONS

1. The psalm describes children as a "heritage" and "reward" from the Lord. How might this perspective transform your approach to parenting, mentoring, or influencing younger generations? In what ways does it challenge cultural attitudes toward children?

_____

_____

2. Consider the metaphor of children as "arrows." What qualities are you intentionally forming in the young people within your sphere of influence? How are you preparing them to eventually "fly" beyond your direct control?

_____

_____

3. The passage suggests that children extend our influence into contexts and generations we cannot personally reach. What specific values, practices, or beliefs do you most want to transmit to future generations? What practical steps might help ensure this transmission?

_____

_____

4. The imagery of "releasing arrows" implies both careful preparation and eventual letting go. Where do you struggle with the tension between guiding younger generations and allowing them the freedom to follow their own calling? How might you grow in this area?

_____

_____

5. Beyond biological parenting, how might God be calling you to invest in younger generations through mentoring, teaching, creating sustainable institutions, or other forms of spiritual legacy? What first step could you take toward this investment?

_____

_____

6. This psalm presents children as sources of blessing, security, and honor. How does this perspective challenge or confirm your faith community's approach to younger generations? What one change might help your community better honor children as divine heritage?

PRAYER FOR TODAY

Gracious Giver of Life,

Today I pause on this pilgrimage to acknowledge with wonder the truth that children are indeed a heritage from You—precious gifts entrusted to our care rather than possessions to control or projects to perfect. Thank You for the privilege of participating in Your creative and redemptive work through influencing younger generations.

Forgive me for the times I've viewed children primarily through the lens of inconvenience, interruption, or extension of my own ego. Transform my perspective to see each young person as bearing Your image and carrying unique potential for Your kingdom purposes.

Grant me wisdom as I "craft arrows" through my influence on younger generations. Show me how to balance intentional guidance with respect for their God-given uniqueness. Help me transmit not just information but living faith—not merely what I say I believe but what my life actually demonstrates matters most.

Give me courage for the necessary releasing of these "arrows" toward targets You have appointed, which may differ from my preferences or expectations. When I am tempted to control or manipulate outcomes for those in my care, remind me that true legacy requires the faith to release what I have nurtured into Your capable hands.

Expand my vision of spiritual parenthood beyond biological family. Open my eyes to opportunities for mentoring, teaching, encouraging, and investing in young lives within my sphere of influence. Use me as an instrument of Your blessing for those who will journey on when my own pilgrimage has ended.

For those who deeply desire biological children but have experienced infertility or loss, bring comfort and perspective. Help them discover the many ways they can participate in nurturing future generations, and guard their hearts from the lie that their worth or legacy depends on having children of their own.

For those actively parenting or mentoring young people who are currently struggling or making choices that bring pain, grant perseverance and hope. Remind them that Your work often unfolds slowly, and that many arrows follow curved trajectories before reaching their intended target.

And for Your church, renew our collective commitment to younger generations. May we never see investment in children and youth as optional or peripheral, but recognize it as central to our covenant faithfulness. Guide us in creating communities where all generations journey together toward deeper knowledge of You.

In the name of Jesus Christ, who welcomed children and warned against causing them to stumble, Amen.

Day 17

The Blessed Life

"Blessed is everyone who fears the LORD, who walks in his ways! You shall eat the fruit of the labor of your hands; you shall be blessed, and it shall be well with you. Your wife will be like a fruitful vine within your house; your children will be like olive shoots around your table. Behold, thus shall the man be blessed who fears the LORD." — Psalm 128:1-4

HISTORICAL CONTEXT

As our pilgrimage through the Songs of Ascent continues, we encounter in Psalm 128 a beautiful portrait of the blessed life that flows from reverence for God. This psalm builds naturally upon the themes of Psalm 127, moving from the futility of self-reliant labor and the blessing of children to a more comprehensive vision of God-centered flourishing.

For the ancient pilgrims traveling to Jerusalem, this song would have reinforced the connection between worship and daily life. The journey to the temple wasn't merely a religious obligation disconnected from ordinary existence but the renewal of a covenant relationship that shaped every dimension of life—work, family, community, and legacy.

The imagery in this psalm draws deeply from agricultural and domestic life in ancient Israel. The references to eating "the fruit of the labor of your hands," a wife like a "fruitful vine," and children like "olive shoots" would have resonated with a people whose livelihood and security were tied to the land. Vines and olive trees were particularly significant crops, requiring years of cultivation before yielding their full harvest—a powerful metaphor for the patient nurturing of family relationships.

The psalm was likely sung as families made the pilgrimage together, reinforcing the understanding that faith was not merely individual but communal and generational. As they approached Jerusalem and caught sight of the temple, this song reminded pilgrims that true worship extends beyond ritual observance to encompass a life oriented around reverence for God.

MEDITATION: THE FOUNDATION OF BLESSING

"Blessed is everyone who fears the LORD, who walks in his ways!"

The psalm opens with a declaration of blessing (יְרֵשֵׁא, ashrei)—a state of profound well-being and divine favor. Significantly, this blessing is not arbitrary or capricious but connected to a specific orientation of heart and life: the fear of the Lord and walking in His ways.

The "fear of the LORD" (הְוֹהְי תאְרִי, yirat YHWH) represents not cringing terror but reverential awe that acknowledges God's transcendent holiness, power, and authority. This concept appears repeatedly in wisdom literature as the foundation of true wisdom (Proverbs 1:7) and the beginning of knowledge (Proverbs 9:10). It describes a proper relationship to God that recognizes both His majesty and our dependence.

This fear is not merely theoretical or emotional but practical, expressed through "walking in his ways." The Hebrew conception of "walking" (הְלָךְ, halak) as metaphor for living emphasizes that faith is not static but dynamic, not merely beliefs held but a path followed. The blessed life doesn't emerge from occasional religious observances but from a consistent journey in the direction of divine instruction.

Notice the inclusive nature of this blessing: "everyone who fears the LORD." Though the psalm later adopts masculine pronouns reflecting its ancient patriarchal context, its opening establishes that the fundamental prerequisites for blessing—reverence for God and obedience to His ways—are available to all regardless of gender, social status, or circumstance.

THE AUTHENTIC PROSPERITY OF THE BLESSED LIFE

"You shall eat the fruit of the labor of your hands; you shall be blessed, and it shall be well with you."

The psalm now describes specific manifestations of blessing, beginning with the satisfaction of enjoying the fruits of one's labor. In an agricultural society where crop failures, political instability, or foreign invasion could easily separate workers from the results of their efforts, the ability to "eat the fruit of the labor of your hands" represented significant blessing.

This blessing stands in stark contrast to the "anxious toil" described in Psalm 127:2. While the self-reliant laborer works feverishly but finds no lasting satisfaction, the one who fears the Lord works faithfully and experiences the genuine prosperity of sufficiency and contentment.

The phrase "it shall be well with you" (הַל בּוֹטוּ, vetov lakh) suggests more than mere material provision. The Hebrew concept of "good" (בּוֹט, tov) encompasses harmony, appropriateness, and flourishing in its fullest sense. The blessed life isn't characterized merely by abundance but by well-being—a state where various aspects of life exist in proper relationship to each other and to God's design.

This prosperity differs significantly from contemporary materialistic conceptions that focus exclusively on financial wealth or status symbols. The blessed life described here centers on meaningful work, sustainable provision, harmonious relationships, and generational continuity— elements that contribute to genuine human flourishing rather than superficial success.

THE RELATIONAL DIMENSION OF BLESSING

"Your wife will be like a fruitful vine within your house; your children will be like olive shoots around your table."

The psalm now turns to the domestic sphere, using agricultural metaphors to describe family relationships. The comparison of a wife to a "fruitful vine" evokes images of beauty, productivity, cultivation, and joy. Vineyards required substantial investment and care, producing fruit that not only provided sustenance but also celebration. Similarly, the blessed marriage described here isn't merely functional but flourishing, characterized by growth and delight.

The location "within your house" suggests both protection and centrality. In ancient Near Eastern architecture, interior courtyards often featured trellised vines providing both shade and fruit. The image places the wife not at the margins of family life but at its heart, integral to its structure and essential to its flourishing.

Children compared to "olive shoots around your table" continue the agricultural imagery. Olive trees were among the most valuable plants in ancient Israel, providing oil for cooking, lighting, medicine, and religious rituals. Young olive shoots sprouting around a mature tree represented both present vitality and future resource. Similarly, children gathered around the family table symbolize both current joy and future security.

The table itself represents more than merely a piece of furniture for dining. In ancient Near Eastern culture, sharing meals created and reinforced community bonds. The table served as the center of family teaching, storytelling, and identity formation. The blessed life includes not just biological reproduction but relational cohesion—the creation of spaces where values and faith can be transmitted across generations.

THE CIRCULAR NATURE OF BLESSING

"Behold, thus shall the man be blessed who fears the LORD."

The psalm concludes this section with a statement that circles back to its opening declaration, creating a sense of completeness. The word "behold" (הִנֵּה, hinneh) calls attention to the full picture of blessing that has been painted—meaningful work, material sufficiency, marital fruitfulness, and family continuity. All these emerge from the foundational posture of fearing the Lord.

This circular structure reinforces the consistent biblical theme that blessing flows from right relationship with God. The fear of the Lord doesn't merely add spiritual dimension to an otherwise secular prosperity but forms the very root system from which true flourishing grows.

APPLICATION: CULTIVATING THE BLESSED LIFE

As we continue our pilgrimage toward deeper intimacy with God, Psalm 128:1-4 invites us to examine our understanding of blessing and the role of reverence in shaping a life of authentic prosperity. While the specific expressions of blessing may differ across cultural and historical contexts, the fundamental principle remains: genuine flourishing emerges from lives oriented around the fear of the Lord.

Begin by reflecting on your conception of the "blessed life." How has contemporary culture shaped your understanding of prosperity and success? The psalm presents a vision of blessing that includes meaningful work, sufficient provision, harmonious relationships, and generational impact—elements that transcend materialistic definitions of success. Consider how this fuller vision might reshape your priorities and aspirations.

Next, examine your understanding of what it means to "fear the LORD." This reverential awe exists in the balance point between unhealthy terror and casual familiarity. It acknowledges both God's transcendent holiness and His intimate love, producing neither paralyzing dread nor presumptuous entitlement but humble confidence. How might cultivating this posture transform your approach to both worship and daily decisions?

Consider how "walking in his ways" manifests in your specific life context. While the ancient Israelites understood this primarily through Torah observance, followers of Christ recognize Jesus himself as the embodiment of God's way (John 14:6). Walking in God's ways today involves both following Christ's example and obeying His teachings. Identify one specific area where greater alignment with God's ways might lead to increased flourishing in your life or relationships.

Reflect on the agricultural metaphors used for family relationships. Both vines and olive trees require patient cultivation over years before reaching full productivity. Similarly, flourishing relationships demand consistent investment, appropriate boundaries, seasonal pruning, and regular nourishment. What practices might help you cultivate greater fruitfulness in your key relationships, whether in marriage, parenting, extended family, or spiritual family?

Finally, consider the communal dimension of blessing emphasized in this psalm. The blessed life is not solitary but shared around tables where stories are told, identity is formed, and faith is transmitted. How might you create or strengthen such spaces in your home or community? What tables—literal or metaphorical—can become sites of blessing where others experience belonging, nourishment, and formation?

Like the ancient pilgrims who sang this psalm as they journeyed toward Jerusalem, may you discover that the path of reverence leads not to diminishment but to genuine flourishing—a blessed life characterized not by the hollow success of self-reliance but by the authentic prosperity that flows from right relationship with God.

REFLECTION QUESTIONS

1. The psalm connects blessing directly to "the fear of the LORD." How would you describe this reverential awe in your own words? In what areas of your life do you find it easier or more difficult to maintain this posture toward God?

_____

_____

2. Consider the phrase "you shall eat the fruit of the labor of your hands." How does this image of blessing differ from contemporary definitions of success? Where in your life do you experience the satisfaction of meaningful work and appropriate reward?

_____

_____

3. The agricultural metaphors of vines and olive shoots suggest that relational flourishing requires patient cultivation over time. What specific practices help you nurture fruitfulness in your key relationships? Where might you need to invest more consistently?

_____

_____

4. The psalm portrays the table as a central gathering place for family. What role does shared meals or other gathering rituals play in your home or community? How might you strengthen these opportunities for connection and formation?

---

5. The blessed life described in this psalm emerges from "walking in his ways." What would it look like in your specific context to more fully align your path with God's ways? What obstacle most hinders this alignment?

---

6. This psalm presents a vision of blessing that includes work, home, and family functioning in harmony rather than competition. Where do you experience tension between these different domains of life? How might the fear of the Lord help integrate these areas into a more cohesive whole?

PRAYER FOR TODAY

God of True Blessing,

Today I come before You with the words of the psalmist echoing in my heart: "Blessed is everyone who fears the LORD, who walks in his ways." Thank You for this invitation to authentic prosperity—not the hollow success offered by our culture but the genuine flourishing that flows from right relationship with You.

Cultivate within me a proper fear of Your name—not cringing terror but reverent awe that acknowledges both Your transcendent holiness and Your intimate love. Deliver me from both casual familiarity that diminishes Your majesty and paralyzing dread that fails to trust Your goodness. Help me approach You with the humble confidence that characterizes those who truly know You.

Align my steps with Your ways. Where cultural values, personal desires, or ingrained habits have led me onto divergent paths, gently redirect my course. Give me courage to follow the example and teachings of Jesus, even when His way contradicts more comfortable or conventional routes. Thank You for the gift of meaningful work. Help me approach my labor—whether paid or unpaid, recognized or hidden—as worship and service rather than merely as means to material gain or status. Grant me the blessing of eating the fruit of the labor of my hands—finding appropriate satisfaction in work well done without making productivity my primary identity.

For the relationships You have entrusted to me—in marriage, family, friendship, church, and community—I ask Your blessing of fruitfulness. Like a skilled gardener tending vines and olive trees, help me cultivate these relationships with patience, appropriate boundaries, seasonal pruning, and regular nourishment. Show me where my relational practices need adjustment to promote greater flourishing.

Bless the tables around which I gather with others. Whether in my home, church, workplace, or wider community, transform these gathering spaces into sites of belonging, nourishment, formation, and joy. Help me create environments where faith can be naturally shared and where Your presence is welcomed.

For those journeying alongside me who struggle to see blessing in their current circumstances—those facing financial hardship, relational brokenness, work challenges, or family difficulties—grant perspective and hope. Remind them that Your blessing operates on a different timeline and according to different metrics than worldly success. Meet their immediate needs even as You work toward their ultimate flourishing.

As I continue this pilgrimage, keep before me the vision of the truly blessed life—not wealth without purpose or achievement without love, but the integrated flourishing that emerges when every dimension of life is lived in reverent response to Your grace.

In the name of Jesus Christ, who came that we might have life abundantly, Amen.

Day 18

Generations of Blessing

"The LORD bless you from Zion! May you see the prosperity of Jerusalem all the days of your life! May you see your children's children! Peace be upon Israel!" — Psalm 128:5-6

HISTORICAL CONTEXT

As our pilgrimage through the Songs of Ascent continues, we encounter the concluding verses of Psalm 128, which expand the vision of blessing beyond individual and family prosperity to encompass community longevity and intergenerational flourishing. These verses transition the psalm from personal blessing to communal and multigenerational concerns, reflecting the interconnected nature of covenant faith.

For the ancient pilgrims journeying to Jerusalem, these verses would have had profound resonance. The mention of "Zion"—a name for Jerusalem emphasizing its status as God's dwelling place—would have taken on immediate significance as they approached the physical city where God's presence was specially manifested in the temple. The prayer for "the prosperity of Jerusalem" connected individual well-being with national flourishing in a society where religious and civic identity were inseparable.

The blessing of seeing "your children's children" reflected both the cultural value placed on lineage and the practical reality that longevity was not guaranteed in a world of high infant mortality, dangerous childbirth, frequent warfare, and limited medical knowledge. Living long enough to see grandchildren represented both divine favor and the continuation of covenant promises through multiple generations.

The final phrase, "Peace be upon Israel," concludes not just this psalm but several others in the Songs of Ascent (see also Psalms 125:5 and 131:3). For pilgrims singing these words as they traveled toward Jerusalem, this benediction unified their individual journeys with the broader covenant community extending across both geography and time. The Hebrew word for "peace" (שָׁלוֹם, shalom) conveyed not merely the absence of conflict but comprehensive well-being—the flourishing of the entire community in harmony with God's purposes.

MEDITATION: THE SOURCE AND SCOPE OF BLESSING

"The LORD bless you from Zion!"

The psalm shifts here from descriptive statements about blessing to a direct invocation of blessing. This reflects the liturgical function of these songs, which not only described the blessed life but actively conferred blessing through communal pronouncement. The change from "Blessed is everyone who fears the LORD" (verse 1) to "The LORD bless you" (verse 5) moves from general principle to personal application.

The source of this blessing is clearly identified: "The LORD... from Zion." While ancient Near Eastern peoples typically associated deities with specific locations, for Israel, Zion represented not God's limitation to one place but His choice to make His presence specially accessible there. The temple on Mount Zion functioned as the meeting place between heaven and earth, the visible sign of God's covenant presence among His people.

For pilgrims making the ascent to Jerusalem, this blessing reminded them that they were journeying not merely toward a geographical location but toward encounter with the living God. Their pilgrimage represented both physical travel and spiritual movement toward the Source of all blessing.

For us today, this phrase reminds us that genuine blessing flows not from impersonal cosmic forces or our own efforts but from relationship with the personal God who makes Himself known and accessible to His people. While we no longer identify God's presence exclusively with a physical temple (John 4:21-24), we continue to seek blessing through deliberate movement toward God in worship, prayer, Scripture, and community.

EXTENDING THE TIMEFRAME OF BLESSING

"May you see the prosperity of Jerusalem all the days of your life! May you see your children's children!"

These parallel statements extend the timeframe of blessing across both community history and family generations. The prayer to "see the prosperity of Jerusalem" connects individual well-being with communal flourishing. The Hebrew word translated "prosperity" (בוט, tuv) conveys goodness in its fullest sense—not merely economic success but moral excellence, beauty, and appropriate function.

This prayer acknowledges that personal blessing cannot be separated from community wellness. In biblical perspective, the truly good life is never purely individual but always embedded in social contexts. We flourish not in isolation but in healthy connection with others who share common values and commitments.

The phrase "all the days of your life" introduces a temporal dimension, recognizing that genuine prosperity must be sustainable rather than fleeting. This contrasts with conceptions of success focused on momentary achievements or temporary advantages. The blessed life unfolds across decades, proving durable through various seasons and challenges.

The parallel blessing—"May you see your children's children"—further extends this temporal horizon beyond one's own lifespan. This represents both longevity (living long enough to see grandchildren) and legacy (establishing values and faith that continue through subsequent generations). The truly blessed life overflows its individual container to nourish future generations. For the ancient Israelites, seeing grandchildren had practical significance for family security and inheritance continuity. But beyond these pragmatic concerns, this blessing expresses the human yearning to participate in something that outlasts our limited lifespan—to plant trees whose shade we will not sit under, to begin stories whose conclusions we will not witness.

THE CULMINATION IN COMMUNAL PEACE

"Peace be upon Israel!"

The psalm concludes with this benediction that widens the circle of blessing to encompass the entire covenant community. The Hebrew word "shalom" encompasses far more than the absence of conflict—it describes wholeness, harmony, right relationship, and comprehensive flourishing. This final blessing reveals that the ultimate goal of individual and family blessing is the wellness of the larger community.

For pilgrims singing this as they approached Jerusalem, this phrase would have reminded them that their individual journeys were part of a collective movement toward covenant renewal. Their private devotion contributed to public good. Their personal transformation participated in communal restoration.

This benediction also acknowledges that true peace requires divine action. Peace is wished "upon" Israel (לְעַ, 'al), suggesting something that descends from above rather than emerging naturally from human dynamics. While human choices and systems certainly affect communal well-being, ultimate shalom depends on divine grace rather than human achievement.

APPLICATION: LIVING BEYOND OUR LIFETIME

As we continue our spiritual pilgrimage, these verses invite us to extend our vision beyond immediate concerns to embrace multigenerational perspectives on faith and flourishing. In a culture often characterized by short-term thinking and individual achievement, this expanded timeframe challenges us to consider how our current choices shape future realities we may never personally witness.

Begin by reflecting on your sources of blessing. The psalm locates blessing as flowing "from Zion"—the place of God's revealed presence. While we no longer associate God with a single geographical location, we still need intentional practices that position us to receive divine blessing. Consider what disciplines, relationships, or environments consistently connect you with God's presence and provision. How might you more deliberately orient your life toward these sources of blessing?

Next, examine how you balance individual flourishing with community wellness. The psalm connects personal blessing with "seeing the prosperity of Jerusalem"—experiencing the flourishing of the larger community. In what ways does your pursuit of blessing contribute to or detract from the well-being of your various communities—family, church, neighborhood, workplace, nation? Where might God be inviting you to align your personal goals more fully with community needs?

Consider how your decisions and investments reflect different timeframes. The blessing of seeing "the prosperity of Jerusalem all the days of your life" suggests sustainable flourishing rather than short-term gain. Evaluate your current choices through this longer lens. Are you building relationships, institutions, and practices that can endure across decades, or pursuing successes that may prove fleeting?

Reflect on your investment in future generations. The blessing of seeing "your children's children" invites us to consider our legacy beyond our lifespan. Whether through biological offspring, mentoring relationships, institutional leadership, or creative contributions, how are you investing in those who will follow you? What values, practices, and resources are you transmitting that might outlast your physical presence?

Finally, consider how you contribute to "peace upon Israel"—the comprehensive well-being of your communities. This may involve working for justice, fostering reconciliation, creating beauty, preserving wisdom, or cultivating environments where diverse individuals can flourish together. What specific contribution might God be calling you to make toward the shalom of the communities where He has placed you?

Like the ancient pilgrims who sang this psalm as they approached Jerusalem, we journey not merely as isolated individuals but as members of communities extending across both geography and time. Our personal transformation participates in collective renewal that began before our birth and will continue after our death. Today, may you live and pray with awareness of the generations who preceded you and those who will follow, finding your place in God's multigenerational work of blessing.

REFLECTION QUESTIONS

1. The psalm locates blessing as flowing "from Zion"—the place of God's revealed presence. What practices, relationships, or environments most consistently connect you with God's presence? How might you more intentionally position yourself to receive divine blessing?

_____

_____

2. Consider the prayer to "see the prosperity of Jerusalem all the days of your life." How do you balance personal flourishing with the well-being of your communities (family, church, neighborhood, workplace, nation)? Where might tension exist between these concerns?

_____

_____

3. The blessing of seeing "your children's children" speaks to legacy beyond our lifetime. Beyond biological offspring, what spiritual, creative, institutional, or relational legacies are you cultivating? What would you most want to be remembered for by future generations?

_____

_____

4. This psalm extends our vision across both community history and family generations. How does this multigenerational perspective challenge contemporary tendencies toward individualism and short-term thinking? What might change if you consistently viewed your life through this longer lens?

_____

_____

5. The final benediction—"Peace be upon Israel"—acknowledges that community flourishing requires divine action. Where do you see tension between human responsibility and divine sovereignty in creating shalom? How do you participate in God's work while recognizing your limitations?

_____

_____

6. The pilgrims who sang this psalm were physically journeying toward Jerusalem. What "Jerusalem" might you be traveling toward in your current season—what goal or destination represents encounter with God's presence? How does this psalm reshape your understanding of that journey?

_____

_____

PRAYER FOR TODAY

God of Generations,

Today I pause on this pilgrimage to lift my eyes beyond my immediate concerns and limited lifespan. Thank You for the expansive vision of Psalm 128, which reminds me that true blessing flows from Your presence, encompasses community flourishing, and extends across generations. Enlarge my perspective to see beyond momentary challenges and achievements to Your eternal purposes unfolding across centuries.

I receive with gratitude Your blessing "from Zion"—not from a physical location but from Your very presence made accessible through Christ. Draw me consistently toward the sources of genuine blessing: Your Word, Your Spirit, Your people, Your creation. When I am tempted to seek prosperity from lesser sources or through my own striving alone, redirect my attention to You as the Fountain of all good gifts.

May I see the prosperity of the communities where You have placed me—my family, church, neighborhood, workplace, and nation. Free me from the illusion that I can flourish while those around me struggle. Show me how my gifts, resources, and influence might contribute to collective well-being rather than merely personal advantage. Where I have prioritized individual gain at community expense, forgive me and reshape my values.

Grant me the blessing of generational vision—the ability to see beyond my own lifetime and invest in those who will follow. Whether through parenting, mentoring, creating, building, teaching, or simply living faithfully, help me contribute something of value to future generations. Guard me against both the pride that seeks to control outcomes beyond my death and the short-sightedness that neglects responsibility toward tomorrow's inhabitants of this world.

For the specific communities You have entrusted to my care: [pause to name them], I pray for comprehensive shalom—not merely absence of conflict but positive flourishing in harmony with Your purposes. Show me my particular role in cultivating this peace, whether through reconciliation, justice work, beauty creation, wisdom preservation, or environment nurturing. Help me neither overestimate nor underestimate my responsibility.

For those who preceded me in faith—grandparents, parents, mentors, teachers, and spiritual ancestors—I give thanks. Their faithfulness created the context for my own journey. For those who will follow—children, grandchildren, students, and spiritual descendants—I pray for Your continued covenant faithfulness. May the blessings I have received flow through me to them, and may they surpass me in faith, love, and fruitfulness.

As I continue this pilgrimage, remind me daily that I travel not alone but as part of Your people stretching across generations. May this awareness both humble me regarding my own importance and inspire me regarding my contribution to Your unfolding story.

Peace be upon Your people, from this generation to the next.

In the name of Jesus Christ, the same yesterday, today, and forever, Amen.

Day 19

Refined by Affliction

"They have greatly oppressed me from my youth," let Israel say; "they have greatly oppressed me from my youth, but they have not gained the victory over me. Plowers have plowed my back and made their furrows long. But the LORD is righteous; he has cut me free from the cords of the wicked." — Psalm 129:1-4

HISTORICAL CONTEXT

As our pilgrimage continues toward Jerusalem, we encounter Psalm 129—a song that acknowledges the painful history of God's people while simultaneously celebrating their endurance. This psalm belongs to the collective memory of Israel, recounting centuries of opposition and persecution that began with slavery in Egypt and continued through numerous invasions, exiles, and subjugations.

The image of plowers making long furrows on the back is particularly striking. It evokes the marks of the whip on the back of a slave or prisoner—deep, parallel wounds that permanently scar the flesh. The psalmist uses this vivid metaphor to describe the repeated suffering Israel endured. Yet remarkably, this is not primarily a psalm of complaint but of resilient faith. It celebrates not just survival but the divine intervention that has preserved God's people despite relentless opposition.

The pilgrims singing this psalm as they approached Jerusalem would likely have reflected on their national history—how Egypt, Assyria, Babylon, and other powers had attempted to destroy them, yet here they were, still journeying to worship in the holy city. The psalm reminded them that their story was not primarily defined by suffering but by divine deliverance.

MEDITATION: THE REFINING POWER OF AFFLICTION

"They have greatly oppressed me from my youth..."

There is profound honesty in this opening declaration. The pilgrim journey does not deny or minimize suffering—it acknowledges it directly. The repetition of this line emphasizes the intensity and duration of the affliction. This was no momentary discomfort but sustained opposition from "youth" onward.

When we face prolonged seasons of suffering, whether through illness, relationship conflict, workplace hostility, or systematic discrimination, we often question its purpose. Why would God allow such persistent pain? The psalm doesn't provide easy answers, but it does reveal a perspective that transforms how we view affliction.

Notice that the suffering described isn't random or meaningless. The image of plowing suggests intention and design. A farmer plows with purpose—to prepare soil for planting and eventual harvest. What the oppressors intended for destruction, God repurposes for cultivation. The very furrows cut into Israel's back become channels for new growth.

This agricultural metaphor offers a profound spiritual truth: opposition, when endured with faith, doesn't destroy us but deepens us. It creates capacity for greater fruitfulness. The theologian Charles Spurgeon wrote, "The spade of trouble digs the reservoir of comfort deeper, and makes more room for consolation." Our suffering, viewed through the lens of faith, becomes not just something to endure but something that expands our capacity to experience God's presence and bear spiritual fruit.

THE TESTIMONY OF ENDURANCE

"...but they have not gained the victory over me."

Here is the triumphant counterpoint to suffering—the declaration that despite all attempts to destroy, the oppressors have failed. This is not mere survival but a profound spiritual victory. The Hebrew phrase suggests not just continuing to exist but continuing to thrive.

What enables such resilience? The psalm points to divine intervention: "But the LORD is righteous; he has cut me free from the cords of the wicked." The image shifts from agricultural to captivity—Israel was bound like an animal, restricted and controlled, but God severed these restraints.

This testimony reminds us that endurance in suffering is not primarily about our strength or determination. Rather, it flows from God's righteous character and faithful action. When we can no longer bear the weight of our circumstances, when the furrows seem too deep and the cords too tight, God intervenes with liberating power.

The Christian tradition has always recognized that suffering, while never good in itself, can be transformative when experienced within relationship with God. The Apostle Paul understood this paradox when he wrote of his own afflictions: "We are hard pressed on every side, but not crushed; perplexed, but not in despair; persecuted, but not abandoned; struck down, but not destroyed" (2 Corinthians 4:8-9). Like the psalmist, Paul recognized that opposition had not gained the victory over him because God's sustaining power was greater than his suffering.

APPLICATION: FINDING PURPOSE IN PERSECUTION

As modern pilgrims, we may experience different forms of opposition than ancient Israel, but the dynamic remains the same. Whether facing subtle cultural hostility to faith, workplace discrimination, family resistance, or in some parts of the world, outright persecution, followers of Christ continue to experience the "plowing" described in this psalm.

The question is not whether we will face opposition but how we will interpret and respond to it. Will we see only meaningless suffering, or will we discern the refining work of God even in our pain? Will we allow affliction to embitter us, or will we permit it to create deeper furrows of faith in which God can plant seeds of greater fruitfulness?

The psalm challenges us to reframe our understanding of opposition. The very forces that seek to destroy our faith often unintentionally strengthen it. History repeatedly demonstrates this paradox—the church has often grown most vigorously during periods of persecution. As Tertullian famously observed in the second century, "The blood of the martyrs is the seed of the church."

Your current struggles, whatever form they take, are not evidence of God's absence but opportunities for God's refining work. Each furrow of pain, when surrendered to God, becomes a channel for grace. Each cord of restriction, when cut by divine intervention, becomes a testimony to God's faithfulness.

As you continue this pilgrim journey, carry this psalm's perspective with you. Let it reshape how you view opposition. Rather than asking, "Why am I suffering?" perhaps the better question is, "How is God using this suffering to deepen my capacity for faith, hope, and love?" The plowing you endure today is preparing the soil of your soul for tomorrow's harvest.

REFLECTION QUESTIONS

1. The psalm speaks of oppression "from my youth." What long-term challenges or opposition have you faced in your life? How have these experiences shaped your character and faith?

_____

_____

2. Consider the image of plowers making furrows on the back. What "furrows" has suffering created in your life? How might God be using these channels for new growth?

_____

_____

3. The psalmist declares, "they have not gained the victory over me." In what ways have you experienced spiritual victory even in the midst of difficult circumstances? What enabled you to endure?

_____

_____

4. The psalm attributes deliverance to God's righteousness: "But the LORD is righteous; he has cut me free." Recall a time when you experienced God's intervention in a difficult situation. How did this experience affect your trust in God?

_____

_____

5. How does knowing that others throughout history have endured suffering for their faith strengthen your own resolve when facing opposition? Who are the specific examples (biblical or historical) that inspire you?

_____

_____

6. If you're journeying through this devotional with others, discuss how your community can better support those currently experiencing opposition or persecution. What practical steps can you take to stand with brothers and sisters facing affliction?

PRAYER FOR TODAY

Righteous God,

I come before You today acknowledging both the reality of suffering in this world and Your sovereign power over it. Like Israel of old, I have experienced furrows plowed across my life—wounds that have left their mark and times when opposition seemed overwhelming.

Thank You that the story doesn't end with the plowing. Thank You that what others intend for harm, You can transform for growth. Help me to see the afflictions I face not merely as painful events to endure but as channels You can use to deepen my faith and increase my fruitfulness.

When I feel bound by circumstances, relationships, or my own fears, be the righteous God who cuts me free. Remind me that no opposition can ultimately prevail against Your purposes in my life. Guard my heart against bitterness when I suffer, and instead, fill those furrows with the seeds of hope, patience, and compassion.

For those in our world facing severe persecution for their faith, I ask for Your protection and strength. May their testimony, like the psalmist's, be one of endurance rather than defeat. Use their witness to inspire others and to advance Your kingdom.

As I continue this journey toward Your presence, transform how I view the difficulties I encounter. Help me to see even the painful plowing as preparation for harvest, trusting that You are working all things together for good for those who love You and are called according to Your purpose.

In the name of Jesus Christ, who endured the cross for the joy set before Him, Amen.

Day 20

When Enemies Fail

"May all who hate Zion be turned back in shame. May they be like grass on the roof, which withers before it can grow; a reaper cannot fill his hands with it, nor one who gathers fill his arms. May those who pass by not say to them, 'The blessing of the LORD be on you; we bless you in the name of the LORD.'" — Psalm 129:5-8

HISTORICAL CONTEXT

As we continue our pilgrim journey through the Songs of Ascent, we encounter the second half of Psalm 129, which takes a striking turn. Having recounted Israel's history of enduring oppression in verses 1-4, the psalmist now addresses the fate of those who oppose God's people. These verses reflect the ancient Near Eastern understanding of justice, where calling for the downfall of enemies was not merely personal vindictiveness but a cry for divine restoration of moral order.

For the Hebrew pilgrims journeying to Jerusalem, these words would resonate deeply. They had experienced generations of hostility from surrounding nations who "hated Zion"—who despised not just Israel as a people but the very covenant relationship between God and His chosen ones. The pilgrims singing this psalm weren't simply expressing resentment toward personal enemies; they were appealing to God's covenant faithfulness. To attack Zion was to attack God's dwelling place, His chosen city, and by extension, to oppose God Himself.

The agricultural metaphor of grass withering on the rooftop would be immediately recognizable to these travelers. In ancient Palestine, thin layers of soil would collect on flat rooftops, allowing seeds blown by the wind to sprout quickly. However, with shallow roots and no protection from the sun, these plants would wither before reaching maturity—a vivid image of the temporary nature of those who set themselves against God's purposes.

MEDITATION: THE QUESTION OF JUSTICE

"May all who hate Zion be turned back in shame."

This opening line of the second half of our psalm presents us with one of the most challenging aspects of the biblical tradition: the prayer for justice against enemies. Modern readers often struggle with such sentiments, wondering how they align with New Testament teachings about loving enemies and blessing those who persecute us. Yet dismissing these verses as merely primitive or pre-Christian misses their theological depth and spiritual wisdom.

At its core, this prayer recognizes something essential: justice matters. When people suffer under oppression and injustice, it is right to long for correction. The psalmist doesn't seek personal revenge but appeals to God as the ultimate arbiter of justice. This is crucial—the desire for enemies to "be turned back in shame" is not a call for the psalmist to take matters into his own hands but a recognition that judgment belongs to God alone.

The Hebrew word for "shame" (וִשְׁבִי, yevoshu) suggests not humiliation for its own sake but a reorienting awareness that forces one to reconsider one's path. When those who oppose God's people "turn back in shame," they are confronted with the futility of their opposition to God's purposes. There is even a redemptive possibility in such shame—it can become the first step toward repentance and transformation.

What the psalmist models is neither bitter vengeance nor passive acceptance of evil, but rather a third way: entrusting justice to God while maintaining hope that even enemies might eventually recognize their error. This approach frees us from both the poison of hatred and the weight of administering justice ourselves.

THE FATE OF OPPOSITION

"May they be like grass on the roof, which withers before it can grow..."

The psalm's central metaphor offers profound insight into the ultimate fate of opposition to God's purposes. The image of grass sprouting on rooftops speaks to impressive but ultimately unsustainable beginnings. What appears to be rapid success—the quick sprouting of seeds in shallow soil—lacks the depth needed for lasting growth.

This metaphor serves not only as a judgment but as a discernment tool for our own lives. Any endeavor, relationship, or ambition rooted in opposition to God's character and commands may show initial promise but ultimately lacks the foundation for meaningful fruition. The psalm invites us to examine the roots of our own desires and pursuits: Are they planted in the deep soil of God's truth and love, or in the shallow ground of self-interest, pride, or animosity?

The detail that "a reaper cannot fill his hands with it" speaks to the ultimate futility of evil. Despite its temporary appearance of thriving, opposition to God's purposes produces no lasting harvest. The history of God's people repeatedly demonstrates this principle—empires that persecuted believers have crumbled, while the community of faith endures. As Jesus would later tell his disciples, "Heaven and earth will pass away, but my words will never pass away" (Matthew 24:35).

THE WITHHELD BLESSING

"May those who pass by not say to them, 'The blessing of the LORD be on you...'"

The psalm concludes with what might initially seem like a minor detail but is actually a profound statement about community boundaries. In ancient agricultural communities, harvesters would exchange blessings as they passed each other in the fields—a beautiful custom acknowledging their shared dependence on God's provision. The psalmist suggests that those who actively oppose God's people place themselves outside this circle of blessing.

This isn't petty exclusion but a recognition of spiritual reality: those who persistently set themselves against God's purposes separate themselves from the flow of divine blessing. The withholding of the customary blessing isn't primarily punishment but acknowledgment of a self-chosen separation.

Yet importantly, this withheld blessing is presented as a prayer, not a personal action. The psalmist doesn't instruct God's people to curse their enemies or treat them with contempt. Rather, he places the entire matter of justice and consequences into God's hands. This approach preserves both the seriousness of opposition to God and the purity of heart for the believer.

APPLICATION: ENTRUSTING JUSTICE TO GOD

As modern pilgrims, we face a crucial question: How do we deal righteously with those who oppose us, particularly when that opposition stems from our faith commitment? The psalm offers several principles to guide us.

First, we must acknowledge the reality of opposition. Following Christ doesn't exempt us from experiencing hostility. Jesus himself warned, "If the world hates you, keep in mind that it hated me first" (John 15:18). Denying or minimizing opposition doesn't strengthen our faith but prevents us from developing the spiritual resources to respond wisely.

Second, we must distinguish between personal vengeance and divine justice. The psalm doesn't call for believers to punish enemies but entrusts their fate to God. This aligns perfectly with Paul's teaching: "Do not take revenge, my dear friends, but leave room for God's wrath, for it is written: 'It is mine to avenge; I will repay,' says the Lord" (Romans 12:19). When we surrender our desire for personal vindication, we free ourselves from the consuming power of bitterness.

Third, we can maintain hope for our opponents' transformation. While the psalm speaks of enemies being "turned back," this very turning can become an opportunity for repentance. Throughout biblical history, opponents of God's people sometimes became their greatest allies—Saul becoming Paul stands as the most dramatic example. Our prayers regarding enemies should always leave room for this possibility.

Finally, we must guard our hearts against bitterness while still acknowledging the pain of opposition. The psalmist doesn't deny suffering but places it in the larger context of God's ultimate justice. Bitterness doesn't harm our enemies; it only poisons our own spirits. As Hebrews 12:15 warns, we must "See to it that no one falls short of the grace of God and that no bitter root grows up to cause trouble and defile many."

As you continue your pilgrim journey, you will likely encounter opposition in various forms. When that happens, resist both the temptation to seek personal revenge and the pressure to pretend injustice doesn't matter. Instead, follow the psalmist's example: acknowledge the reality of opposition, entrust justice to God, maintain hope for transformation, and guard your heart against bitterness. This approach doesn't guarantee freedom from suffering, but it does promise freedom in suffering—the liberty to continue your journey toward God's presence with an undefiled heart.

REFLECTION QUESTIONS

1. Think about a time when you faced opposition because of your faith or values. How did you respond? In what ways did your response align with or differ from the approach suggested in this psalm?

---

2. The psalm uses the metaphor of grass on the roof to describe the temporary nature of opposition to God's purposes. What examples have you observed of seemingly powerful opposition that ultimately proved unsustainable?

_____

_____

3. How do you reconcile the psalm's prayer concerning enemies with Jesus' command to love our enemies and pray for those who persecute us (Matthew 5:44)? Are these necessarily in conflict, or can they be harmonized?

_____

_____

4. The psalm emphasizes entrusting justice to God rather than taking it into our own hands. What specific practices help you surrender your desire for vindication when you've been wronged?

_____

_____

5. Consider the "withheld blessing" mentioned in verses 7-8. How do you discern when to maintain healthy boundaries with those who oppose you while still maintaining a heart of love and hope for their transformation?

_____

_____

6. If you're journeying through this devotional with others, discuss how your community can support members facing opposition while helping them guard against bitterness. What does this kind of support look like in practice?

_____

_____

PRAYER FOR TODAY

Righteous God,

In a world where opposition to Your ways sometimes seems to flourish, I come before You with the honest cry of my heart. When I face hostility because of my faith, when I experience injustice, when those who oppose You seem to prosper, grant me the wisdom to respond as this psalm teaches.

Help me to acknowledge the reality of opposition without being defined by it. Guard my heart against the poison of bitterness and the temptation of personal revenge. Remind me that judgment belongs to You alone, and that Your justice, while sometimes delayed in my limited perspective, is ultimately perfect and complete.

For those who actively oppose You and Your people, I pray not for their destruction but for their transformation. May they, like Paul who once persecuted the church, encounter Your truth in ways that change the direction of their lives. Turn them back not merely in shame but toward Your grace.

When I am tempted to take justice into my own hands, remind me of Christ who, "when they hurled their insults at him, he did not retaliate; when he suffered, he made no threats. Instead, he entrusted himself to him who judges justly" (1 Peter 2:23). Give me the strength to follow His example.

As I continue this pilgrim journey, keep my heart pure and my steps steady. Help me to maintain firm boundaries where needed without building walls of hostility. And even in seasons of opposition, let my life bear fruit that lasts—not like grass on the rooftop but like a tree planted by streams of water.

I trust Your perfect justice and Your perfect timing, even when I cannot see how all things will work together for good. In this trust, I find peace that transcends circumstances and freedom that no opposition can take away.

In the name of Jesus Christ, our Righteous Advocate, Amen.

PART III: THE VALLEY OF SHADOWS (Days 21-30)

Day 21

The Cry from the Depths

"Out of the depths I cry to you, LORD; Lord, hear my voice.
Let your ears be attentive to my cry for mercy." — Psalm 130:1-2

HISTORICAL CONTEXT

As our pilgrimage through the Songs of Ascent continues, we arrive at Psalm 130, one of the most profound expressions of human suffering and divine hope in Scripture. This psalm has been cherished throughout history as one of the seven penitential psalms and is traditionally known by its Latin title, De Profundis ("Out of the depths").

For the ancient Hebrew pilgrims making their way to Jerusalem, this song would resonate with both personal and collective experiences of despair. The "depths" (מִיְקְמֶעַמ, ma'amakim) evoked multiple layers of meaning—the literal depths of the valleys they traversed on their upward journey to Jerusalem, the metaphorical depths of national calamities like exile and oppression, and the spiritual depths of personal sin and alienation from God.

This psalm likely originated during or after the Babylonian exile, a period when Israel experienced profound national trauma. Jerusalem had been destroyed, the temple razed, and many people forcibly relocated to Babylon. In such circumstances, the journey from despair to hope was not merely spiritual rhetoric but urgent existential necessity. The pilgrims singing this song as they approached Jerusalem were enacting physically what the psalm describes spiritually—an ascent from the depths toward divine presence.

MEDITATION: THE DEPTHS OF HUMAN EXPERIENCE

"Out of the depths I cry to you, LORD..."

The psalm begins with unflinching honesty. There is no pretense, no spiritual posturing, no attempt to appear more whole or holy than the psalmist actually feels. Instead, we encounter a voice calling out from the lowest places of human experience.

What are these "depths" from which the psalmist cries? The Hebrew word suggests something far below normal ground level—the deep places where light struggles to penetrate and where one feels overwhelmed, as if drowning. While the specific circumstances remain unnamed (allowing each of us to fill in our own experiences), the image conveys profound suffering, whether from external circumstances, internal anguish, or spiritual alienation.

The Christian tradition has identified various "depths" from which believers cry out:

The depths of sin and guilt, where we recognize our moral failures and their consequences for ourselves and others.

The depths of suffering, where illness, loss, betrayal, or injustice plunge us into pain that seems beyond endurance.

The depths of doubt and confusion, where cherished certainties dissolve and God seems distant or silent.

The depths of depression and despair, where emotional darkness envelops us and hope seems impossibly remote.

What makes this psalm so powerful is its insistence that these depths—whatever their specific nature—are not places beyond God's hearing or beyond legitimate spiritual expression. The psalmist doesn't wait to pray until emerging from the depths; the cry comes from within them. This challenges the common assumption that we must somehow compose ourselves, resolve our negative emotions, or achieve some minimal level of spiritual equilibrium before approaching God.

The message is revolutionary: There is no depth so low that it disqualifies us from prayer. There is no anguish so great, no doubt so severe, no sin so grave that it places us beyond the reach of divine hearing. We need not pretend to be standing when we are drowning. We can call out to God exactly as we are, from exactly where we are.

THE NATURE OF THE CRY

"...Lord, hear my voice. Let your ears be attentive to my cry for mercy."

Notice the directness of the psalmist's address. These are not carefully composed theological formulations but the urgent words of someone drowning and calling for rescue. The doubled address—"LORD" (the divine name, YHWH) and "Lord" (Adonai)—suggests both intimacy and reverence, personal relationship and recognition of divine sovereignty. Even from the depths, the psalmist remembers to whom he speaks.

The request itself is elemental: "hear my voice." Before asking for specific resolution, comfort, or guidance, the psalmist simply asks to be heard. This reveals a profound human need—to know that our suffering registers with someone who cares, that our cries don't simply dissipate in an indifferent universe. The worst form of suffering is often not the pain itself but the isolation it creates, the sense that we suffer alone and unheard.

The Hebrew phrase translated "cry for mercy" (לְנוּנְתָּ, tachanunan) conveys not just a request but a plea for grace—an appeal not based on the petitioner's worthiness but on the character of the one addressed. Even in desperation, the psalmist recognizes that divine response comes not as earned right but as generous gift. There is humility here alongside the urgency.

What the psalmist models is neither stoic suppression of pain nor unrestrained emotional catharsis, but something more profound: authentic prayer that brings the full reality of human experience into conscious relationship with God. This cry from the depths serves not only as expression of pain but as affirmation of trust. After all, we only cry out to those we believe might hear and respond.

APPLICATION: PRAYING FROM OUR DEPTHS

As modern pilgrims, we too encounter depths along our journey. Sometimes these arise suddenly through external circumstances—a devastating diagnosis, the loss of a relationship, professional failure, or global upheaval. Other times they develop gradually as internal struggles with doubt, disappointment, or disillusionment erode our spiritual foundations. Regardless of their source, these depths present us with a fundamental choice: Will we cry out from them, or will we allow them to silence us?

Many forces conspire to keep us silent in our suffering. Cultural stoicism suggests that emotional restraint demonstrates strength. Religious perfectionism implies that negative emotions reflect spiritual failure. Fear whispers that voicing our darkest thoughts might scandalize others or even offend God. The result? Many believers suffer in silence, putting on brave spiritual faces while drowning inside.

The psalmist offers a different way—a path of courageous vulnerability that refuses to compartmentalize life into "presentable" and "unpresentable" aspects before God. This approach doesn't promise immediate resolution of suffering, but it does protect us from the additional burden of spiritual pretense. It creates space for authentic relationship with God and with others who might join us in our journey through the depths.

Learning to pray from our depths involves several spiritual practices:

First, we must give ourselves permission to acknowledge the depths. This sounds simple but proves challenging in religious environments that subtly reward perpetual positivity. The psalmist reminds us that naming our reality before God isn't faithlessness but the precondition for authentic faith.

Second, we must resist the temptation to spiritualize or theologize prematurely. While Scripture encourages us to give thanks in all circumstances (1 Thessalonians 5:18), rushing to spiritual platitudes before fully expressing our pain often short-circuits genuine healing. The psalmist doesn't begin with theological explanation but with raw expression.

Third, we must direct our cry toward God rather than simply into the void. The difference between despair and lament is not the depth of the emotion but its direction. Despair curves inward upon itself; lament reaches outward toward a God believed to be listening. Even when divine presence feels most absent, orienting our pain toward God constitutes an act of stubborn hope.

Finally, we must make space for others to cry from their depths without attempting to silence or "fix" them. Communities that cannot accommodate expressions of suffering inevitably become superficial. By contrast, communities that create safe space for authentic lament foster genuine spiritual intimacy and growth.

As you continue your pilgrim journey, remember that the path to Jerusalem—to deeper communion with God and others—sometimes leads through the valleys. When you find yourself in those depths, resist both the impulse to deny them and the temptation to remain in them indefinitely. Instead, follow the psalmist's example: cry out honestly, direct that cry to the God who hears, and trust that even your darkest moments can become the soil from which authentic faith grows.

REFLECTION QUESTIONS

1. Reflect on a time when you experienced being in "the depths." What were the circumstances, and how did that experience affect your relationship with God and others?

_____

_____

2. What makes it difficult for you to cry out to God from places of pain, confusion, or doubt? What voices—internal or external—try to silence your authentic expression?

_____

_____

3. The psalmist addresses God directly even from the depths. How does your prayer language change when you're suffering? Do you find yourself speaking to God, about God, or withdrawing from prayer altogether?

_____

_____

4. Consider the simple request "hear my voice." Why do you think being heard is so important in times of suffering? How might the assurance that God hears change how we experience our depths?

_____

_____

5. How comfortable is your faith community with expressions of lament and spiritual struggle? What would need to change for your community to become safer for people experiencing the depths?

_____

_____

6. If you're journeying through this devotional with others, consider sharing about a current "depth" in your life (to whatever degree feels appropriate). How might mutual vulnerability strengthen your connections with God and with each other?

PRAYER FOR TODAY

God of the Depths,

Today I come to You as I am, without pretense or polish. You who formed the deep places of the earth know also the deep places of my heart—the wounds that still ache, the fears that keep me awake, the doubts that sometimes cloud my faith, and the regrets that haunt quiet moments. Out of my particular depths, I cry to You today. [Take a moment to name your specific "depths" before God.] I don't come with eloquent words or theological certainty, just the raw cry of a heart that needs to know it's heard.

Thank You that I don't need to clean myself up, sort myself out, or find the right spiritual words before approaching You. Thank You that Jesus Christ has torn the temple curtain, giving me direct access to Your presence not because of my worthiness but because of His.

When the depths threaten to overwhelm me, help me remember that no water rises higher than Your love, no darkness penetrates deeper than Your light, and no suffering takes me beyond the reach of Your comfort. Remind me that You are not distant from my pain but present within it, just as Your Son entered the depths of human suffering and death before rising to new life.

For others around me who dwell in their own depths today, give me the wisdom to be present without premature problem-solving, to listen without judging, and to walk alongside without trying to rush them to higher ground. Help me create space for authentic expression in my relationships, just as You create space for me.

I trust that even this journey through the depths is part of my pilgrimage toward Your presence. Like the ancient travelers climbing toward Jerusalem through valleys and ravines, lead me upward one step at a time, hearing my cry and sustaining me by Your mercy.

In the name of Jesus Christ, who descended to the depths that we might rise with Him, Amen.

Day 22

Beyond Guilt

"If you, LORD, kept a record of sins, Lord, who could stand? But with you there is forgiveness, so that we can, with reverence, serve you." — *Psalm 130:3-4*

HISTORICAL CONTEXT

As our pilgrimage through the Songs of Ascent continues, we remain in the profound terrain of Psalm 130. Having cried out from the depths in verses 1-2, the psalmist now moves to confront the reality of human sin and divine forgiveness. This progression is significant—from honest expression of suffering to honest assessment of moral failing.

For the ancient Hebrew pilgrims journeying to Jerusalem, these verses would resonate with both personal and collective experience. The temple toward which they traveled was not merely a place of celebration but of atonement. Its elaborate sacrificial system served as a constant reminder that the relationship between humanity and God required addressing the reality of sin.

The historical context of this psalm likely ties to Israel's experience of exile. The prophets had consistently interpreted national calamity as divine judgment for covenant unfaithfulness. As Jeremiah lamented, "Your sins have deprived you of good" (Jeremiah 5:25). Yet alongside judgment came the prophetic promise of forgiveness and restoration. As the returning exiles made their pilgrim journey to a rebuilt Jerusalem, they carried this dual awareness—the gravity of sin and the greater reality of divine mercy.

This historical setting enriches our understanding of these verses. The psalmist isn't engaged in abstract theological reflection but expressing the lived experience of a people who had witnessed both the consequences of moral failure and the wonder of undeserved restoration.

MEDITATION: THE WEIGHT OF SIN

"If you, LORD, kept a record of sins, Lord, who could stand?"

The psalmist poses a question that cuts to the heart of the human condition. The Hebrew word translated "kept a record" (רָמַשׁ, shamar) suggests careful observation and preservation. It evokes the image of God as meticulous accountant, noting every moral debt, every failure, every falling short of divine standards. The question acknowledges a sobering reality: if our standing before God depended on our moral performance, none of us would remain upright.

Notice the inclusive nature of this recognition. The psalmist doesn't divide humanity into the exceptionally sinful and the relatively righteous. The question assumes universal moral vulnerability—"who could stand?" This corresponds to the broader biblical witness that "all have sinned and fall short of the glory of God" (Romans 3:23). The psalmist recognizes that moral failure isn't just a problem for particularly egregious offenders but the shared human condition.

What makes this verse so powerful is its unflinching honesty about the gravity of sin. Modern culture often minimizes moral failure, recasting it as mere mistake, psychological maladjustment, or understandable response to social conditioning. While these perspectives contain partial truths, they fail to capture the profound spiritual dimension of sin—its character as rebellion against our created purpose and rupture in our relationship with God.

The psalmist doesn't soften this reality. The question acknowledges that sin carries consequences weighty enough to crush us completely—to make it impossible to "stand" before God. This is not divine vindictiveness but the natural outcome when finite creatures set themselves against the infinite source of life and goodness. As C.S. Lewis observed, "It is not that God is going to punish us for our sins; they are the punishment."

Yet this brutal honesty about sin becomes, paradoxically, the gateway to hope. Only when we abandon pretense about our moral condition do we create space to receive what comes next.

THE WONDER OF FORGIVENESS

"But with you there is forgiveness, so that we can, with reverence, serve you."

The simplicity of this declaration belies its revolutionary impact. With one word—"But"—the entire trajectory changes. The psalmist pivots from the crushing weight of sin to the liberating reality of forgiveness. The Hebrew conjunction (כִּי, ki) introduces not merely a contrast but a foundation-shaking revelation: the God who has every right to keep a record of sins chooses instead to extend forgiveness.

This isn't grudging pardon or reluctant tolerance. The phrase "with you there is forgiveness" suggests forgiveness as essential divine attribute rather than occasional divine action. Forgiveness isn't something God does sometimes, against his better judgment; it flows from who God is essentially. As Moses would hear at Sinai, God is "compassionate and gracious, slow to anger, abounding in love and faithfulness, maintaining love to thousands, and forgiving wickedness, rebellion and sin" (Exodus 34:6-7).

What makes this forgiveness so remarkable is that it doesn't minimize the reality of sin but addresses it directly. Unlike human tendency to address wrongdoing by denying it ("It wasn't that bad"), minimizing it ("Everyone makes mistakes"), or excusing it ("You had good reasons"), divine forgiveness acknowledges the full weight of sin and absorbs its consequences. As the prophet Isaiah would declare, "We all, like sheep, have gone astray, each of us has turned to our own way; and the LORD has laid on him the iniquity of us all" (Isaiah 53:6).

The purpose of this forgiveness is noteworthy: "so that we can, with reverence, serve you." Forgiveness isn't primarily about relieving our guilt feelings or improving our self-esteem, though these may be welcome side effects. Its deepest purpose is restoration of relationship and purpose. We are forgiven not merely to feel better but to live differently—to serve God with reverence (הָאֵרְיֹ, yirah), a Hebrew word suggesting both awe and loving respect.

This reveals a profound paradox: true freedom comes not from moral autonomy but from forgiveness that enables righteous living. Contrary to the fear that grace leads to moral license, the psalmist recognizes that genuine forgiveness produces not casual presumption but reverent service. As Dietrich Bonhoeffer would later observe, what looks like "cheap grace" ultimately proves more expensive than legalism, for it fails to achieve its transformative purpose.

APPLICATION: LIVING BEYOND GUILT

As modern pilgrims, we journey through a culture simultaneously obsessed with and confused about guilt and shame. On one hand, social media amplifies call-out culture, where moral failings become grounds for permanent ostracism. On the other hand, therapeutic impulses encourage us to reject "toxic guilt" and embrace unconditional self-acceptance. Navigating between moralism and moral relativism, many find themselves either crushed by shame or numbed through denial of objective moral standards.

The psalmist offers a different path—one that acknowledges the reality of sin without allowing it to become our defining identity. This approach invites several spiritual practices for living beyond guilt while taking moral responsibility seriously:

First, we must develop the courage to confront our sin honestly. The journey beyond guilt begins not with self-acquittal but with truthful self-assessment. When we rationalize, minimize, or project blame for our moral failures, we remain stuck in patterns that harm ourselves and others. Only when we name our sin as sin—seeing it as God sees it—can we experience the transformative power of authentic forgiveness.

Second, we must learn to distinguish between false guilt and genuine conviction. False guilt manifests as vague, persistent feelings of moral inadequacy disconnected from specific actions or attitudes. By contrast, genuine conviction, while sometimes painful, focuses on specific behaviors contrary to love of God and neighbor, always with the goal of restoration rather than condemnation. As the Apostle Paul noted, "Godly sorrow brings repentance that leads to salvation and leaves no regret, but worldly sorrow brings death" (2 Corinthians 7:10).

Third, we must actively receive and internalize God's forgiveness. Many believers intellectually affirm divine forgiveness while emotionally living as if their sins remain counted against them. We may find ourselves repeatedly confessing already-forgiven sins, maintaining emotional penance through persistent guilt feelings, or psychologically separating ourselves from the community with thoughts like "If they knew the real me, they wouldn't accept me." Moving beyond guilt requires the often-difficult practice of believing that God's assessment of us—as forgiven and beloved—outweighs both our self-condemnation and others' potential judgment.

Fourth, we must allow forgiveness to transform our identity and purpose. The psalmist recognizes that divine forgiveness isn't primarily about changing how we feel but about changing how we live. When we truly grasp that "there is now no condemnation for those who are in Christ Jesus" (Romans 8:1), we find ourselves freed not for moral independence but for "reverent service." Being forgiven becomes not the end of our spiritual journey but the beginning of a new way of living characterized by gratitude, freedom, and joyful obedience.

As you continue your pilgrim journey, remember that confronting your sin honestly isn't meant to leave you mired in shame but to connect you with the God whose forgiveness defines reality more fundamentally than your failures ever could. Your moral inventory, while important, was never meant to be your permanent address. You were created to live beyond guilt—not by denying its reality but by embracing the greater reality of divine forgiveness that transforms both identity and purpose.

REFLECTION QUESTIONS

1. The psalmist asks, "If you, LORD, kept a record of sins, Lord, who could stand?" What makes it difficult for you to acknowledge the full reality of your sin? How might honest self-assessment actually create space for deeper experience of grace?

_____

_____

2. Consider the statement "with you there is forgiveness." How does understanding forgiveness as essential to God's character (rather than occasional divine action) change how you approach God after moral failure?

_____

_____

3. What is the difference between feeling sorry for your sins and truly repenting of them? How might genuine repentance lead not to persistent guilt but to freedom and transformation?

_____

_____

4. The psalm suggests that divine forgiveness leads to reverent service. In what ways has experiencing God's forgiveness changed how you live? Are there areas where guilt still dominates where forgiveness could lead to freedom?

_____

_____

5. How do you distinguish between the Holy Spirit's genuine conviction about sin and false guilt that comes from other sources? What practices help you respond appropriately to each?

_____

_____

6. If you're journeying through this devotional with others, consider how your community handles sin and forgiveness. Does your community create space for honest confession without condemnation? How might you foster an environment where people experience both truth and grace?

PRAYER FOR TODAY

Merciful God,

I come before You today with the psalmist's words echoing in my heart: "If you, LORD, kept a record of sins, Lord, who could stand?" I acknowledge that if my relationship with You depended on my moral performance, I would have no hope. My thoughts, words, and actions fall short of Your perfect standards in ways both obvious and subtle.

Thank You that this is not the end of the story. Thank You for the transformative truth that "with You there is forgiveness." I receive again today the freedom that comes not from denying my sin but from bringing it into the light of Your grace. Thank You that Your forgiveness is not reluctant or grudging but flows from Your very nature as a God of steadfast love.

Help me to live in the liberating tension of these verses—honest about my sin yet confident in Your forgiveness. Guard me from both self-justifying pride and self-condemning shame. When I sin, give me courage to confront it directly rather than hiding in denial or rationalization. When I confess, help me to fully receive the forgiveness You so freely offer.

Transform my identity by Your grace. When voices within and without try to define me by my failures, remind me that You see me through the lens of forgiveness. And let this undeserved mercy lead not to casual presumption but to reverent service. May gratitude for all You've forgiven motivate me more powerfully than fear of judgment ever could.

For others struggling with shame and guilt, I pray for the healing encounter with Your forgiveness that moves them beyond self-condemnation into freedom. For our community, I ask for wisdom to create spaces where sin can be honestly acknowledged and forgiveness genuinely experienced.

As I continue this pilgrim journey toward deeper communion with You, let each stumbling step be redeemed by the knowledge that Your forgiveness makes it possible, once again, for me to stand.

In the name of Jesus Christ, who bore our sins that we might become the righteousness of God, Amen.

Day 23

Watching for Dawn

"I wait for the LORD, my whole being waits, and in his word I put my hope.
I wait for the Lord more than watchmen wait for the morning, more than watchmen wait for the
morning." — Psalm 130:5-6

HISTORICAL CONTEXT

As our pilgrimage through the Songs of Ascent continues, we remain in Psalm 130, now focusing on verses 5-6. Having cried from the depths (vv. 1-2) and reflected on sin and forgiveness (vv. 3-4), the psalmist now enters the challenging terrain of waiting. This progression reveals spiritual wisdom—the journey from crisis through confession now leads to the patient posture of anticipation.

For the ancient Hebrew pilgrims journeying to Jerusalem, these verses would resonate in multiple dimensions. Physically, their pilgrim journey involved periods of waiting—resting between stages of travel, waiting for traveling companions, or waiting outside the city gates until morning when they would open. Historically, Israel was a people formed through waiting—four hundred years in Egyptian captivity, forty years in wilderness wandering, seventy years in Babylonian exile. Their national consciousness was shaped by the tension between divine promise and delayed fulfillment.

The image of watchmen waiting for morning carries particular significance. In ancient walled cities, night watchmen would guard the community during the vulnerable hours of darkness. Their task combined vigilance against danger with anticipation of dawn. These hours before sunrise were often the coldest and darkest of the night, when enemies might attack and when the watchman's own resolve would be most tested. Yet with absolute certainty, they knew morning would eventually come.

The historical realities of temple worship also inform these verses. The Levitical priests maintained perpetual watches in the temple, with assignments changing at daybreak. The morning sacrifice—when divine presence would again be tangibly sought—began at the first rays of dawn. For pilgrims approaching Jerusalem, this liturgical rhythm of darkness yielding to divine encounter shaped their understanding of spiritual waiting.

MEDITATION: THE DISCIPLINE OF WAITING

"I wait for the LORD, my whole being waits..."

The Hebrew word for "wait" (הָוָק, qavah) suggests more than passive resignation or marking time. It carries connotations of gathering together, collecting oneself, and maintaining hopeful tension—like a bow drawn back, storing energy for future release. This is not the waiting of abandoned hope but the waiting of focused anticipation.

Notice the intensity conveyed by "my whole being waits." The Hebrew יַשׁפַּנ (nephesh) refers to the complete person—body, mind, emotions, and will. This waiting engages every dimension of human experience. It is not compartmentalized religiosity but wholehearted devotion. The psalmist doesn't merely think about waiting or perform waiting rituals; his entire being participates in this posture of suspended anticipation.

Such waiting constitutes one of faith's most difficult disciplines. Human nature craves immediate resolution. We prefer answered prayers to prolonged petition, clear guidance to extended discernment, tangible blessing to promises not yet fulfilled. Our technological culture compounds this impatience, training us to expect instant results, immediate information, and on-demand services. The spiritual muscle of waiting atrophies when not deliberately exercised.

Yet throughout Scripture, waiting emerges as essential to spiritual formation. Abraham waited twenty-five years for the promised son. Joseph waited thirteen years from dream to fulfillment. Moses waited forty years in Midian before his burning bush encounter. Jesus himself waited thirty years before beginning public ministry. These periods weren't empty delays but preparation—soil being prepared for eventual harvest.

What distinguishes spiritual waiting from mere delay is its object and foundation. The psalmist doesn't wait for circumstances to improve or feelings to change but for the Lord himself—divine presence, action, and revelation. This personal focus transforms waiting from frustration to relationship, from empty delay to pregnant anticipation.

THE FOUNDATION OF WAITING

"...and in his word I put my hope."

Here the psalmist reveals what sustains this difficult discipline. Waiting without foundation collapses into despair; waiting anchored in divine promise maintains its tension even through prolonged darkness. The Hebrew term translated "word" (רָבָד, davar) encompasses not just verbal communication but active, creative divine expression—the same term used in Genesis when God speaks creation into existence.

This grounding in divine communication provides stability when subjective feelings fluctuate and circumstances disappoint. The psalmist doesn't say, "in my feelings I put my hope" or "in improved circumstances I put my hope," but "in his word I put my hope." This objective anchor holds firm precisely when subjective experiences seem to contradict divine goodness.

For contemporary believers, this foundation takes multiple forms—Scripture's eternal truths, personal promises discerned through prayer, prophetic words from the community of faith, or the abiding promise of Christ's presence. What unites these varied expressions is their source in divine faithfulness rather than human wishful thinking.

The connection between waiting and hope reveals profound spiritual wisdom. Hope without waiting becomes superficial optimism—the expectation that good things will happen quickly and easily. Waiting without hope becomes fatalistic endurance—grimly bearing what cannot be changed. But waiting grounded in hope creates the spiritual conditions for transformation, allowing divine timing to unfold while maintaining confident expectation.

THE INTENSITY OF WAITING

"I wait for the Lord more than watchmen wait for the morning, more than watchmen wait for the morning."

The psalm's repetition—stating twice that the waiting exceeds that of watchmen for morning—underscores the intensity of this spiritual posture. This isn't casual waiting but urgent expectation. The watchmen provide the perfect analogy, for their waiting combines absolute certainty (morning will definitely come) with unknown timing (the exact moment remains beyond their control).

What makes the watchmen's waiting so intense? Several factors: First, their waiting serves purpose beyond themselves—the city's safety depends on their vigilance. Second, their waiting occurs during darkness, when visibility is limited and danger increased. Third, their waiting maintains alertness rather than passive resignation—they scan the horizon for both threats and signs of dawn. Finally, their waiting anchors itself in natural law—the absolute certainty that night eventually yields to day.

The repetition of this image—"more than watchmen wait for the morning, more than watchmen wait for the morning"—creates a rhythm that mimics the watchman's experience. We can almost feel the tension of repeated checking the eastern sky, the mounting anticipation as hours pass, the mixture of weariness and hope that characterizes the final hours before dawn.

Yet remarkably, the psalmist claims to wait for the Lord with even greater intensity. This comparison elevates spiritual anticipation above even the most urgent earthly waiting. It suggests that divine encounter matters more than physical dawn, that spiritual deliverance outweighs natural rhythms. The God who created morning itself is worth more focused anticipation than the morning.

APPLICATION: CULTIVATING SPIRITUAL PATIENCE

As modern pilgrims, we encounter numerous seasons that require waiting—periods of unanswered prayer, unclear guidance, spiritual dryness, or delayed fulfillment of deeply held desires. These seasons test our faith precisely because they create space between divine promise and human experience, between what we believe about God and what we currently feel.

Learning to wait well requires intentional spiritual practices:

First, we must distinguish between passive resignation and active anticipation. Biblical waiting never surrenders hope but maintains spiritual alertness. Like the watchmen scanning the horizon, we continue looking for signs of divine movement even when darkness persists. This active waiting involves continuing spiritual disciplines, maintaining hopeful conversation with God, and remaining engaged with the community of faith even when immediate reward seems absent.

Second, we must anchor our waiting in objective divine promises rather than subjective feelings or circumstances. When God seems silent or distant, Scripture reminds us that divine faithfulness transcends our perceptions. As Jeremiah proclaimed even amid national catastrophe, "Because of the LORD's great love we are not consumed, for his compassions never fail. They are new every morning; great is your faithfulness" (Lamentations 3:22-23). This anchoring in divine character sustains hope when immediate evidence seems contradictory.

Third, we must recognize waiting as formational rather than accidental. The delays we experience aren't divine oversight or cosmic punishment but opportunities for spiritual deepening. Just as precious metals require prolonged heating to remove impurities, certain aspects of spiritual maturity emerge only through extended waiting. Impatience short-circuits this formation; faithful waiting allows it to complete its work. As James writes, "Let perseverance finish its work so that you may be mature and complete, not lacking anything" (James 1:4).

Fourth, we must maintain community during seasons of waiting. The Hebrew pilgrims sang this psalm together, reminding each other that they weren't waiting alone. When individual faith falters, the community continues hoping on our behalf. Their testimony reminds us that darkness eventually yields to dawn, that divine silence doesn't equal divine absence. As the theologian Dietrich Bonhoeffer wrote from prison, "By gracious powers so wonderfully sheltered...I wait the day that thou shalt make."

As you continue your pilgrim journey, remember that waiting constitutes not an interruption of spiritual progress but an essential component of it. The waiting itself—the seemingly empty space between promise and fulfillment—forms your capacity to receive what God eventually brings. Like the watchmen certain of morning's arrival, maintain your vigilance with the absolute assurance that divine faithfulness outlasts even the darkest night.

REFLECTION QUESTIONS

1. The psalm describes waiting with one's "whole being." What aspects of waiting—physical, emotional, intellectual, or spiritual—do you find most challenging? How might a more integrated approach to waiting transform your experience?

_____

_____

2. Consider the phrase "in his word I put my hope." What specific divine promises or scriptural truths anchor your hope during seasons of waiting? How might you more intentionally ground yourself in these foundations?

_____

_____

3. The image of watchmen anticipating dawn suggests both certainty (morning will definitely come) and uncertainty (the exact timing remains unknown). How does this tension appear in your own seasons of spiritual waiting? How do you balance confident expectation with acceptance of divine timing?

_____

_____

4. Reflect on a significant period of waiting in your spiritual journey. What formation occurred during that time that likely wouldn't have happened through immediate fulfillment? How did that waiting shape your understanding of God and yourself?

_____

_____

5. The psalm repeats the watchmen image twice, emphasizing the intensity of waiting. What practices help you maintain spiritual alertness and expectation when God seems silent or distant? What causes your attention to drift during these seasons?

_____

_____

6. If you're journeying through this devotional with others, discuss how your community supports its members during seasons of waiting. How might you better bear one another's burdens when divine timing doesn't match human expectation?

_____

_____

PRAYER FOR TODAY

Patient God,

In a world of instant downloads and overnight delivery, I come to You acknowledging my struggle with waiting. My natural impatience chafes against Your divine timing. Too often I mistake Your pace for absence, Your silence for indifference, Your delays for denial. Forgive my hurried heart that wants fulfillment without formation, answers without deepening, and dawn without the night's vigil.

Today I choose to wait for You with my whole being—not just my thoughts or words but my emotions, choices, and physical practices. Like the watchmen of old, I fix my attention on the horizon of possibility, trusting absolutely in Your appearance while surrendering control of the timing. I anchor this waiting not in my shifting feelings but in Your unchanging word, the promises that hold firm even when my perception suggests otherwise.

In this current season of waiting [take a moment to name your specific area of waiting], grant me the patience that doesn't merely endure but actively anticipates. Protect me from both the despair that surrenders hope and the presumption that demands immediate resolution. Help me recognize this interval not as wasted time but as sacred space where deeper formation occurs.

For others waiting alongside me, I pray for strengthened faith and sustained hope. May we encourage one another with testimonies of Your faithfulness, reminding each other that no night lasts forever, no silence remains unbroken. When individual faith falters, may our community continue watching for dawn on behalf of those in deepest darkness.

I wait for You, Lord, more than watchmen wait for morning—with greater certainty, deeper longing, and more focused attention. Even in this waiting, I thank You for Your presence that never actually leaves, Your purposes that continue unfolding, and Your promises that remain unbroken even when unfelt.

In the name of Jesus Christ, who waited thirty years for ministry, three days for resurrection, and who now waits expectantly for the complete fulfillment of Your kingdom, Amen.

Day 24

Abundant Redemption

"Israel, put your hope in the LORD, for with the LORD is unfailing love and with him is full redemption. He himself will redeem Israel from all their sins." — Psalm 130:7-8

HISTORICAL CONTEXT

As our pilgrimage through the Songs of Ascent continues, we come to the culmination of Psalm 130. Having moved from personal cry (vv. 1-2) through confession (vv. 3-4) and waiting (vv. 5-6), the psalm now broadens to encompass the entire community. This expansion from individual to communal perspective reflects the journey of the Hebrew pilgrims themselves—individuals and families traveling from various locations, gradually merging into larger caravans, and finally joining the full assembly of worshippers in Jerusalem.

For these ancient pilgrims, the language of redemption would evoke multiple layers of meaning. At its most basic level, the Hebrew term for redemption (תּוּדְפ, pedut) described the payment of a price to secure someone's freedom—whether ransoming a prisoner of war, purchasing a slave's liberty, or reclaiming family property. This economic metaphor carried profound theological significance in Israel's collective experience.

The defining redemption in Israel's history was the Exodus—God's dramatic liberation of His people from Egyptian slavery. The Passover ritual, celebrated annually in Jerusalem, commemorated this redemption with tangible elements and narrated memory. Just as God had instructed the first generation to place lamb's blood on their doorposts, securing their freedom through substitutionary sacrifice, each subsequent generation participated in this redemptive memory through ritual reenactment.

The context of exile and return would add another dimension to the psalm's redemption language. For those who composed and first sang these Songs of Ascent after the Babylonian captivity, "full redemption" represented not just spiritual cleansing but national restoration—the return to the land, the rebuilding of Jerusalem and the temple, and the reestablishment of covenant community. Their pilgrim journey to Jerusalem enacted physically what God had accomplished historically.

MEDITATION: THE FULLNESS OF REDEMPTION

"...with the LORD is unfailing love and with him is full redemption."

The psalmist makes a remarkable claim—not just that God offers redemption but that with Him is "full redemption" (תוּדְּפ, pedut). The Hebrew suggests completeness, abundance, and sufficiency. This is not partial liberation or temporary relief but comprehensive restoration. The qualifier "full" indicates that God's redemptive work exceeds expectations and addresses every dimension of human need.

This fullness stands in stark contrast to the limited redemptions available through human effort or systems. Political reforms may change external conditions but cannot transform hearts. Psychological insights may bring understanding but cannot atone for moral failure. Economic prosperity may improve material circumstances but cannot satisfy spiritual longing. Even religious rituals, while potentially meaningful, cannot themselves generate the reality they symbolize.

The juxtaposition of "unfailing love" (דֶסֶח, chesed) and "full redemption" reveals their intimate connection. Divine redemption flows from divine character. God redeems not from reluctant obligation but from faithful love. This covenant love—steadfast, reliable, and generous—ensures that redemption remains available despite human waywardness. As the prophet Jeremiah proclaimed even amid national catastrophe, "Because of the LORD's great love we are not consumed, for his compassions never fail" (Lamentations 3:22).

What makes this redemption "full" is its comprehensive scope. While forgiveness of sins forms its core (as verse 8 emphasizes), biblical redemption extends beyond spiritual pardon to include physical healing, emotional restoration, relational reconciliation, and eventually cosmic renewal. The Hebrew vision of salvation never separated spiritual redemption from embodied wholeness or individual restoration from communal flourishing.

This comprehensive understanding appears throughout Scripture. Isaiah envisions redemption encompassing rebuilt cities, healed bodies, restored relationships, and transformed nature itself (Isaiah 65:17-25). Jesus demonstrates this fullness by combining forgiveness with physical healing, social reintegration, and restored dignity (Mark 2:1-12; Luke 8:43-48; John 8:1-11). Paul extends redemption's scope to include "our bodies" (Romans 8:23) and ultimately "all things" (Colossians 1:20). Biblical redemption leaves nothing unredeemed.

THE SOURCE OF REDEMPTION

"He himself will redeem Israel from all their sins."

The emphatic personal language here—"He himself"—highlights divine initiative and action in redemption. The psalmist doesn't say Israel will redeem itself through moral improvement, ritual precision, or accumulated merit. Nor does he suggest that redemption comes through abstract principles or impersonal forces. Rather, redemption flows directly from divine agency.

This personal emphasis contradicts both ancient and modern tendencies to depersonalize spiritual reality. Ancient paganism often viewed the divine as impersonal cosmic forces requiring appeasement through mechanical rituals. Modern spirituality similarly tends toward abstract principles—energy, consciousness, or universal laws—rather than relationship with a personal redeemer. Against these tendencies, the psalmist insists that redemption comes through personal encounter with the covenantal God who acts decisively in history.

The verb "will redeem" places this action in the future, creating tension with the earlier statement that redemption already exists "with him." This paradox reflects the "already but not yet" nature of divine redemption—secured in principle but unfolding in practice, present in promise while awaiting complete fulfillment. The Hebrew pilgrims experienced this tension as they journeyed toward Jerusalem—already redeemed through covenant relationship, yet still moving toward fuller participation in that redemption.

The specific focus on redemption "from all their sins" identifies both the core problem requiring redemption and the comprehensive scope of divine solution. Sin—understood biblically as not just moral infraction but fractured relationship with God, others, and creation—provides the fundamental diagnosis. The qualifying "all" emphasizes that no dimension of this fundamental distortion lies beyond redemptive reach.

APPLICATION: COMMUNAL DIMENSIONS OF REDEMPTION

Modern Western Christianity often understands redemption primarily through individualistic lenses—personal salvation securing one's eternal destiny. While this perspective contains truth, it represents a significant narrowing of biblical redemption. The psalmist's movement from individual cry to communal hope invites us to recover the fuller dimensions of God's redemptive work.

Notice how the psalm begins with "I" language (vv. 1-6) but concludes with "Israel" (vv. 7-8). This expansion reflects a profoundly biblical understanding: while redemption personally addresses individual need, it simultaneously creates redeemed community. We are not saved in isolation but incorporated into covenant people whose shared life manifests redemption's transformative power. As Peter would later write, we become "a chosen people, a royal priesthood, a holy nation, God's special possession" precisely to "declare the praises of him who called you out of darkness into his wonderful light" (1 Peter 2:9).

Embracing redemption's communal dimensions involves several spiritual practices:

First, we must recognize salvation as incorporation rather than mere individualistic transaction. When God redeems us, He doesn't merely change our eternal destination but incorporates us into His covenant community. Our redemption finds expression and completion through our connection with others similarly redeemed. As Dietrich Bonhoeffer observed, "Christianity means community through Jesus Christ and in Jesus Christ."

Second, we must expand our prayers beyond personal concerns to embrace the redemptive needs of our communities. The psalmist moves from individual petitions to communal focus: "Israel, put your hope in the LORD... He himself will redeem Israel from all their sins." This broadening perspective doesn't diminish personal relationship with God but situates it within larger redemptive purposes. Our prayers mature as they increasingly encompass others' redemptive needs.

Third, we must allow redemption to address both internal and external dimensions of life. The Hebrew understanding of redemption never separated spiritual transformation from social justice, personal holiness from communal flourishing. Jesus embodied this integration by both forgiving sins and confronting oppressive systems, healing individual bodies and challenging societal structures that perpetuated suffering. Our participation in redemption similarly embraces both inner renewal and outward reformation.

Fourth, we must live as witnesses to redemption's reality in contexts still awaiting its fullness. The tension between "with him is full redemption" (present reality) and "He himself will redeem" (future promise) creates the space where Christian testimony becomes most critical. We live as those already experiencing redemption's firstfruits while acknowledging and addressing the brokenness still evident around us. This "already but not yet" posture avoids both naive triumphalism ("everything is already perfect") and cynical despair ("nothing can really change").

As you continue your pilgrim journey, remember that the God who hears your personal cry from the depths (v. 1) is simultaneously working redemption on cosmic scale. Your individual story of salvation finds both meaning and completion as it merges with the larger story of God redeeming a people, restoring creation, and renewing all things. This expansive vision doesn't diminish the wonder of personal redemption but magnifies it, revealing your story as one crucial thread in the grand tapestry of divine redemption.

REFLECTION QUESTIONS

1. The psalm moves from individual focus ("I wait for the LORD") to communal emphasis ("Israel, put your hope in the LORD"). How does your own understanding of redemption balance personal and communal dimensions? Which aspect tends to receive more emphasis in your spiritual life?

_____

_____

2. Consider the phrase "full redemption." What areas of your life or our world might you have considered beyond redemption's reach? How might embracing redemption's fullness expand your prayers and expectations?

_____

_____

3. The psalmist connects redemption directly to God's "unfailing love" (דֶסֶח, chesed). How does understanding redemption as flowing from God's character rather than merely His power change how you approach Him when seeking restoration?

_____

_____

4. What is the relationship between forgiveness of sins and broader dimensions of redemption like physical healing, emotional wholeness, relational reconciliation, and social justice? How has this relationship played out in your own experience of God's redemptive work?

_____

_____

5. The psalm places redemption both in present reality ("with him is redemption") and future promise ("He himself will redeem"). Where do you experience this tension between the "already" and "not yet" aspects of redemption in your life and community?

_____

_____

6. If you're journeying through this devotional with others, discuss how your community might more effectively embody and witness to God's "full redemption." What specific needs—spiritual, relational, physical, or social—is God calling you to address together?

PRAYER FOR TODAY

God of Abundant Redemption,

Today I marvel at the fullness of Your saving work. Thank You that Your redemption extends beyond narrow religious categories to encompass every dimension of brokenness in my life and in our world. Thank You that with You is not partial or temporary relief but complete and enduring restoration.

I acknowledge my tendency to shrink redemption to fit my limited expectations—to seek spiritual salvation while neglecting physical needs, to pursue personal transformation while ignoring systemic injustice, or to focus on future hope while neglecting present healing. Forgive me for domesticating the wild reach of Your redemptive love. Expand my vision to embrace the comprehensive scope of what You have done, are doing, and will complete in Christ.

As the psalmist moved from individual cry to communal hope, help me similarly broaden my spiritual perspective. Remind me that my story finds its deepest meaning as part of Your larger redemptive narrative. When I'm tempted toward spiritual individualism, draw me back into meaningful connection with Your covenant community, where redemption is not just believed but embodied through our shared life.

For those areas in my life that seem most resistant to change—persistent struggles, deep wounds, seemingly intractable conflicts—I claim the promise of Your "full redemption." Nothing lies beyond the reach of Your restoring grace. With the psalmist, I put my hope in Your unfailing love, trusting that You who began this good work will carry it to completion.

For our community and world, I pray for manifestations of Your redemption that address both personal sin and systemic brokenness. Make us agents of Your comprehensive restoration—people who forgive as we have been forgiven, who heal as we have been healed, who liberate as we have been liberated. May our communal life offer a foretaste of the complete redemption that awaits creation.

I rest today in the confidence that redemption ultimately depends not on human effort but on Your faithful initiative: "He himself will redeem." All my hope is in You, the God whose love never fails and whose redemption leaves nothing unredeemed.

In the name of Jesus Christ, through whom and for whom all things are being reconciled and made new, Amen.

Day 25

The Weaned Child

*"My heart is not proud, LORD, my eyes are not haughty; I do not concern myself with g
reat matters or things too wonderful for me. But I have calmed and quieted myself, I am like a weaned child
with its mother; like a weaned child I am content. Israel, put your hope in the LORD both now and
forevermore." — Psalm 131:1-3*

HISTORICAL CONTEXT

As our pilgrimage through the Songs of Ascent continues, we encounter Psalm 131—one of the shortest yet most profound songs in this collection. After the emotional intensity of Psalm 130, with its cry from the depths and longing for redemption, this psalm offers a striking contrast—a quiet, centered simplicity that reflects spiritual maturity.

For the ancient Hebrew pilgrims journeying to Jerusalem, this psalm would resonate with the physical and spiritual contours of their ascent. Physically, as they approached Jerusalem, the terrain became increasingly imposing. The city itself sat upon Mount Zion, with the temple at its highest point. Looking up at these heights might naturally evoke feelings of smallness and humility—a physical reminder of one's place in relation to divine majesty.

The historical attribution to David connects this psalm to Israel's greatest king—a man who experienced both extraordinary triumph and devastating failure. That such a powerful leader would compose these words of humility and contentment carries special significance. In ancient Near Eastern culture, kings typically projected images of grandeur and self-sufficiency. David's willingness to compare himself to a weaned child—dependent and content in that dependence—would strike the original audience as a profound subversion of royal expectations.

The image of the weaned child would resonate deeply in ancient agricultural communities where weaning represented a significant developmental milestone, typically occurring between ages two and four. Before weaning, a child relates to the mother primarily as source of nourishment and immediate gratification. After weaning, the relationship transforms—still characterized by dependence and intimacy but no longer driven by urgent demand. The child learns to find comfort in the mother's presence rather than just her provision.

MEDITATION: THE SIMPLICITY OF HUMILITY

"My heart is not proud, LORD, my eyes are not haughty..."

The psalm begins with striking directness—a negative confession that establishes spiritual orientation. The Hebrew terms for "proud" (הַבְּנ, gabah) and "haughty" (סוּר, rum) both convey elevation or lifting up. Pride fundamentally involves self-elevation—placing oneself above proper position in relation to God and others.

Notice that the psalmist addresses this confession directly to God: "LORD, my heart is not proud." This is not public virtue-signaling but intimate spiritual assessment before divine presence. The sequence is significant—"heart" before "eyes." Biblical spirituality consistently moves from internal reality to external expression. Pride begins in the heart's orientation before manifesting in the eyes' perspective.

The humility described here doesn't involve self-deprecation or false modesty but accurate self-perception. As C.S. Lewis observed, "Humility is not thinking less of yourself but thinking of yourself less." The psalmist has discovered the paradoxical freedom that comes from abandoning self-importance—the spaciousness that emerges when we release the exhausting project of self-promotion.

This humility stands in stark contrast to contemporary culture's emphasis on self-assertion, personal branding, and curated public image. Social media platforms reward performative identity and carefully constructed personas. Career advancement often requires strategic self-promotion. Even religious environments sometimes measure spiritual maturity by knowledge accumulation, ministry visibility, or platform size.

Against these currents, the psalmist offers a radical alternative—the simplicity of accurate self-assessment before God. This creates space for genuine relationship uncomplicated by constant positioning and impression management. The humble heart finds rest precisely because it stops the exhausting work of trying to appear more significant than it is

THE BOUNDARIES OF KNOWLEDGE

"I do not concern myself with great matters or things too wonderful for me."

This remarkable statement acknowledges the limits of human understanding with neither frustration nor resignation but peaceful acceptance. The Hebrew phrase for "great matters" (תּוֹלְדֹּג, gedolot) suggests things beyond one's capacity or appropriate sphere. The psalmist has discovered the freedom that comes from accepting finitude rather than constantly pushing against it.

This doesn't advocate for willful ignorance or anti-intellectualism. David himself was a sophisticated thinker, poet, and strategist. Rather, it suggests a wisdom that recognizes which questions we are equipped to answer and which mysteries exceed our capacity. It acknowledges that some divine realities remain "too wonderful" (תּוֹאָלְפִנ, nifla'ot)—literally too marvelous or extraordinary—for complete human comprehension.

How countercultural this spiritual posture appears in our information-saturated age! Contemporary culture often assumes that with sufficient data and processing power, all mysteries become solvable puzzles. Religious discourse sometimes mirrors this assumption, attempting to systematize divine mystery into comprehensive theological frameworks that leave no questions unanswered.

The psalmist offers an alternative—intellectual humility that makes peace with mystery rather than demanding mastery. This posture doesn't abandon the pursuit of understanding but recognizes its proper limits. It finds contentment not in comprehensive explanation but in relational trust. As the psalmist will continue, this acceptance of limits becomes the foundation for profound spiritual rest.

THE QUIET SOUL

"But I have calmed and quieted myself, I am like a weaned child with its mother; like a weaned child I am content."

Here the psalm shifts from what the psalmist does not do to what he actively practices. The Hebrew verbs "calmed" (יתִיּוִשׁ, shiviti) and "quieted" (יתִּמַמוֹד, domamti) suggest deliberate spiritual discipline—not passive resignation but intentional cultivation of internal stillness. This reframes spiritual maturity not as achieving ever-greater heights but as developing ever-deeper capacity for restful presence.

The comparison to a weaned child provides the psalm's central metaphor and its most profound insight. Unlike a nursing infant who relates to the mother primarily as source of nourishment, the weaned child has developed capacity for relationship beyond immediate need-fulfillment. The child still depends completely on the mother but has matured beyond the demanding urgency of infancy.

This metaphor offers a powerful corrective to both immature and overly complicated spirituality. Immature faith often relates to God primarily as divine problem-solver or blessing-dispenser—the spiritual equivalent of a nursing infant, content only when immediate needs receive satisfaction. Conversely, overly complicated faith often substitutes intellectual complexity or religious activity for simple presence—the spiritual equivalent of an adolescent trying too hard to appear grown-up.

The weaned child represents the middle path of mature simplicity. Still fully dependent yet peacefully content, the weaned child finds security not in constant consumption but in assured presence. This child doesn't demand constant stimulation or immediate gratification but has developed capacity to rest quietly in relationship itself.

APPLICATION: CULTIVATING SPIRITUAL CONTENTMENT

As modern pilgrims, we journey through landscapes that constantly undermine the spiritual contentment this psalm describes. Consumer capitalism depends on creating perpetual discontent while promising satisfaction through the next purchase. Social media platforms engender constant comparison while rewarding performative identity. Even religious environments sometimes measure spiritual growth by activity, knowledge, or emotional intensity rather than deepening capacity for restful presence.

Against these currents, Psalm 131 offers a vision of spiritual maturity characterized not by achievement but by contentment, not by acquisition but by simplicity, not by certainty but by trust. Cultivating this mature simplicity involves several spiritual practices:

First, we must practice regular self-assessment regarding pride and pretension. The psalmist's opening confession—"My heart is not proud, LORD, my eyes are not haughty"—models this examination. Where do we find ourselves striving for recognition beyond our appropriate place? Where does concern for appearance or reputation drive our choices? Where do we feel compelled to appear more knowledgeable, successful, or spiritual than we actually are? This honest inventory before God creates space for genuine humility.

Second, we must identify and release questions and concerns beyond our capacity. The psalmist's refusal to preoccupy himself with "great matters or things too wonderful" models this discernment. Which theological puzzles, personal circumstances, or future uncertainties are we frantically trying to solve when wisdom might involve accepting their mystery? What would change if we redirected the energy spent on unanswerable questions toward deepening trust in the One who holds the answers?

Third, we must intentionally practice internal stillness. The psalmist's statement "I have calmed and quieted myself" suggests deliberate spiritual discipline rather than passive waiting for peace to arrive. Practices like contemplative prayer, scripture meditation, technology sabbaths, and scheduled silence create space for the soul's quieting. These disciplines don't earn God's presence but develop our capacity to recognize and rest in the presence always available.

Fourth, we must reframe our understanding of spiritual maturity. The weaned child metaphor invites us to see growth not primarily through acquisition (of knowledge, experiences, or spiritual credentials) but through developing capacity for peaceful presence even when immediate desires go unmet. Maturity appears not in constant spiritual stimulation but in deepening contentment with simple relationship.

As you continue your pilgrim journey, consider what "weaning" your soul might involve in this season. Which perceived spiritual needs might actually be expressions of immature demand for immediate gratification? What would change if you found contentment not in constant spiritual consumption but in simple presence with the God who holds you as a mother holds her child? The journey toward Jerusalem—toward deeper communion with God and others— often involves not adding complexity but discovering simplicity.

REFLECTION QUESTIONS

The psalm begins with a confession directly to God: "My heart is not proud, LORD, my eyes are not haughty." What areas of pride or pretension in your life might benefit from similar honest assessment before God? How might acknowledging these tendencies create space for greater spiritual peace?

_____

_____

Consider the statement "I do not concern myself with great matters or things too wonderful for me." What questions, concerns, or circumstances are you trying to figure out that might be beyond your current capacity? What would change if you released these to God rather than demanding immediate understanding?

The psalmist describes actively calming and quieting his soul. What specific practices help you cultivate internal stillness? When do you find it most difficult to quiet your soul, and what might these difficulties reveal about your spiritual development?

Reflect on the metaphor of the weaned child. In what ways might your relationship with God still resemble a nursing infant—demanding immediate satisfaction of perceived needs? What might spiritual "weaning" look like in your current season?

The psalm concludes by expanding from personal practice to communal invitation: "Israel, put your hope in the LORD." How might your personal cultivation of spiritual contentment impact your relationships and community? How does mature simplicity create space for deeper connection with others?

If you're journeying through this devotional with others, discuss how your community either supports or hinders the spiritual contentment this psalm describes. What practices might you adopt together to cultivate more restful presence with God and each other?

PRAYER FOR TODAY

Faithful God,

Today I come before You with the psalmist's words echoing in my heart: "My heart is not proud, LORD, my eyes are not haughty." Yet even as I speak these words, I recognize how often pride distorts my perception and complicates my relationship with You and others. I confess the ways I've elevated myself through comparison, positioned myself through pretense, or exhausted myself through constant self-promotion.

Forgive me for concerning myself with matters too great for me—trying to solve every mystery, answer every question, control every outcome. I release these burdens of omniscience and omnipotence that were never mine to carry. In their place, I receive the liberating truth of my limitations and the corresponding invitation to trust Your unlimited wisdom and power.

Teach me the art of calming and quieting my soul. In a world of constant noise and perpetual urgency, show me how to create space for stillness. When my soul resembles a fussy infant—demanding immediate gratification of every desire—wean me toward the more mature contentment of resting in Your presence whether my perceived needs receive immediate satisfaction or not.

Like a weaned child with its mother, help me find security not in what You provide but in who You are. Transform my relationship with You from transaction to communion, from consumption to presence. When I'm tempted toward spiritual complexity or performative maturity, draw me back to the profound simplicity of being held by Love itself.

For others on this pilgrim journey, especially those traveling alongside me through this devotional, I pray for similar contentment. When our souls grow restless with comparison, discontent, or spiritual ambition, remind us of our shared identity as Your beloved children. Help us create community that values being over doing, presence over performance, and depth over appearance.

I put my hope in You, LORD, now and forevermore. Not in my understanding, achievements, or spiritual progress, but in Your unfailing love that holds me more securely than I could ever hold myself.

In the name of Jesus Christ, who modeled perfect humility while offering perfect rest, Amen.

Day 26

David's Devotion

"LORD, remember David and all his self-denial. He swore an oath to the LORD, he made a vow to the Mighty One of Jacob: 'I will not enter my house or go to my bed, I will allow no sleep to my eyes or slumber to my eyelids, till I find a place for the LORD, a dwelling for the Mighty One of Jacob.'" — Psalm 132:1-5

HISTORICAL CONTEXT

As our pilgrimage through the Songs of Ascent continues, we encounter Psalm 132, the longest and perhaps most historically grounded song in this collection. After the quiet simplicity of Psalm 131, with its image of the contented weaned child, this psalm introduces a dramatically different spiritual posture—intense devotion and passionate commitment.

For the ancient Hebrew pilgrims journeying to Jerusalem, these verses would resonate profoundly with their national identity and sacred history. The psalm refers to a pivotal moment in Israel's development as a unified kingdom—David's determination to establish a permanent dwelling place for the Ark of the Covenant, the physical symbol of God's presence among His people.

Before David's time, the Ark had known a tumultuous history. Captured by the Philistines, then returned; housed temporarily in various locations; but never settled in a permanent sanctuary as originally intended. 2 Samuel 6-7 recounts how David brought the Ark to Jerusalem with great celebration and immediately expressed desire to build a "house" for God—a proper temple to replace the portable tabernacle that had served since wilderness wandering. While God ultimately assigned the temple construction to Solomon, David's son, the passion behind the project originated with David himself.

The pilgrims singing this psalm would be journeying toward the temple that stood as the fulfillment of David's vision. Many would have traveled great distances, enduring significant hardship to reach Jerusalem. Their physical journey mirrored the spiritual devotion expressed in these verses—prioritizing worship above comfort, convenience, and personal concerns.

MEDITATION: THE NATURE OF DEVOTION

"LORD, remember David and all his self-denial."

The psalm begins with a remarkable request—that God would remember not just David himself but specifically his "self-denial" (וְתוֹנַע, unnoto). This Hebrew term suggests affliction, humility, and willingness to suffer discomfort for a greater purpose. The psalmist doesn't appeal to David's accomplishments, victories, or royal status, but to his self-sacrificial devotion.

This opening sets the tone for the entire psalm. Before recounting David's vow, the psalmist establishes that true devotion involves costs willingly embraced. The Hebrew concept of zealousness for God never involved merely emotional intensity or verbal profession but consistently manifested in concrete actions that prioritized divine concerns above personal comfort.

David's devotion provides a striking counterpoint to contemporary spirituality that often emphasizes personal fulfillment, emotional comfort, and convenient religious practice. His commitment didn't emerge from calculating what might benefit him personally but from a consuming passion for God's presence and glory. As he would later write, "Zeal for your house consumes me" (Psalm 69:9)—a declaration Jesus would embody when cleansing the temple (John 2:17).

This devotional intensity raises important questions for modern believers. Has the emphasis on God's love and acceptance—vital theological truths—sometimes overshadowed the corresponding biblical emphasis on reverent devotion? Has the legitimate desire to avoid legalism sometimes led to casual approaches to spiritual commitment? David's example invites us to consider whether true spiritual maturity involves not just peaceful contentment (as in Psalm 131) but also passionate commitment that rearranges priorities and accepts personal costs.

THE POWER OF A VOW

"He swore an oath to the LORD, he made a vow to the Mighty One of Jacob..."

The psalm continues by recounting David's formal commitment—a solemn vow made to "the Mighty One of Jacob." This divine title, relatively rare in Scripture, emphasizes God's power and faithfulness demonstrated through Israel's history. By invoking this specific name, David connects his personal devotion to the larger covenant story—his individual commitment flows from and contributes to the ongoing relationship between God and His people.

The practice of making vows appears frequently in Hebrew spirituality. Unlike casual promises or general intentions, biblical vows involved formal commitments made directly to God, often with specific conditions and consequences. Numbers 30 outlines the binding nature of such vows, emphasizing their seriousness. What makes David's vow remarkable isn't just its content but its motivation—not obligation or crisis but zealous love for God's presence.

The formality of David's commitment—"he swore an oath" (עָבְשַׁנ, nishba) and "made a vow" (רַדָנ, nadar)—reflects an often-overlooked aspect of mature spirituality: the role of deliberate, binding commitment in spiritual formation. While divine-human relationship ultimately flows from grace rather than contractual obligation, the biblical witness consistently includes space for formal promises that provide structure and accountability to spiritual intentions.

This raises important questions about the place of formal commitment in contemporary spirituality. Has the legitimate emphasis on relationship sometimes diminished the complementary biblical emphasis on covenant? Have appropriate reactions against legalism sometimes weakened appreciation for the spiritual formation that occurs through binding commitments? David's example suggests that freedom and commitment aren't opposed but complementary—he freely bound himself through vows precisely because his devotion ran so deep.

THE CONTENT OF COMMITMENT

"I will not enter my house or go to my bed, I will allow no sleep to my eyes or slumber to my eyelids, till I find a place for the LORD, a dwelling for the Mighty One of Jacob."

Now the psalm reveals the specific content of David's vow, and its intensity is breathtaking. He commits to postpone basic physical needs—shelter, comfort, and even sleep—until he has secured "a place for the LORD." The poetic parallelism—house/bed, sleep/slumber, place/dwelling—emphasizes the comprehensive nature of this commitment.

While the language contains poetic hyperbole, its essential meaning remains clear: David placed securing God's dwelling above his own basic comforts. The historical fulfillment of this vow appears in 2 Samuel 6, where David refuses to bring the Ark into his own house until proper preparations are made, declaring, "How can the ark of the LORD come to me?" (2 Samuel 6:9). His reverence forbade casual or convenient approaches to divine presence.

What motivated such extraordinary devotion? David understood something fundamental about divine-human relationship: where God's presence dwells, blessing flows. His passion for establishing a "place for the LORD" wasn't mere religious obligation but recognition that divine presence constitutes the ultimate good for both individuals and communities. As he would write elsewhere, "You make known to me the path of life; you will fill me with joy in your presence, with eternal pleasures at your right hand" (Psalm 16:11).

This understanding challenges utilitarian approaches to spirituality that value divine presence primarily for its benefits rather than for its inherent worth. David sought God's dwelling not merely for what it would provide (though he understood its benefits) but because he recognized that reverent love for God rightfully claims highest priority. His devotion flowed not from calculation but from conviction—the settled certainty that nothing deserves greater commitment than creating space for divine presence.

APPLICATION: CULTIVATING SPIRITUAL PASSION

As modern pilgrims, we journey through cultural landscapes often hostile to the kind of devotion this psalm describes. Consumerism promotes comfort as ultimate value and convenience as non-negotiable expectation. Individualism encourages us to prioritize personal preferences above communal concerns. Even religious environments sometimes repackage faith as means to personal fulfillment rather than response to divine worthiness.

Against these currents, Psalm 132 offers a vision of spirituality characterized by passionate commitment and concrete sacrifice for sacred purpose. Cultivating this devotional intensity involves several spiritual practices:

First, we must reconnect with awe as foundation for authentic devotion. David's extraordinary commitment flowed from extraordinary reverence—recognition of who God is and what His presence means. Contemporary spirituality sometimes emphasizes divine accessibility (a vital truth) while underemphasizing divine transcendence. Practices that restore appropriate awe—contemplating creation's vastness, studying God's attributes, worshiping with reverent communities—create soil from which genuine devotion grows.

Second, we must reexamine our understanding of spiritual formation. David's vow reminds us that spiritual growth involves not just internal development but external commitments. While legalism always threatens to reduce faith to rule-following, the biblical witness consistently includes space for formal promises that provide structure and accountability to spiritual intentions. Consider what specific commitments might support your spiritual growth—sabbath practices, financial generosity, service commitments, or daily disciplines—and how formalizing these might deepen their formative impact.

Third, we must recover theological vision regarding sacred space. While New Testament teaching clearly expands divine dwelling beyond physical structures (1 Corinthians 3:16, 6:19), the underlying principle remains: creating and maintaining space for divine presence constitutes a fundamental spiritual priority. This applies to physical spaces (church buildings, worship environments, retreat centers), temporal spaces (sabbath days, prayer times, liturgical seasons), and relational spaces (Christian communities, mentoring relationships, service opportunities). David's passion for "a place for the LORD" invites us to consider what spaces for divine presence we might help establish or maintain.

Fourth, we must allow devotional intensity to reshape practical priorities. David's commitment reached beyond sentiment or intention to concrete actions—postponing personal comfort until sacred space was secured. Similarly, authentic spiritual passion inevitably affects everyday decisions about time, money, energy, and attention. Where do your actual priorities (revealed by calendar and bank statement rather than stated intentions) align with your professed devotion? Where might reordering be needed?

As you continue your pilgrim journey, consider what might change if David's devotional intensity found expression in your spiritual life. This doesn't necessarily mean dramatic gestures or extreme practices but rather reorienting priorities around a central conviction: that creating space for divine presence constitutes life's highest purpose. The Hebrew pilgrims singing this psalm on their journey to Jerusalem embodied this conviction through their physical travel. What journey—literal or metaphorical—might your devotion inspire?

REFLECTION QUESTIONS

1. The psalm begins by highlighting David's "self-denial" rather than his accomplishments or status. When have you experienced spiritual growth through willingly embraced discomfort or sacrifice? What distinguishes healthy spiritual self-denial from unhealthy asceticism?

2. David made a formal vow regarding his devotion to creating space for God's presence. What role do formal commitments play in your spiritual life? How might intentional promises (whether private or public) support your spiritual formation?

3. David prioritized establishing "a place for the LORD" above his own comfort. What spaces for divine presence (physical, temporal, or relational) are you currently helping to create or maintain? What obstacles or competing priorities make this challenging?

_____

_____

4. The psalm portrays devotion that affects concrete priorities and daily decisions. How does your spiritual passion currently influence practical matters like use of time, money, and energy? Where might greater alignment be needed?

_____

_____

5. David's devotion focused specifically on the Ark of the Covenant—the physical symbol of God's presence among His people. What helps you connect with divine presence in tangible ways? How might strengthening these connections deepen your devotional life?

_____

_____

6. If you're journeying through this devotional with others, discuss how your community might collectively express devotion similar to David's. What shared commitments, projects, or priorities might emerge from passionate desire for God's dwelling place?

_____

_____

PRAYER FOR TODAY

God of David's Devotion,

I come before You today humbled by the passion and commitment described in this psalm. When I consider David's zeal for Your dwelling place—his willingness to postpone comfort and rest until he secured a place for Your presence—I recognize both the beauty of such devotion and how frequently my own priorities fall short of this standard.

Rekindle in me a passion for Your presence that transcends casual religious observance. Where my spirituality has become comfortable, convenient, or primarily self-serving, restore the holy fire that consumed David. Help me to love You not just for Your benefits but for who You are—the Mighty One whose presence constitutes life's greatest treasure.

I recognize that meaningful devotion involves not just sentiment but commitment, not just intention but action. Give me courage to make and keep specific promises that align my life more fully with my professed values. Show me what "places" for Your presence I might help establish or maintain—physical spaces, temporal rhythms, or relational contexts where divine glory can dwell more fully.

Guard me from both legalism that reduces devotion to rule-following and casualness that diminishes reverent commitment. Instead, lead me to the holy ground where freedom and devotion meet, where love expresses itself through willing sacrifice, and where passion produces concrete priorities that honor You.

For my community of faith, I pray for renewed zeal for Your dwelling place. Where religious routine has replaced genuine devotion, breathe fresh fire. Where comfort has become higher priority than mission, realign our collective vision. Help us encourage one another toward the kind of commitment this psalm describes—not through guilt or obligation but through contagious passion for Your presence.

As I continue this pilgrim journey, may my steps be motivated by David-like devotion—the settled conviction that nothing deserves greater commitment than creating space for divine presence in my life and world.

In the name of Jesus Christ, who embodied perfect zeal for Your house, Amen.

Day 27

Finding God's Dwelling

"We heard it in Ephrathah, we came upon it in the fields of Jaar: 'Let us go to his dwelling place, let us worship at his footstool, saying, "Arise, LORD, and come to your resting place, you and the ark of your might." May your priests be clothed with your righteousness; may your faithful people sing for joy.'" — Psalm 132:6-9

HISTORICAL CONTEXT

As our pilgrimage through the Songs of Ascent continues, we remain in Psalm 132, now focusing on verses 6-9. Having recalled David's passionate vow to establish a dwelling place for God (vv. 1-5), the psalm now narrates the fulfillment of that commitment and its implications for worship.

For the ancient Hebrew pilgrims journeying to Jerusalem, these verses would resonate with both historical memory and present experience. The geographical references—Ephrathah (the region around Bethlehem) and the "fields of Jaar" (likely referring to Kiriath Jearim)—recall specific locations in the Ark's journey. After being captured by the Philistines and then returned to Israel, the Ark remained at Kiriath Jearim for twenty years (1 Samuel 7:1-2) before David brought it to Jerusalem (2 Samuel 6).

This historical narrative held profound significance for pilgrims traveling to Jerusalem. Just as the Ark had journeyed from place to place before finding its "resting place" in the temple, so these worshippers physically journeyed from various locations toward the same sacred destination. Their pilgrimage reenacted the sacred history they celebrated—the movement from scattered locations to the central place of divine presence.

The theological context is equally important. In ancient Near Eastern understanding, divine presence wasn't abstract or purely spiritual but manifested in particular locations and contexts. While acknowledging God's transcendence and omnipresence (as expressed in 1 Kings 8:27: "But will God really dwell on earth? The heavens, even the highest heaven, cannot contain you.

How much less this temple I have built!"), Israelite worship simultaneously emphasized the reality of specific divine dwelling—the temple as the place where heaven and earth intersected, where divine presence became specially accessible.

MEDITATION: THE JOURNEY TOWARD PRESENCE

"We heard it in Ephrathah, we came upon it in the fields of Jaar..."

The psalm begins this section with collective memory—"we heard... we came upon." These aren't merely historical facts being recited but communal experience being remembered and reenacted. The Hebrew verb for "came upon" (הוֹנֶאְצָמ, metsa'nuha) suggests discovery or encounter rather than mere intellectual information. This wasn't theoretical knowledge about divine presence but actual finding of the place where God could be met.

This journey from hearing to discovering provides a profound metaphor for spiritual experience. Faith often begins with secondhand knowledge—reports from others about divine reality. We hear testimonies, read Scripture, absorb teaching. But authentic spiritual life requires moving beyond hearing to firsthand encounter—actually "coming upon" divine presence ourselves. The pilgrims singing this psalm were enacting physically what must happen spiritually—moving from distant hearing to direct encounter.

The geographical movements described trace not just the Ark's literal journey but the spiritual progression from scattered, fragmented religious experience toward centered, integrated encounter. Ephrathah and Jaar represent the periphery—places of temporary divine presence— while Jerusalem represents the center where God's presence becomes established and accessible. This movement from periphery to center mirrors the spiritual journey from occasional, disconnected encounters with God toward consistent, integrated relationship.

What makes this section particularly poignant is the nature of the discovery. After David's intense vow—refusing comfort until finding "a place for the LORD" (v. 5)—the psalm reveals that this discovery involved collective wisdom and communal journey. The pronouns shift from singular ("he swore") to plural ("we heard... we came"). Divine dwelling becomes known not through isolated pursuit but through shared pilgrimage. This reminds us that authentic encounter with God often requires both individual passion and communal practice, both personal devotion and participation in the collective journey of faith.

THE NATURE OF WORSHIP

"Let us go to his dwelling place, let us worship at his footstool, saying..."

Having recalled the journey toward divine presence, the psalm now describes the appropriate response to that presence—worship. The Hebrew term for "worship" (הִשְׁתַּחֲוָה, nishtachaweh) literally means to bow down or prostrate oneself. This physical posture symbolizes spiritual reality—recognition of divine greatness and human dependence. True worship flows from accurate perception of the divine-human relationship.

The reference to God's "footstool" further emphasizes this relational dynamic. In ancient Near Eastern royal imagery, the king's footstool symbolized dominion—enemies were often depicted as being beneath the ruler's feet. By approaching this "footstool" (the Ark and temple), worshippers acknowledged divine sovereignty while simultaneously accepting the remarkable invitation to approach the cosmic King's throne room.

What makes biblical worship distinctive is this combination of reverence and intimacy. Unlike pagan approaches that either domesticated deity through manipulative rituals or kept gods at fearful distance, Hebrew worship maintained creative tension—God as both transcendent sovereign and accessible covenant partner. The invitation to "go to his dwelling place" reflects divine initiative in creating space for relationship. God establishes dwelling places not because divine nature requires containment but because human nature needs tangible connection points.

This understanding of worship challenges both ancient and contemporary misconceptions. Against magical thinking that attempts to control divine power, the psalm depicts worship as response to God's prior initiative. Against abstract spirituality that dismisses embodied practice, it affirms concrete locations and physical expressions. Against privatized religion, it emphasizes communal approach to divine presence. The worshippers say "Let us go" and "Let us worship"—plural verbs indicating collective action rather than merely individual devotion.

THE INVITATION TO DIVINE PRESENCE

"Arise, LORD, and come to your resting place, you and the ark of your might."

Here the psalm takes a remarkable turn—the worshippers who have journeyed to find God's dwelling now invite God to arise and enter that dwelling. This reflects profound theological understanding. While the temple represented divine presence, ancient Israelites maintained clear distinction between the building itself and the living God it was designed to house. The structure provided the context for encounter but required divine decision to fill it with presence.

The prayer "Arise, LORD, and come" acknowledges divine freedom. Unlike pagan conceptions where gods could be manipulated or controlled through correct ritual, biblical faith recognized divine sovereignty. God couldn't be summoned on demand but could be reverently invited. This invitation expresses both humble acknowledgment of dependence and confident expectation based on covenant relationship.

The reference to God's "resting place" (מְנוּחָתֶךָ, menuchatekha) adds another dimension. While human religious impulse often focuses on securing divine help for human projects, this prayer recognizes God's own desires and purposes. The temple isn't merely for human benefit but provides space for divine "rest"—not in the sense of fatigue but of satisfied accomplishment and established presence. True worship aligns with divine purposes rather than merely seeking to harness divine power for human agendas.

The phrase "you and the ark of your might" reflects theological sophistication—distinguishing between the ark as symbol and God as reality while simultaneously acknowledging their connection. The ark represented divine presence and power but was never confused with God Himself. This balanced understanding avoided both superstitious veneration of religious objects and disconnected spirituality that dismissed physical symbols. The ark provided tangible focus for worship without becoming an idol.

MANIFESTATIONS OF DIVINE PRESENCE

"May your priests be clothed with your righteousness; may your faithful people sing for joy."

The psalm concludes this section by identifying two manifestations of authentic divine presence—righteous leadership and joyful community. These aren't merely pleasant religious features but evidence that God has indeed "arisen" and "come" to dwell among His people.

The prayer for priests "clothed with righteousness" recognizes that divine presence transforms religious leaders. The Hebrew term for "righteousness" (צֶדֶק, tsedeq) encompasses both moral integrity and correct relationship—living rightly with both God and others. This righteousness isn't merely human achievement but divine endowment, something God provides as covering and protection. Where divine presence authentically manifests, religious leadership displays character that transcends mere professionalism or technique.

Similarly, the prayer for the faithful to "sing for joy" identifies authentic spiritual emotion as evidence of divine presence. The Hebrew term (וּנְנְרִי, yerannenu) suggests not polite religious appreciation but spontaneous, exuberant response to divine goodness. Where God truly dwells, communities experience joy that transcends circumstantial happiness—a deeper gladness rooted in divine character and presence rather than temporary conditions.

These twin manifestations—righteous leadership and joyful community—provide important criteria for discerning authentic divine presence. Religious contexts may feature impressive buildings, elaborate rituals, or emotional experiences, but without transformed character and genuine joy, these remain empty forms rather than true divine dwelling.

APPLICATION: DISCERNING DIVINE PRESENCE

As modern pilgrims, we journey through diverse religious landscapes, each claiming to offer authentic connection with God. From traditional sanctuaries to contemporary worship venues, from established liturgies to innovative spiritual practices, from organized congregations to informal gatherings—we face countless options for seeking divine encounter. How do we discern where God truly dwells?

Psalm 132:6-9 offers several principles for this discernment:

First, we must recognize that finding God's dwelling involves both hearing and seeing, both received wisdom and personal discovery. The psalm's language—"We heard it... we came upon it"—suggests the complementary roles of tradition and experience. Authentic spirituality neither dismisses inherited wisdom in favor of purely subjective experience nor substitutes second-hand knowledge for personal encounter. Rather, it allows received testimony to guide toward firsthand discovery. Consider how your spiritual journey integrates these elements—how tradition informs experience and experience enlivens tradition.

Second, we must understand that divine presence manifests through communal pilgrimage rather than merely individualistic pursuit. Throughout this psalm section, plural pronouns dominate—"we heard... we came... let us go... let us worship." While personal devotion remains essential (as David's vow in verses 1-5 demonstrates), full experience of divine dwelling occurs through shared journey and collective worship. Where contemporary spirituality often emphasizes private practice disconnected from community, the psalm reminds us that finding God's dwelling place typically involves journeying alongside others. Consider how your pursuit of divine presence balances individual and communal dimensions.

Third, we must approach divine presence with both reverent humility and confident expectation. The worship described involves both prostration "at his footstool" (acknowledging divine transcendence) and bold invitation for God to "arise and come" (expressing covenant intimacy). Where religious contexts emphasize only transcendence, they risk creating distant, fearful spirituality. Where they emphasize only intimacy, they risk presumptuous casualness that diminishes divine holiness. Authentic encounter maintains creative tension between these dimensions. Consider how your spiritual practices reflect both reverence and relationship.

Fourth, we must evaluate spiritual contexts not primarily by their forms or feelings but by their fruits—specifically, righteous leadership and joyful community. The psalm identifies these as evidence that God has indeed responded to the invitation to "arise and come." Religious environments may feature impressive aesthetics, engaging presentations, or emotional experiences without necessarily manifesting divine presence. The questions that matter most are: Does this context produce leaders characterized by authentic righteousness (not just skill or charisma)? Does it cultivate communities marked by genuine joy (not just enthusiasm or entertainment)? Consider how these criteria might inform your discernment of where God truly dwells.

As you continue your pilgrim journey, remember that finding God's dwelling place involves movement—both physical and spiritual—from where you currently are toward where divine presence manifests. Like the ancient Hebrew pilgrims, you may need to leave familiar territory, join others on the journey, and prepare your heart for encounter. The promise embedded in this psalm is that such pilgrimage ultimately leads to discovery—"we came upon it"—genuine experience of the God who desires to dwell among His people.

REFLECTION QUESTIONS

The psalm describes movement from "hearing about" divine presence to "coming upon" it. How has your spiritual journey progressed from secondhand knowledge to firsthand encounter? What helped facilitate this progression?

_____

_____

Consider the communal language throughout this passage—"we heard... we came... let us go... let us worship." How does your pursuit of divine presence balance individual and communal dimensions? What might need rebalancing in your current spiritual practice?

_____

_____

The worshippers approach God's "footstool" (acknowledging divine transcendence) while simultaneously inviting God to "arise and come" (expressing covenant intimacy). How do your spiritual practices reflect both reverence and relationship? Which aspect might need strengthening?

_____

_____

The psalm identifies righteous leadership and joyful community as evidence of authentic divine presence. How do these criteria help you discern contexts where God truly dwells? How might they challenge popular measures of "successful" religious environments?

The geographical references in verse 6 recall specific locations in the Ark's journey before reaching its ultimate destination. What "temporary dwelling places" has God used in your spiritual journey? How did these prepare you for deeper encounter?

If you're journeying through this devotional with others, discuss how your community might more intentionally create space for divine presence. What practices or priorities might help your group become a more authentic "dwelling place" for God?

PRAYER FOR TODAY

God of Dwelling Places,

I come before You today as a pilgrim seeking authentic encounter with Your presence. Like the ancient worshippers who journeyed toward Jerusalem, I long to move beyond merely hearing about You to genuinely coming upon Your dwelling place. Guide my steps from the periphery of religious information toward the center of transformative relationship.

Thank You for the various ways You've made Your presence accessible—through Scripture that reveals Your character, through creation that displays Your glory, through communities that embody Your love, through Spirit-filled moments that transcend ordinary experience. Help me discern where and how You're inviting me to encounter You in this season of my journey.

I approach Your presence with both reverence and confidence—bowing at Your footstool in acknowledgment of Your transcendent holiness while also boldly inviting You to arise and come, believing Your covenant promises. Guard me from both casual presumption that diminishes Your greatness and distant formality that forgets Your intimate love.

Transform the contexts where I worship and serve into authentic dwelling places for Your presence. Clothe our leaders with Your righteousness—not mere professionalism or charisma but genuine Christ-likeness that reflects Your character. Fill our community with genuine joy—not manufactured emotion or shallow enthusiasm but deep gladness rooted in Your goodness and grace.

For others on this pilgrim journey, especially those traveling alongside me through this devotional, I pray for similar encounter with Your dwelling presence. When the journey seems long or the destination unclear, remind us that You are both the path and the destination, both the journey and the home toward which we travel.

I set my heart toward Your dwelling place, trusting that as I seek, I will find—not because of my spiritual skill but because You desire to be found, not because I've earned Your presence but because You delight in making Yourself known.

In the name of Jesus Christ, who tabernacled among us and who promised His abiding presence, Amen.

Day 28

The Davidic Covenant

*"For the sake of your servant David, do not reject your anointed one. The LORD s
wore an oath to David, a sure oath he will not revoke: 'One of your own descendants I will place on your
throne.
If your sons keep my covenant and the statutes I teach them, then their sons will sit on your throne for ever
and ever.'"* — Psalm 132:10-12

HISTORICAL CONTEXT

As our forty-day pilgrimage continues, we encounter a psalm deeply rooted in Israel's national
memory and covenant hope. Psalm 132 stands apart in the Songs of Ascent as the longest and
most historically specific, focusing on David and God's promises to him.

This psalm likely accompanied pilgrims as they approached Jerusalem, the city David established
as Israel's capital and spiritual center. It recounts David's determination to find a dwelling place
for God (verses 1-5) and celebrates the ark's journey to Jerusalem (verses 6-9). Our focus today
is on verses 10-12, which highlight the covenant God made with David—a promise that shaped
Israel's understanding of their future and ultimately points to the coming Messiah.

The Davidic Covenant, recorded in 2 Samuel 7, was God's promise that David's dynasty would
endure forever. This covenant became fundamental to Israel's national identity and messianic
hope. When pilgrims sang these words approaching Jerusalem, they weren't merely recalling
history—they were affirming their trust in God's enduring promises, even in times when those
promises seemed unfulfilled or distant.

For the original singers of this psalm, the covenant may have seemed broken. The Babylonian
exile had ended the Davidic monarchy, and even after return from exile, no Davidic king sat on
Israel's throne. Yet this psalm stubbornly clings to God's oath, modeling faithful remembrance
in the face of apparent contradiction.

MEDITATION: COVENANT AS RELATIONSHIP

"The LORD swore an oath to David, a sure oath he will not revoke..."

At its heart, covenant is about relationship. While modern minds might think of covenants in primarily legal terms—like contracts or agreements—biblical covenants established bonds of loyalty, commitment, and mutual obligation that went far beyond transactional arrangements.

The Hebrew word for "oath" (הָעוּבְש, shevuah) shares its root with the number seven (עָבְש, sheva), the number of completion and fullness. When God "swore" to David, He was binding Himself completely to this promise. Unlike human promises that often prove fragile and conditional, God's oath is "sure" and one "he will not revoke."

This unbreakable commitment reflects God's character. Throughout Scripture, God identifies Himself as the covenant-keeping God whose faithfulness endures despite human unfaithfulness. The psalmist appeals to this divine loyalty, asking God to act "for the sake of your servant David"—not because David was perfect, but because God had bound Himself to David in covenant love.

We often approach our relationship with God as if it depends entirely on our performance—as if one misstep might cause God to abandon us. The Davidic covenant reminds us that God's commitment to us precedes and outlasts our commitment to Him. Before we ever choose God, He has chosen us. Before we pledge our loyalty, He has pledged His to us.

THE COVENANT'S CONTENT

"One of your own descendants I will place on your throne."

God's promise to David was specific and tangible: his family line would continue on the throne of Israel. This wasn't merely about political succession but about God's ongoing work in history through a particular family. The promise carried immense significance for a nation whose identity was inseparable from their covenant relationship with God.

For the pilgrim approaching Jerusalem, this promise would have stirred complex emotions. If singing during the monarchy, it would affirm the legitimacy of the current king. If singing after exile, when no Davidic king reigned, it would express faith that God's purposes remained intact despite appearances to the contrary.

The New Testament reveals that this covenant finds its ultimate fulfillment in Jesus Christ, the "Son of David" (Matthew 1:1) who establishes an eternal kingdom. The angel Gabriel announced

to Mary that her son would receive "the throne of his father David, and he will reign over Jacob's descendants forever; his kingdom will never end" (Luke 1:32-33).

This covenant thread running from David through history to Jesus reveals how God works through particular people and circumstances to accomplish universal purposes. The covenant with one man and his family ultimately blesses all nations through the Messiah who comes from David's line.

THE COVENANT'S CONDITION

"If your sons keep my covenant and the statutes I teach them, then their sons will sit on your throne for ever and ever."

Here we encounter a tension that appears throughout Scripture: the interplay between God's unconditional promises and conditional human response. God's oath to David is "sure" and will not be revoked, yet continued blessing depends on the faithfulness of David's descendants.

This wasn't a contradiction but a reflection of relationship's dual nature. God's commitment to the covenant was absolute, but its full expression in history required human participation. When David's descendants rejected God's ways, they didn't nullify the covenant but temporarily interrupted its full blessing.

Israel's history demonstrated this reality. Solomon's idolatry led to the kingdom's division. Later kings' unfaithfulness resulted in exile. Yet God preserved a "remnant" of David's line, maintaining His covenant despite human failure, until the perfect Son of David arrived to establish the eternal kingdom.

This tension offers profound insight for our spiritual journeys. God's commitment to us in Christ is absolute—nothing "will be able to separate us from the love of God" (Romans 8:39). Yet our experience of covenant blessing depends on our response. Like David's descendants, we can choose to live within or outside the fullness of covenant relationship.

APPLICATION: LIVING COVENANT LIVES

As pilgrims journeying toward Jerusalem, we're called to live as covenant people—those who understand both God's unshakable commitment to us and our responsibility within that relationship.

First, we embrace the security of God's covenant faithfulness. In a world of broken promises and conditional acceptance, God offers unwavering commitment. When you fail, when you wander, when you feel unworthy of God's love—remember the God who swore an oath He will not revoke. Your relationship with Him doesn't depend on perfect performance but on His perfect faithfulness
.

Second, we recognize our covenant responsibility. God's commitment doesn't negate human response but invites it. The descendants of David had to "keep my covenant and the statutes I teach them" to experience the fullness of covenant blessing. Similarly, Jesus told his disciples, "If you love me, keep my commands" (John 14:15). Our obedience doesn't earn God's love but expresses our love in response to His.

Finally, we recognize that we're part of something larger than ourselves. The Davidic covenant wasn't just about one family but about God's redemptive purpose for all humanity. When pilgrims sang this psalm, they located their individual journeys within God's grand narrative. Our spiritual pilgrimage today likewise finds meaning as part of God's ongoing covenant work in the world—a work that began long before us and will continue long after.

Today, as you journey toward Jerusalem, receive the assurance of God's unwavering commitment to you in Christ, embrace your covenant responsibilities with gratitude rather than obligation, and find your place in the grand story of God's redemptive work through history.

REFLECTION QUESTIONS

1. How does understanding God's covenant faithfulness to David affect your perception of God's commitment to you? In what areas of your life do you struggle to trust God's unwavering faithfulness?

_____

_____

2. The psalm reveals tension between God's unconditional oath and the conditions of obedience. How do you understand the relationship between God's grace and your responsibility in your spiritual journey?

3. David's descendants often failed to uphold their covenant obligations, yet God remained faithful. How have you experienced God's faithfulness despite your own failures or unfaithfulness?

_____

_____

4. The pilgrims sang this psalm even when no Davidic king sat on Israel's throne, believing God's promise despite circumstances. What promises of God are you clinging to even when circumstances seem to contradict them?

_____

_____

5. Jesus is the ultimate fulfillment of the Davidic covenant. How does seeing Jesus as the "Son of David" and eternal king shape your understanding of who He is and what He came to accomplish?

_____

_____

6. If you're journeying through this devotional with others, discuss how covenant relationships (with God and each other) differ from the transactional relationships that often characterize our modern world. How might you cultivate more covenant-centered relationships in your community?

_____

_____

PRAYER FOR TODAY

Covenant-keeping God,

Today I stand in awe of Your faithfulness that spans generations. You who swore an oath to David and fulfilled it perfectly in Jesus Christ—teach me to trust the unshakable nature of Your promises to me.

Thank You that my relationship with You isn't based on my perfect performance but on Your perfect commitment. When I feel unworthy of Your love or fear I've strayed too far, remind me of the covenant You've established—not one that depends on my strength but on Yours.

Yet Lord, I also embrace my covenant responsibilities. Help me to respond to Your faithfulness with faithful obedience—not from obligation but from love and gratitude. When obedience feels difficult, strengthen me with the knowledge that Your commands are always for my flourishing. As I continue this pilgrimage toward Jerusalem, help me to see my small story as part of Your grand narrative. Use me as You used David—not because I am perfect, but because You are faithful. Help me to live today as a covenant person, secure in Your promises and committed to Your purposes.

I pray this in the name of Jesus Christ, the Son of David and my eternal King, Amen.

Day 29

God's Chosen Resting Place

"For the LORD has chosen Zion, he has desired it for his dwelling, saying, 'This is my resting place for ever and ever; here I will sit enthroned, for I have desired it. I will bless her with abundant provisions; her poor I will satisfy with food. I will clothe her priests with salvation, and her faithful people will ever sing for joy.'" — Psalm 132:13-16

HISTORICAL CONTEXT

As our forty-day pilgrimage continues, we remain with Psalm 132, shifting our focus from the Davidic covenant to God's choice of Zion as His dwelling place. While yesterday we examined God's promises to David, today we explore God's commitment to a place—Jerusalem, specifically Mount Zion, where the temple stood.

For ancient Israelite pilgrims ascending to Jerusalem for festivals, these verses carried profound significance. They weren't merely approaching a religious site or national capital; they were drawing near to what they understood as God's chosen resting place on earth. The temple represented the meeting point between heaven and earth, the place where God's presence was uniquely manifest.

The concept of God having a "dwelling place" emerged from Israel's wilderness experience with the tabernacle and found permanent expression in Solomon's temple. After Solomon completed the temple, 2 Chronicles 7:1-3 records how "the glory of the LORD filled the temple" in a visible manifestation confirming God's presence. Even after the Babylonian destruction of Solomon's temple and the building of the second temple, Jews continued to regard Jerusalem as God's chosen dwelling.

For pilgrims making their ascent, these verses weren't abstract theology but lived experience. With each step toward Jerusalem, they were approaching the place where heaven and earth converged—where God had chosen to make His presence known in a unique way.

MEDITATION: GOD'S INTENTIONAL CHOICE

"For the LORD has chosen Zion, he has desired it for his dwelling..."

Consider the language used here: God "chose" and "desired" Zion. These are verbs of intentionality and affection. The Hebrew word for "desired" (אָוָה, avah) conveys longing or yearning—the same word used in Song of Songs to describe romantic desire. This isn't the language of cold divine calculation but of passionate divine preference.

Why does this matter? Because it reveals something extraordinary about our God: He desires to be present with His people. The Creator of galaxies and atoms, the One who exists beyond time and space, intentionally chooses to locate His presence in ways we can experience. The God revealed in Scripture isn't distant and uninvolved but seeks proximity and relationship.

This divine choice of Zion wasn't arbitrary. Jerusalem held no inherent sacredness before God chose it. It wasn't the tallest mountain or most naturally defensible location. God's choice transformed what was ordinary into something extraordinary. This pattern appears throughout Scripture: God consistently takes what seems ordinary—people, places, objects—and imbues them with sacred significance through His presence.

This reveals a profound truth: holiness in Scripture isn't primarily about inherent qualities but about relationship to God. What makes something or someone holy is God's presence and purpose, not intrinsic characteristics. Zion became holy because God chose it, not because it possessed special qualities that attracted God.

THE NATURE OF GOD'S DWELLING

"This is my resting place for ever and ever; here I will sit enthroned..."

The image of God "resting" and being "enthroned" creates a powerful picture of divine presence that is both intimate and majestic. The term "resting place" (הַמְּנוּחָה, menuchah) denotes not merely cessation from activity but a settled contentment. It echoes Genesis 2:2, where God rested after creation—not from exhaustion but in satisfaction with what He had made.

When God calls Zion His "resting place forever," He's expressing commitment to permanent presence with His people. This doesn't mean God is confined to one location—Solomon himself acknowledged in 1 Kings 8:27, "But will God really dwell on earth? The heavens, even the highest heaven, cannot contain you. How much less this temple I have built!" Rather, God accommodates to human limitations by making His infinite presence accessible in specific ways.

Simultaneously, God describes Himself as "enthroned" in Zion. This royal imagery reminds us that God's intimate presence doesn't diminish His sovereignty. He comes close not by becoming less than He is but by enabling us to experience more of who He is. Divine closeness doesn't require divine diminishment.

For the pilgrim singing this psalm, these images created the expectation of encountering both God's intimate presence and sovereign majesty in Jerusalem—the place where heaven's King had established His throne room on earth.

THE CONSEQUENCES OF GOD'S PRESENCE

"I will bless her with abundant provisions; her poor I will satisfy with food. I will clothe her priests with salvation, and her faithful people will ever sing for joy."

God's presence isn't merely symbolic or spiritual—it transforms material reality. Notice how the consequences of God's dwelling involve meeting tangible human needs: provision for the poor, clothing for priests, joy for the faithful. When God establishes His presence, human flourishing follows.

First, God promises "abundant provisions" with specific mention of satisfying the poor with food. Divine presence addresses social inequities and physical needs. Throughout Scripture, true worship of God consistently connects with justice for the vulnerable. Isaiah 58 makes this explicit, condemning religious observance disconnected from caring for the hungry and oppressed.

Second, God promises to "clothe her priests with salvation." Priests mediated between God and people, representing both to each other through sacrificial worship. Their clothing symbolized their identity and role. God's promise to clothe them with salvation suggests that divine presence transforms religious functionaries into genuine carriers of God's deliverance. When God dwells among His people, religious roles become filled with authentic spiritual power.

Finally, God promises joy for the faithful—not as a temporary emotion but as a sustained response to divine presence. The Hebrew suggests ongoing, perpetual singing. This isn't forced cheerfulness but the natural human response to experiencing God's presence. As Augustine famously observed, "You have made us for yourself, O Lord, and our hearts are restless until they rest in you." When God chooses to dwell with us, our hearts find their true resting place too.

APPLICATION: LIVING IN GOD'S CHOSEN DWELLING PLACE

As pilgrims journeying toward Jerusalem, we recognize that God's chosen dwelling place has expanded beyond a geographical location. Through Christ, God's presence is no longer confined to a physical temple. Paul asks in 1 Corinthians 3:16, "Don't you know that you yourselves are God's temple and that God's Spirit dwells in your midst?" And again in 1 Corinthians 6:19, "Your bodies are temples of the Holy Spirit."

This reality transforms how we understand sacred space. First, we recognize our individual bodies as places God has chosen for His dwelling. This elevates the dignity of human physicality and reminds us to honor God with our bodies. It also means God's presence travels with us wherever we go—we're never separated from sacred space.

Second, we understand the gathered community of believers as God's temple. When Jesus said, "Where two or three gather in my name, there am I with them" (Matthew 18:20), He was extending the promise of divine presence beyond Jerusalem to any place His followers gather. Our communities become "Zion"—places God has chosen for His dwelling.

Finally, we anticipate the ultimate fulfillment described in Revelation 21:3: "God's dwelling place is now among the people, and he will dwell with them." The trajectory of Scripture moves toward perfect communion between God and humanity, where the entire created order becomes God's temple.

As you continue your pilgrimage today, consider the implications of being God's chosen dwelling place. How does God's presence in you address tangible needs around you? How does His presence clothe you with salvation? How does His presence generate authentic joy? The same God who chose Zion has now chosen you—not because of your inherent qualities but because of His desire for relationship with you.

Today, let your life become a place where others encounter the transformative power of God's presence.

REFLECTION QUESTIONS

1. God "chose" and "desired" Zion for His dwelling place. What does it mean to you personally that God desires to dwell with His people? How does this shape your understanding of who God is?

   _____

   _____

2. The passage shows how God's presence addresses practical human needs like provision, clothing, and joy. In what specific ways have you experienced God's presence meeting tangible needs in your life?

   _____

   _____

3. Scripture teaches that believers individually and collectively are now God's temple. How conscious are you of being God's dwelling place throughout your daily activities? What might change if you lived with greater awareness of this reality?

   _____

   _____

4. God's choice of Zion transformed an ordinary place into sacred space. What ordinary aspects of your life might God be transforming through His presence? How might seemingly mundane spaces or activities become sacred when viewed through this lens?

   _____

   _____

5. The passage promises that God's faithful people "will ever sing for joy." How would you describe the relationship between experiencing God's presence and experiencing joy? What obstacles might prevent you from experiencing this joy fully?

   _____

   _____

6. If you're journeying through this devotional with others, discuss how your community might more intentionally embody its identity as God's dwelling place. How might you create space for God's presence to address needs, clothe with salvation, and generate joy within your group?

PRAYER FOR TODAY

Dwelling God,

I stand in awe today that You—Creator of all things, sovereign over the universe—desire to make Your home with me. Thank You for choosing to rest in places where I can experience Your presence. Thank You that through Christ, I have become Your temple, Your chosen dwelling place.

Forgive me for the times I've treated Your presence casually or forgotten the sacred dignity of being Your temple. Forgive me for seeking Your presence only in special buildings or formal worship while neglecting to recognize You dwelling within me and my community.

As Your temple, Lord, make me a place where Your transforming presence is evident. Use me to provide for those in need around me. Clothe me with the salvation that changes how I live and relate to others. Fill me with authentic joy that witnesses to Your goodness.

Help me to create space in my life for Your presence to dwell fully—through silence, Scripture, worship, and communion with other believers. May my life become a place where others encounter You.

And as I journey with others, make us collectively a dwelling place that reflects Your character. Build us together into a spiritual house where the poor find provision, where people find salvation, and where joy overflows in genuine worship.

I pray this in the name of Jesus Christ, who made Your dwelling among us, Amen.

Day 30

The Horn of David

Psalm 132:17-18 "Here I will make a horn grow for David and set up a lamp for my anointed one. I will clothe his enemies with shame, but his head will be adorned with a radiant crown." — Psalm 132:17-18

HISTORICAL CONTEXT

As our forty-day pilgrimage approaches its final stages, we conclude our meditation on Psalm 132 with verses that look forward in hope and anticipation. These final verses of the psalm shift from God's past promises to future fulfillment—from what God has done to what God will yet do.

For the ancient pilgrims climbing toward Jerusalem, these words carried profound messianic significance. The "horn" and "lamp" imagery directly connected to Israel's hope for a coming deliverer from David's line who would restore God's kingdom. When they sang of God making "a horn grow for David," they were expressing faith in the continued vitality of God's covenant promises, even when present circumstances seemed to contradict them.

During periods when the Davidic dynasty ruled in Jerusalem, these verses would have reinforced the legitimacy of the current king while also pointing beyond him to the ideal Davidic ruler yet to come. During and after the exile, when no descendant of David sat on the throne, these words would have sustained Israel's hope that God had not abandoned His covenant promises despite apparent evidence to the contrary.

The imagery of "horn," "lamp," "anointed one," and "crown" drew from Israel's rich symbolic tradition. The horn represented strength and power in ancient Near Eastern culture (as in Deuteronomy 33:17). The lamp recalled God's promise that David's dynasty would always have a light burning in Jerusalem (1 Kings 11:36). The anointed one (messiah in Hebrew) pointed to the consecrated king. The crown symbolized royal authority and splendor.

Together, these symbols created a vivid picture of the coming Messiah who would fulfill God's promises to David and establish God's reign on earth.

MEDITATION: THE HORN OF DAVID

"Here I will make a horn grow for David..."

The Hebrew word for "horn" (נֶרֶק, qeren) appears throughout Scripture as a powerful symbol of strength, victory, and authority. When animals like bulls or rams lowered their horns, they demonstrated their power and readiness for battle. The altar in God's temple had horns at its four corners, representing God's power to save those who took refuge there.

God's promise to "make a horn grow for David" signified the emergence of a powerful leader from David's lineage—one who would embody divine strength and authority. The verb "grow" suggests organic development, indicating that this horn wouldn't appear suddenly but would emerge in God's perfect timing from seemingly barren circumstances.

This imagery spoke directly to Israel's deepest hopes. Would God's promises to David fail? Would foreign powers permanently dominate God's people? Would Israel's story end in defeat? The horn imagery answered with resounding hope: God would raise up strength from David's line. What appeared dead would sprout with new life.

For Christians, this horn imagery finds its fulfillment in Jesus Christ. When Zechariah, father of John the Baptist, prophesied in Luke 1:69, he celebrated that God had "raised up a horn of salvation for us in the house of his servant David." Zechariah recognized in the coming of Jesus the very horn that Psalm 132 had promised centuries earlier.

The horn symbolism reminds us that God's strength often emerges from what appears weak and insignificant. Jesus wasn't born in a palace but a stable. He didn't lead an army but gathered fishermen and tax collectors. He didn't seize power but submitted to death on a cross. Yet through this apparent weakness, God displayed ultimate strength. As Paul wrote, "God chose the weak things of the world to shame the strong" (1 Corinthians 1:27).

THE LAMP FOR THE ANOINTED ONE

"...and set up a lamp for my anointed one."

The lamp imagery connects to God's promise to maintain David's dynasty. In 2 Samuel 21:17, David is called the "lamp of Israel," and in 1 Kings 11:36, God promises to maintain a lamp for David in Jerusalem. Lamps in the ancient world provided both light and continuity—a household's lamp was kept burning continuously as a symbol of the family's ongoing life and prosperity.

God's promise to "set up a lamp" conveyed the assurance that David's line would not be extinguished, even when it seemed to flicker and fade. Throughout Israel's darkest periods—division, exile, foreign domination—this promise sustained hope that God would preserve the Davidic line until the perfect king emerged.

Jesus identified himself as "the light of the world" (John 8:12), claiming a title that resonated with this messianic lamp imagery. The Gospel of John declares that in Jesus, "The true light that gives light to everyone was coming into the world" (John 1:9). The lamp God promised for His anointed one now illuminates the entire world through Christ.

This lamp imagery speaks powerfully to our spiritual journey. We may pass through dark valleys where God's presence seems distant and His promises uncertain. In those moments, this verse reminds us that God preserves the light of hope even in the darkest circumstances. As Jesus told his disciples, "You are the light of the world" (Matthew 5:14), extending this lamp imagery to all who follow Him. We now carry the light of Christ into dark places, continuing the messianic mission.

THE CONTRAST OF DESTINIES

"I will clothe his enemies with shame, but his head will be adorned with a radiant crown."

The psalm concludes with a striking contrast between two destinies—shame for enemies and glory for God's anointed one. This juxtaposition addresses the apparent contradiction between God's promises and Israel's historical experience. Despite God's covenant with David, Israel often suffered defeat and humiliation. This verse assures that the final chapter has not been written—ultimate vindication awaits God's anointed one.

The imagery of clothing suggests complete covering or identity. God's enemies will be wrapped in shame—their opposition exposed as foolish and their defeat complete. Meanwhile, God's anointed will wear a crown described as "radiant" or "shining"—a striking visual representation of vindicated faithfulness.

For Christians, this contrast points to Christ's resurrection and ascension following his crucifixion. What appeared to be defeat became victory. Those who opposed God's Messiah found themselves opposing God's purposes, while Christ received "the crown of glory that will never fade away" (1 Peter 5:4).

This contrast also points ahead to the final consummation of history described in Revelation, where Christ returns as conquering King, wearing "many crowns" (Revelation 19:12). The One once crowned with thorns will be crowned with glory, fulfilling perfectly the destiny promised to David's horn.

APPLICATION: LIVING IN MESSIANIC HOPE

As pilgrims journeying toward Jerusalem, we live between the "already" and "not yet" of messianic fulfillment. Christ, the horn of David, has already come, establishing God's kingdom through his life, death, and resurrection. Yet we await the full manifestation of that kingdom when Christ returns to complete what he began.

This tension defines the Christian life. We celebrate the horn that has already grown from David's line while longing for its complete expression. We walk in the light of the lamp already lit while awaiting the day when "the city does not need the sun or the moon to shine on it, for the glory of God gives it light, and the Lamb is its lamp" (Revelation 21:23).

Living in messianic hope means, first, recognizing Jesus as the fulfillment of God's promises to David. The horn and lamp imagery finds its perfect expression in Christ, who embodies divine strength and illumination. Our faith isn't grounded in abstract principles but in God's concrete actions in history, culminating in Jesus Christ.

Second, living in messianic hope means participating in Christ's ongoing work. Jesus doesn't merely fulfill these verses individually; he fulfills them through his body, the church. Paul describes believers as "fellow heirs with Christ" (Romans 8:17), sharing in both his suffering and glory. We become extensions of the horn's strength and the lamp's light in our broken world.

Finally, living in messianic hope means maintaining confident expectation amid apparent contradictions. Like the ancient pilgrims who sang this psalm when no Davidic king reigned, we hold to God's promises even when circumstances seem to deny them. We trust that the One who began the good work of kingdom restoration will carry it to completion (Philippians 1:6).

Today, as you continue your pilgrimage, remember that you journey not only toward the Jerusalem of personal spiritual growth but toward the New Jerusalem where God's promises find their complete fulfillment. The horn has grown; the lamp is lit; the crown awaits. Live today as a citizen of that coming kingdom, drawing strength from its King.

REFLECTION QUESTIONS

1. The "horn of David" symbolizes strength emerging from apparent weakness. In what areas of your life do you need to trust God's strength to emerge from situations that seem weak or hopeless?

_____

_____

2. Jesus identified himself as "the light of the world" and called his followers to be "the light of the world." How are you currently reflecting Christ's light in your family, workplace, or community? Where might God be calling you to bring light into darkness

_____

_____

3. The psalm contrasts the destiny of God's enemies (shame) with the destiny of God's anointed (crowned with glory). How does this future hope influence how you respond to current opposition or difficulties in your faith journey?

_____

_____

4. Christians live between the "already" of Christ's first coming and the "not yet" of his return. How do you experience this tension in your daily life? In what ways do you find it challenging to live as a citizen of God's kingdom while still in this world?

_____

_____

5. The horn and lamp imagery points to God's faithfulness to His promises despite apparent contradictions. What promises of God do you find most difficult to believe in your current circumstances? How might remembering God's faithfulness throughout history strengthen your faith?

_____

_____

6. If you're journeying through this devotional with others, discuss how your community might more effectively embody the strength (horn) and light (lamp) of Christ to your surrounding world. What specific actions could your group take to extend Christ's messianic work?

PRAYER FOR TODAY

Faithful God,

Thank You for the hope extended to us through Your promises to David. Thank You for fulfilling these promises in Jesus Christ, the perfect horn of strength and lamp of light for our world. I praise You for Your unwavering commitment to Your word, even when circumstances seem to contradict it.

Lord Jesus, You are the horn grown from David's line—the strength of God made manifest in what appeared to be weakness. Help me to find my strength not in outward power but in surrender to Your purposes. When I face situations that overwhelm me, remind me that Your strength is made perfect in weakness.

You are also the lamp set up by God—the light that darkness cannot overcome. Illuminate the dark places in my heart, mind, and circumstances. Use me as a carrier of Your light to others who walk in darkness. Show me specific ways I can reflect Your light today in my relationships and responsibilities.

I confess the times I've doubted Your promises when faced with contradicting circumstances. Forgive my lack of faith. Help me to live with confident expectation of Your kingdom's full manifestation, even as I participate in its present reality.

As I continue this pilgrimage, deepen my identification with You—the anointed King whose enemies will be clothed with shame and whose head will be adorned with an eternally radiant crown. May my life today reflect the reality of Your coming kingdom.

I pray this in the name of Jesus Christ, the horn of salvation and light of the world, Amen.

PART IV: THE ARRIVAL
(Days 31-40)

Day 31

The Oil of Unity

"How good and pleasant it is when God's people live together in unity! It is like precious oil poured on the head, running down on the beard, running down on Aaron's beard, down on the collar of his robe." — Psalm 133:1-2

HISTORICAL CONTEXT

As our forty-day pilgrimage progresses, we turn to Psalm 133, one of the briefest Songs of Ascent but also one of the most vivid and profound. This psalm celebrates the beauty of community among God's people—a fitting theme for pilgrims traveling together toward Jerusalem for worship.

For ancient Israelites, the journey to Jerusalem for major festivals wasn't undertaken in isolation. Families, neighbors, and entire villages would form caravans, traveling the roads together for protection and companionship. As they journeyed, these diverse groups—perhaps separated by economic status, tribal affiliation, or social standing in normal life—experienced a unique unity of purpose and identity. The journey itself created community.

Upon arrival in Jerusalem, this sense of unity intensified as pilgrims from across the nation gathered to worship. The divisions that marked everyday life temporarily dissolved in the shared experience of festival celebration. Rich and poor, priest and layperson, people from northern tribes and southern tribes—all came together as the covenant people of God.

This psalm likely arose from these experiences of pilgrimage unity. The psalmist isn't merely describing an abstract ideal but something witnessed and experienced. The exclamation "How good and pleasant it is!" suggests firsthand observation of something beautiful and worthy of celebration.

The historical context also includes the priesthood of Aaron, Israel's first high priest and brother of Moses. The vivid image of oil flowing down Aaron's beard refers to the consecration ceremony described in Exodus 29:7 and Leviticus 8:12, where Moses anointed Aaron by pouring sacred oil on his head. This anointing symbolized Aaron's consecration for service and the endowment of God's Spirit for his priestly duties.

MEDITATION: THE GOODNESS OF UNITY

"How good and pleasant it is when God's people live together in unity!"

The psalm begins with an exclamation rather than an argument. The psalmist doesn't try to convince us of unity's value through logical reasoning but invites us to recognize what we already know intuitively: human hearts are drawn to harmony and connection.

The Hebrew text uses two descriptive terms: "good" (בוֹט, tov) and "pleasant" (םיִעָנ, na'im). "Good" suggests moral rightness and practical benefit, while "pleasant" conveys aesthetic beauty and emotional satisfaction. Together, they present unity as something that is simultaneously right, beneficial, beautiful, and satisfying. Unity among God's people isn't merely a practical strategy for effectiveness; it touches something deep in the human soul.

Notice that the psalm speaks specifically of unity among "brothers" or "God's people." The unity celebrated here isn't generic human togetherness but the specific bond shared by those who recognize the same divine Father. Jesus emphasized this in John 17:20-23, praying for his followers "that all of them may be one, Father, just as you are in me and I am in you." Christian unity isn't merely human agreement but participation in the unity of the Trinity.

The phrase "live together" (תֶבֶש, shevet) in Hebrew suggests not merely proximity but shared life. This isn't about forced uniformity or superficial pleasantness but genuine life together—sharing joys and sorrows, strengths and weaknesses, resources and needs. The early church exemplified this in Acts 2:44-47, where believers "had everything in common" and "broke bread in their homes and ate together with glad and sincere hearts."

In our fragmented and individualistic age, this exclamation stands as both invitation and challenge. Do we recognize how good and pleasant unity truly is? Have we experienced the depth of community God intends for His people? Are we willing to prioritize unity over personal preferences and comfort?

THE OIL OF CONSECRATION

"It is like precious oil poured on the head, running down on the beard, running down on Aaron's beard, down on the collar of his robe."

To help us grasp unity's significance, the psalmist provides a vivid sensory image: consecration oil flowing generously over Aaron's head, beard, and garments. This isn't a small dab of oil but a lavish pouring—so abundant that it runs down from head to clothing.

The oil used to consecrate priests wasn't ordinary olive oil but a special blend containing myrrh, cinnamon, calamus, and cassia mixed with olive oil according to specific proportions (Exodus 30:22-33). This "precious oil" was reserved exclusively for sacred use; using it for common purposes carried serious consequences. By comparing unity to this oil, the psalmist places community in the realm of the sacred.

Aaron's anointing marked his consecration as high priest—setting him apart for service to God and mediation between God and people. Similarly, Christian community isn't merely a human association but a divinely consecrated reality, set apart for sacred purposes. In unity, we're not just enjoying human connection; we're participating in something God has ordained for His glory and our sanctification.

The flowing motion of the oil suggests that unity isn't static but dynamic. Like oil spreading from head to beard to clothing, genuine community extends outward, embracing more people and circumstances. Unity that remains confined to comfortable relationships or convenient occasions hasn't yet fulfilled its purpose. True Christian unity flows outward, crossing boundaries and drawing others into its fragrant embrace.

This flowing quality also suggests abundance. The anointing wasn't meager but generous—oil pouring freely, symbolizing the lavish provision of God's Spirit. Similarly, Christian unity isn't something we must ration carefully but a reality we can enter with abundance. The more freely we give ourselves to community, the more richly we experience its blessing.

Finally, the oil's fragrance provides another dimension to the metaphor. Everyone in proximity to Aaron would have smelled the aromatic oil. Similarly, Christian unity carries a distinctive "aroma" that affects not only those directly involved but also those who witness it. Jesus emphasized this in John 13:35: "By this everyone will know that you are my disciples, if you love one another." Unity becomes a testimony to the world, a fragrant witness to the reality of the gospel.

APPLICATION: CULTIVATING SACRED COMMUNITY

As pilgrims journeying toward Jerusalem, we're called to experience and express the unity this psalm celebrates. Unlike the ancient Israelites who experienced this unity primarily during festival pilgrimages, we're invited into ongoing community through the church—the body of Christ united by His Spirit.

First, we must recognize unity as divine gift rather than human achievement. The oil that consecrated Aaron wasn't something he produced but something he received. Similarly, Christian unity isn't primarily something we create through effort but something we receive through Christ's work and enter through humility. Ephesians 4:3 exhorts us not to create unity but to "make every effort to keep the unity of the Spirit through the bond of peace." The Spirit creates unity; our responsibility is to preserve what God has established.

Second, we cultivate unity by valuing it appropriately. The psalmist calls it "good and pleasant"— worthy of celebration and protection. Too often we treat Christian community as optional or secondary, a nice addition to individual spiritual life rather than essential to it. When we truly value unity as the psalmist did, we'll make decisions that prioritize community over convenience, relationship over personal preference, and harmony over having our own way.

Third, we participate in unity by bringing our authentic selves into community. The oil of Aaron's anointing didn't change his identity but consecrated who he already was for sacred service. Similarly, Christian unity doesn't require uniformity or suppression of our unique personalities and gifts. Rather, it invites the full expression of our true selves in the context of covenant relationship. As Paul explains in 1 Corinthians 12, the body functions best when each distinct part fulfills its role while remaining connected to the whole.

Fourth, we protect unity by addressing division promptly and honestly. The precious oil of Aaron's anointing was carefully guarded against contamination. Similarly, we must guard the precious unity of God's people against the contaminating influences of gossip, unresolved conflict, pride, and exclusivity. Jesus provided clear guidance in Matthew 18:15-20 for addressing conflicts that threaten community. When we follow these principles, we protect the sacred oil of unity from spilling wastefully on the ground.

Today, as you continue your pilgrimage, consider your participation in the community of God's people. Have you experienced the "good and pleasant" reality of genuine unity? Are you contributing to that unity or detracting from it? How might you more fully enter into the sacred community God has established through Christ?

Remember that spiritual ascent isn't a solo journey but a communal pilgrimage. The oil of unity consecrates us not just individually but together for God's purposes in the world.

REFLECTION QUESTIONS

1. The psalmist exclaims about how "good and pleasant" unity is among God's people. Reflect on a time when you experienced this kind of sacred unity in Christian community. What made it particularly meaningful, and how did it affect your spiritual journey?

_____

_____

2. The image of flowing oil suggests unity is dynamic and expansive rather than static and confined. In what ways have you seen unity flow beyond comfortable boundaries in your experience of Christian community? Where might God be inviting you to extend unity further?

_____

_____

3. Aaron received the anointing oil as a gift for his consecration. Similarly, Christian unity is a gift we receive rather than an achievement we create. How does this perspective change your approach to community? What might it mean to receive unity rather than trying to manufacture it?

_____

_____

4. The oil of consecration set Aaron apart for sacred service. How does genuine Christian community set us apart from the patterns of relationship common in the world? What distinctive qualities should mark the unity of God's people?

_____

_____

5. Unity among believers serves as a witness to the world—a fragrant aroma that draws others to Christ. How have you seen Christian unity (or its absence) affect the witness of the church to those outside the faith? What testimony does your own participation in community offer?

_____

_____

6. If you're journeying through this devotional with others, discuss concrete ways your group might more fully embody the unity this psalm celebrates. What practices or commitments might help your community experience the flowing oil of sacred unity?

_____

_____

PRAYER FOR TODAY

Unifying God,

I marvel today at Your desire to see Your people dwell together in unity. Thank You for the gift of community—for brothers and sisters with whom I can share this journey of faith. Thank You for the beauty and goodness of relationships consecrated by Your Spirit.

Forgive me for the times I've devalued unity, prioritizing my preferences over harmony and my convenience over community. Forgive me for contributing to division through pride, impatience, gossip, or withdrawal. Help me to recognize how precious the oil of unity truly is and to guard it accordingly.

Lord Jesus, You prayed that Your followers would be one as You and the Father are one. Pour out Your Spirit afresh on Your church, anointing us with the oil of unity that flows from Your throne. Help us to demonstrate a quality of community that testifies to Your transforming presence.

Show me my place in the body of Christ. Help me to bring my authentic self into community—neither dominating others nor hiding in fear, but offering who I am for the benefit of all. When conflicts arise, give me courage to address them honestly and humility to seek reconciliation quickly.

Extend the flow of unity beyond comfortable boundaries. Use our community to draw others into Your embrace. May the fragrance of our life together attract those who long for genuine connection and belonging.

As I continue this pilgrimage with others, deepen our bonds of affection and commitment. Make us not merely associates but family, united by Your love and consecrated for Your purposes. I pray this in the name of Jesus Christ, who broke down dividing walls to create one new humanity, Amen.

Day 32

Dew of Hermon

"It is as if the dew of Hermon were falling on Mount Zion. For there the LORD bestows his blessing, even life forevermore." — Psalm 133:3

HISTORICAL CONTEXT

As our forty-day pilgrimage continues, we remain with Psalm 133, focusing now on its final verse. Yesterday, we explored the psalmist's first metaphor for unity—the precious anointing oil flowing down Aaron's beard. Today, we encounter a second, equally vivid image—the dew of Mount Hermon falling on Mount Zion.

For the ancient Israelite pilgrims journeying to Jerusalem, this geographical reference carried immediate significance. Mount Hermon stands as the highest peak in the region, rising to over 9,000 feet along what is now the border between Syria and Lebanon. Known for its heavy dew and snowfall, Hermon served as a crucial water source for the Jordan River, providing life-giving moisture to the often arid landscape of Israel.

In contrast, Mount Zion in Jerusalem stands at a much lower elevation in a considerably drier region. While Hermon was known for abundant moisture, Jerusalem depended on carefully collected rainwater stored in cisterns. The notion of Hermon's abundant dew falling on Zion represented an extraordinary blessing—the life-giving abundance of one location miraculously appearing in another.

In the agricultural society of ancient Israel, dew held tremendous importance. During the long dry season from May to October, dew provided the only consistent moisture for crops and vegetation. Without it, plants would wither and die. The Hebrew Scriptures frequently mention dew as a divine blessing (Genesis 27:28, Deuteronomy 33:13) and its withholding as divine judgment (Haggai 1:10).

For pilgrims singing this psalm as they approached Jerusalem, the image of Hermon's dew on Zion would have evoked a powerful vision of God's abundant blessing flowing to His chosen dwelling place. The metaphor connected the natural world they knew intimately with the spiritual reality they were experiencing in community.

MEDITATION: THE DEW OF BLESSING

"It is as if the dew of Hermon were falling on Mount Zion."

Having compared unity to the flowing oil of priestly consecration, the psalmist now employs a second metaphor drawn from nature. Both images—oil and dew—involve downward movement, suggesting that unity, like divine blessing, descends as gift rather than rises as achievement.

The Hebrew construction here suggests something seemingly impossible—the abundant dew characteristic of a distant northern mountain somehow appearing on a southern hill. Geographically, this shouldn't happen. Hermon's dew belongs on Hermon. Yet the psalmist envisions this geographical impossibility as a metaphor for the supernatural blessing that flows when God's people dwell in unity.

This image contains several profound insights about community. First, it suggests that unity creates an environment where blessing that might seem impossible becomes possible. Like Hermon's dew appearing miraculously on Zion, genuine community makes space for God to work in ways that transcend natural expectation.

Second, the dew metaphor emphasizes the gentle, pervasive nature of community's blessing. Unlike rain that falls in visible, sometimes dramatic downpours, dew forms quietly during the night, covering everything with life-sustaining moisture. Similarly, the blessing of unity isn't always dramatic or immediately visible but accumulates gradually, sustaining spiritual life in ways we might not immediately recognize.

Third, dew illustrates unity's refreshing quality. In an arid climate, morning dew brings coolness and relief. It revives what heat and dryness have depleted. In a world parched by conflict, competition, and isolation, the unity of God's people offers similar refreshment—a counterculture of mutual care and genuine connection that revives the human spirit.

Finally, the dew metaphor highlights our dependence on divine provision. Israelite farmers could plow, plant, and tend their crops, but they couldn't produce dew. They depended entirely on God's provision of this essential moisture. Similarly, while we actively participate in building community, the life-giving blessing that flows through unity remains God's gift, not our creation.

THE SOURCE AND NATURE OF BLESSING

"For there the LORD bestows his blessing, even life forevermore."

The psalm concludes by identifying both the source and substance of the blessing that flows through unity. The blessing comes explicitly from "the LORD" (Yahweh)—the covenant God who has committed Himself to His people. The unity of God's people creates a dwelling place for divine blessing, but the blessing itself originates in God's generous character.

The location word "there" connects directly to the unity described in verse 1. Where God's people dwell together in unity—that's where God "bestows his blessing." This doesn't mean God withholds blessing from individuals or that divine favor only appears in community. Rather, it suggests that unity creates a particular environment where God's blessing finds full expression.

The substance of this blessing is specified as "life forevermore" (םייַח, chayyim). This isn't merely extended physical existence but life in its fullest dimension—vibrant, purposeful, and connected to its divine source. Jesus echoed this when he declared, "I have come that they may have life, and have it to the full" (John 10:10).

The Hebrew term translated "forevermore" ('ad-ha'olam) carries connotations of both duration and fullness. It suggests blessing that extends beyond temporal limitations and encompasses the totality of human experience. The psalmist envisions not merely momentary harmony but community that participates in eternal realities.

For Christians, this vision finds its ultimate fulfillment in the eternal community described in Revelation 21-22, where God dwells permanently with His people and "death shall be no more, neither shall there be mourning, nor crying, nor pain anymore" (Revelation 21:4). The unity we experience now, however imperfectly, serves as a foretaste of that eternal community.

APPLICATION: CREATING SPACE FOR DIVINE BLESSING

As pilgrims journeying toward Jerusalem, we're called not only to appreciate unity's beauty (verse 1) and participate in its sacred character (verse 2) but also to recognize it as an environment where divine life flourishes (verse 3). How do we create space for the dew of divine blessing to fall in our communities?

First, we cultivate receptivity. Dew forms when surfaces cool sufficiently to receive moisture from the air. Similarly, community becomes receptive to divine blessing when we cool the heated passions of pride, self-sufficiency, and competition. James 4:6 reminds us that "God opposes the proud but shows favor to the humble." When we humble ourselves before God and each other, we create the conditions where the dew of blessing can form.

Second, we practice attentiveness. Because dew forms gradually and often overnight, it requires attention to notice and appreciate. Similarly, God's blessing through community might not always appear in dramatic manifestations. It often accumulates in small moments of care, encouragement, challenge, and shared purpose. Cultivating attentiveness to these "dew moments" helps us recognize and celebrate divine blessing in community.

Third, we commit to distribution. Dew doesn't fall selectively but covers everything in its reach. Genuine community doesn't restrict blessing to certain members or create insider/outsider dynamics. Instead, it ensures that life-giving resources—whether material support, spiritual encouragement, or opportunities for service—reach everyone. Acts 4:34-35 exemplifies this: "There were no needy persons among them... the money was distributed to anyone who had need."

Fourth, we embrace interdependence. Dew forms through the relationship between earth and sky, vegetation and atmosphere. It requires connection between different elements. Similarly, divine blessing flows most fully when we acknowledge our need for each other and for God. Paul's body metaphor in 1 Corinthians 12 emphasizes this interdependence: "The eye cannot say to the hand, 'I don't need you!'" Blessing flourishes when we acknowledge that we need each other's gifts, perspectives, and presence.

The psalm's progression moves from the recognition of unity's goodness (verse 1) through its sacred character (verse 2) to its life-giving result (verse 3). Similarly, our journey in Christian community progresses from appreciating relationship to recognizing its sacred purpose to experiencing its life-giving power.

Today, as you continue your pilgrimage, consider how you might contribute to creating an environment where God's blessing flows like Hermon's dew. What attitudes or actions might help your community become more receptive to divine life? How might you become more attentive to the ways God is already bestowing blessing through your relationships? Where is God inviting you to more fully participate in the life-giving unity of His people?

Remember that the dew falls not through human engineering but through divine gift. Our role isn't to manufacture blessing but to create conditions where God's life can flourish among us.

REFLECTION QUESTIONS

1. The psalm compares unity's blessing to the impossible scenario of Mount Hermon's dew appearing on Mount Zion. When have you experienced unexpected or seemingly impossible blessing through Christian community? What made this experience particularly meaningful?

_____

_____

2. Dew forms quietly, often unnoticed until morning reveals its presence. What subtle, easily overlooked blessings have you received through your relationships with other believers? How might you become more attentive to these "dew moments" of divine blessing?

_____

_____

3. The psalm states that "there the LORD bestows his blessing"—in the place of unity. What specific qualities of community create an environment where God's blessing flows most freely? How have you seen this in your own experience?

_____

_____

4. The ultimate blessing God bestows is described as "life forevermore." In what specific ways has Christian community contributed to your experience of abundant, purpose-filled life? Where do you see evidence of eternal life breaking into present reality through relationships?

_____

_____

5. Dew forms when surfaces cool sufficiently to receive moisture from the air. Similarly, humility and receptivity in community create conditions for divine blessing. What "cooling" might need to happen in your life or community to become more receptive to God's blessing?

_____

_____

6. If you're journeying through this devotional with others, discuss how your group might more intentionally create space for God's blessing to flow. What practices or commitments would help you become a community where the "dew of Hermon" regularly appears?

_____

_____

PRAYER FOR TODAY

Life-giving God,

I stand in wonder today at the blessing You bestow when Your people dwell together in unity. Thank You for the gift of community—not merely as human companionship but as the environment where Your supernatural life flows like refreshing dew. Thank You for every moment when I've experienced Your presence through the love and care of others.

Forgive me for the times I've taken community for granted or failed to recognize Your blessing flowing through relationships. Forgive me for contributing to disunity through pride, self-sufficiency, critical spirit, or withdrawal. Create in me a heart that values unity as the sacred space where Your life flourishes.

Lord Jesus, You prayed that Your followers' unity would show the world that the Father sent You. Make our communities places where Your life is so evident that others are drawn to You through us. May the impossible become possible among us—may Hermon's dew appear on our Zion as Your supernatural blessing flows contrary to the world's expectations.

Holy Spirit, cultivate in me the qualities that create receptivity to Your blessing—humility instead of pride, gratitude instead of entitlement, generosity instead of self-protection. Make me attentive to the subtle ways You're already at work in my community, bringing life through everyday interactions and shared moments.

Help me to contribute to a community where blessing reaches everyone without favoritism or exclusion. Show me how to use whatever gifts, resources, or influence I have to ensure that all experience the life You bestow.

As I continue this pilgrimage with others, deepen our commitment to creating space where Your life-giving presence can dwell. May we together experience not only momentary blessing but life that connects us to eternity.

I pray this in the name of Jesus Christ, the source of life forevermore, Amen.

Day 33

Night Watches

"Praise the LORD, all you servants of the LORD who minister by night in the house of the LORD. Lift up your hands in the sanctuary and praise the LORD." — Psalm 134:1-2

HISTORICAL CONTEXT

As our forty-day pilgrimage nears its conclusion, we arrive at Psalm 134, the final Song of Ascent. This brief psalm serves as a fitting culmination to the pilgrim's journey, focusing on worship within the sanctuary that was the journey's destination.

For ancient Israelites making the pilgrimage to Jerusalem, this psalm would likely have been sung as they reached the temple itself—the physical goal of their ascent. The specific mention of those who "minister by night" gives us insight into temple practices that many pilgrims might never have witnessed themselves.

According to historical records, the Jerusalem temple operated continuously, with priests and Levites serving in shifts throughout the day and night. 1 Chronicles 9:33 mentions Levitical singers who were "on duty day and night," while verse 27 notes that some Levites "had charge of the gates" and "would spend the night stationed around the house of God." These night ministers maintained the temple's lamps, prepared for morning sacrifices, guarded the sacred precincts, and continued the rhythm of prayer and praise when most of Israel slept.

The phrase "servants of the LORD" specifically designated priests and Levites—those officially consecrated for temple service. While most Israelites supported temple worship through tithes and festival participation, only these designated servants could enter the sacred precincts and perform ritual duties.

For the pilgrims singing this psalm, there would have been a poignant recognition that their journey was temporary. After celebrating the festival, they would return to homes and fields throughout Israel. But the temple servants remained, maintaining the continual worship that represented Israel's covenant relationship with God. The pilgrims' brief, intense worship experience depended on the faithful, often unseen service of these night ministers.

MEDITATION: THE NIGHT MINISTERS

"Praise the LORD, all you servants of the LORD who minister by night in the house of the LORD."

The Hebrew word translated "minister" (םידְמֹע, omdim) literally means "standing." It conveys not just activity but position and readiness—maintaining one's place, remaining alert, being available. These servants stood at their posts through the night hours, when natural human rhythms pull toward sleep and rest.

Why focus specifically on those serving at night? Night in ancient times intensified every challenge. Without electric lighting, darkness severely limited visibility. Night brought heightened vulnerability to threats and dangers. Night also magnified isolation, as most of the community slept. Those serving through these hours faced unique tests of faithfulness and courage.

Night ministry also occurred when almost no one was watching. During daylight hours, the temple bustled with worshippers who could observe, appreciate, and affirm the priests' and Levites' service. But night servants performed their duties when few if any witnessed their faithfulness. Their primary audience was God Himself.

This verse invites us to consider the spiritual significance of serving when no one sees, when affirmation is minimal, when physical challenges are intensified, and when the reward is simply knowing one's place in God's house has been maintained. These night ministers embodied a profound truth: worship doesn't depend on visibility, convenience, or human recognition. True service to God persists when external motivations diminish.

For Christians, this connects directly to Jesus' teaching in Matthew 6:1-6, where he commends religious practices done in secret rather than for public recognition. "Your Father, who sees what is done in secret, will reward you," Jesus promised. The night ministers of the temple prefigured this spiritual principle, finding meaning not in public acclaim but in divine awareness.

THE POSTURE OF PRAISE

"Lift up your hands in the sanctuary and praise the LORD."

Having acknowledged these night ministers, the psalm directs them toward their essential task: praise. The lifted hands described here represented a common posture of prayer and worship in ancient Israel. This physical gesture symbolized openness to God, surrender, and receptivity. Like a child lifting arms to be picked up by a parent, the worshipper extended empty hands toward heaven, expressing both offering and reception.

The Hebrew word for "sanctuary" (שֹׁדֶק, qodesh) literally means "holiness" or "holy place." It designated the temple as set apart from ordinary space—a location where heaven and earth intersected. The night ministers occupied this liminal space, standing at the threshold between the divine and human realms during hours when most people were disconnected from sacred consciousness.

The command to "praise the LORD" (וּכְרָב, barchu) literally means "bless" and suggests active declaration of God's goodness. Even in darkness, isolation, and potential weariness, these servants were called to articulate God's worth and excellence. Their praise maintained the continuous acknowledgment of God's character that was Israel's primary covenant responsibility.

Notice that the psalm doesn't specify elaborate rituals or complex theological declarations. The essence of the night ministers' task was stunningly simple: lift hands and bless God. This simplicity reminds us that at its core, worship doesn't require sophisticated methods or performances. The heart turning toward God in acknowledgment and gratitude constitutes authentic worship's essence.

For the night ministers, this simple act carried profound significance. Their praise ensured that Israel's acknowledgment of God never ceased. Like relay runners passing a baton, they ensured the continuation of worship when others rested. When most of Israel's voices fell silent in sleep, theirs maintained the nation's witness to God's worthiness.

APPLICATION: EMBRACING UNSEEN SERVICE

As pilgrims journeying toward Jerusalem, we recognize in this psalm an invitation to embrace the spiritual value of unseen service and private devotion. While our forty-day pilgrimage has included shared insights and community reflection, this psalm reminds us that much of our spiritual journey occurs in moments no one else witnesses.

First, we're called to recognize the dignity of service that lacks visibility. Contemporary culture often equates value with publicity—social media metrics, public recognition, and observable impact. This psalm subverts such values, highlighting those whose service occurred beyond public awareness. Jesus affirmed this principle when he taught, "Be careful not to practice your righteousness in front of others to be seen by them" (Matthew 6:1). The night ministers remind us that service's value derives not from its visibility but from its alignment with God's purposes.

Second, we're invited to discover worship's power in challenging seasons. Night in this psalm represents more than literal darkness; it symbolizes periods of life marked by difficulty, isolation, or reduced spiritual consolation. During such seasons, worship may feel more like faithful standing than ecstatic experience. The night ministers teach us that praise offered during difficulty carries its own sanctity. As the psalmist wrote elsewhere, "I will bless the LORD at all times" (Psalm 34:1)—not just when circumstances feel favorable.

Third, we're encouraged to maintain spiritual disciplines when external motivations diminish. The night ministers didn't depend on audience energy, community affirmation, or visible outcomes to sustain their service. Similarly, our private prayers, unseen generosity, and faithful presence with those who cannot reciprocate may lack immediate reinforcement. Yet these hidden practices often constitute our most authentic worship, precisely because they continue when no motivation exists except love for God and commitment to His purposes.

Fourth, we're reminded of the value of maintaining sacred rhythms. The night ministers ensured unbroken continuity in Israel's worship. Similarly, our consistent spiritual practices—daily prayer, Scripture reading, Sabbath observance, regular communion—maintain vital connection with God through changing circumstances. These rhythms don't depend on feeling inspired or having exceptional experiences; they express commitment to remaining in relationship with God through all life's seasons.

Today, as you continue your pilgrimage, consider the "night watches" of your own spiritual journey. What faithful service do you offer when no one is watching? How do you maintain worship when circumstances turn challenging? What spiritual disciplines persist not because they bring immediate satisfaction or recognition but because they express your commitment to God? These questions lead us toward mature faith that finds meaning not in visibility or affirmation but in knowing we've maintained our place in God's house, regardless of who notices.

Remember that the God who sees in secret is the same God who rewards faithfulness with deeper relationship and increased capacity for love. The night ministers who lifted hands when no human observed were never truly alone—the One to whom their praise ascended saw every gesture and heard every word. Your unseen faithfulness likewise unfolds in the presence of the God who never slumbers or sleeps.

REFLECTION QUESTIONS

1. The psalm specifically addresses those who serve "by night" when few people would observe their ministry. What aspects of your spiritual life or service occur primarily in private, without public recognition? How do you maintain faithfulness in these areas?

   _____

   _____

2. Night ministry presented unique challenges—darkness, isolation, weariness. What particular challenges do you face in your own "night watches" of faith? How might you embrace these challenges as opportunities for deeper trust rather than obstacles to overcome?

   _____

   _____

3. The posture described in verse 2—lifted hands in the sanctuary—expressed both offering and receptivity toward God. What physical or spiritual postures help you express authentic worship, particularly during difficult seasons? How might you incorporate these more intentionally into your private devotion?

   _____

   _____

4. Jesus taught that the Father "sees what is done in secret" (Matthew 6:4, 6, 18). How does this awareness of God's seeing presence affect your approach to unseen service and private devotion? In what ways might this awareness need to deepen in your spiritual life?

   _____

   _____

5. The night ministers maintained Israel's worship when most of the community slept. In what ways do you contribute to maintaining the ongoing worship and witness of the Christian community, perhaps in ways others might not immediately recognize or appreciate?

---

6. If you're journeying through this devotional with others, discuss how your community might better honor and support the "night ministers" among you—those whose faithful service often occurs beyond public recognition. How might you cultivate greater appreciation for various forms of unseen ministry?

PRAYER FOR TODAY

Seeing God,

Today I recognize that much of my spiritual journey unfolds in moments no one else witnesses— my private prayers, unseen acts of service, faithfulness maintained when no one is watching. Thank You that You see what is done in secret. Thank You that no genuine worship or service escapes Your notice, even when others remain unaware.

Forgive me for the times I've prioritized visible ministry over hidden faithfulness, seeking human recognition rather than Your approval. Forgive me when I've neglected the night watches of my own spiritual life—those consistent disciplines that maintain connection with You even when immediate rewards aren't evident.

Lord Jesus, You modeled perfect faithfulness in unseen moments—rising before dawn to pray, serving those who couldn't reciprocate, maintaining integrity when tempted in private. Help me follow Your example, finding meaning not in visibility or acclaim but in knowing I'm fulfilling my place in Your purposes.

When I face my own night watches—seasons of challenge, isolation, or reduced spiritual consolation—help me lift hands in the sanctuary despite the darkness. When worship feels more like faithful standing than ecstatic experience, remind me that such persistent praise carries its own distinct beauty.

Holy Spirit, sustain those in my community whose service often goes unrecognized—those who pray when others sleep, who maintain our shared spaces, who offer support behind the scenes, who serve in ways that never make announcements or receive applause. Show me how to honor and support these hidden ministers.

As I continue this pilgrimage, deepen my capacity for faithful presence in unseen moments. Help me discover worship's power not just in mountain-top experiences but in valleys of ordinary obedience. May my night watches become opportunities to know You more intimately as the God who neither slumbers nor sleeps.

I pray this in the name of Jesus Christ, who sees every secret and rewards every faithfulness, Amen.

Day 34

Blessing God, Blessed by God

"May the LORD bless you from Zion, he who made heaven and earth." — Psalm 134:3

HISTORICAL CONTEXT

As our forty-day pilgrimage continues through the final Song of Ascent, we focus today on the concluding verse of Psalm 134. This verse completes not only this particular psalm but serves as a fitting culmination to the entire collection of pilgrimage songs.

For ancient Israelite pilgrims, this verse would likely have functioned as a benediction—a final blessing pronounced as they prepared to depart from Jerusalem and return to their homes throughout the land. After days of festival celebration, temple worship, and community fellowship, this blessing would have sent them back to ordinary life with the assurance of God's continued presence.

The historical context reveals an interesting shift in voice between verses 1-2 and verse 3. The first two verses addressed the temple servants directly ("Praise the LORD, all you servants..."), likely spoken by the pilgrims. This final verse, however, appears to be the response of the temple servants to the departing pilgrims ("May the LORD bless you..."). This exchange creates a beautiful liturgical dialogue between those who came to worship temporarily and those who remained in continuous service.

The specific mention of blessing "from Zion" connects to the ancient understanding of Jerusalem, particularly the temple mount, as the place where heaven and earth intersected—where God's presence dwelled in unique intensity. While Israelites affirmed that God was present everywhere (Psalm 139), they recognized certain locations as points of special divine manifestation. Zion represented not just a geographical location but the source of divine blessing flowing out to God's people.

The identification of the LORD as "he who made heaven and earth" grounds this blessing in creation theology. The God who blesses from Zion is not merely a local or national deity but the Creator of all reality. This cosmic perspective places the pilgrimage experience within the largest possible context—connecting the worshippers' brief journey to the grand narrative of creation and redemption.

MEDITATION: THE RECIPROCAL NATURE OF BLESSING

When we compare verse 3 with verses 1-2, a striking pattern emerges: the psalm begins with people blessing God ("Praise/bless the LORD") and concludes with God blessing people ("May the LORD bless you"). This creates a complete circuit of blessing—a sacred exchange between divine and human partners.

The Hebrew word for "bless" (בָּרַךְ, barakh) appears in both directions. When humans bless God, they acknowledge His goodness, declare His worthiness, and express gratitude for His character and actions. When God blesses humans, He bestows favor, provision, protection, and presence. Though the same word is used, the content differs based on the direction—we cannot add anything to God, while He can transform everything about us.

This reciprocal blessing reveals something profound about worship's nature. Authentic worship never flows in only one direction. It creates a responsive pattern where divine initiative and human response continuously interact. God's goodness inspires our praise; our praise opens us further to receive His blessing; His blessing generates more praise. The cycle continues, deepening the relationship with each revolution.

In this cycle, God always retains priority. Notice the concluding description: "he who made heaven and earth." This reminds us that God's capacity to bless infinitely exceeds our own. As Creator, He possesses all resources and authority. Our blessing of God, while meaningful, remains responsive rather than originating. As 1 John 4:19 expresses, "We love because he first loved us." Similarly, we bless because He first blessed us.

Yet despite this asymmetry, the psalm affirms that human blessing of God genuinely matters. The first two verses wouldn't command the night ministers to praise God if their action were insignificant. God genuinely desires and receives the blessing we offer, not because He needs it but because He values relationship that includes both giving and receiving.

THE SOURCE AND SCOPE OF BLESSING

"May the LORD bless you from Zion, he who made heaven and earth."

This benediction identifies both the source and scope of divine blessing. The source is specifically "from Zion"—the place of God's chosen dwelling. For the ancient pilgrims, this had concrete geographical significance. Having ascended to Jerusalem to encounter God's presence, they now carried that blessing back to their everyday lives. The blessing wasn't confined to the temple precincts but extended outward through those who had experienced God's presence.

For Christians, this principle finds fulfillment in Christ, who makes God's presence accessible beyond geographical limitations. As Jesus told the Samaritan woman, true worship would no longer be limited to a specific mountain but would occur "in the Spirit and in truth" (John 4:23-24). The blessing that once flowed from physical Zion now flows from Christ himself, who embodies God's presence among His people.

The scope of blessing is indicated by the Creator title: "he who made heaven and earth." This expansive description prevents us from limiting divine blessing to spiritual experiences detached from material reality. The God who blesses is the same God who created matter, space, and time. His blessing extends to every dimension of human existence—body, soul, relationships, work, and environment.

This cosmic framing also reminds us that blessing ultimately connects to God's purposes for all creation. The pilgrims' journey represented not just personal spiritual experience but participation in God's redemptive work throughout the world. Their blessing carried responsibility—as recipients of divine favor, they were to extend that blessing to others, fulfilling the Abrahamic covenant: "all peoples on earth will be blessed through you" (Genesis 12:3).

APPLICATION: COMPLETING THE CYCLE

As pilgrims nearing the end of our forty-day journey, this verse invites us to consider how we complete the cycle of blessing in our relationship with God and others. How do we receive God's blessing and extend it outward? How does our worship create the continuous circuit where divine giving and human responsiveness interact?

First, we cultivate receptivity to God's blessing. The pilgrims didn't generate blessing themselves but received it "from Zion"—from God's presence. Similarly, we position ourselves to receive what God offers. This receptivity involves both active practices (prayer, Scripture, worship, community) and internal postures (humility, openness, expectancy, gratitude). As Jesus taught in the Beatitudes (Matthew 5:3-12), certain heart orientations particularly align us with divine blessing.

Second, we embrace the comprehensive nature of blessing. The Creator reference reminds us that God's blessing encompasses our whole existence. We sometimes artificially separate "spiritual blessing" from material, relational, or vocational flourishing. But the God who blesses from Zion is the God who made everything. His blessing addresses our physical needs, emotional health, intellectual development, relational connections, and cultural engagement. As we receive this comprehensive blessing, we avoid false spirituality that dismisses earthly concerns as unimportant.

Third, we recognize our role in extending blessing. Israel was blessed not merely for their own sake but to bless others. Similarly, we receive divine blessing as conduits, not endpoints. Peter identifies believers as those who inherit blessing specifically so we can bless others, "not repaying evil with evil or insult with insult, but with blessing" (1 Peter 3:9). The circuit of blessing continues as it flows through us to those around us, particularly to those who cannot repay or reciprocate.

Fourth, we maintain the priority of relationship. The exchanged blessings in this psalm weren't transactional but relational—expressions of covenant connection between God and His people. Similarly, our participation in blessing isn't primarily about obtaining benefits or fulfilling obligations but about deepening relationship with God and others. When blessing becomes merely transactional—serving God to get things from Him—we distort its fundamental nature.

As you continue your pilgrimage today, consider how you participate in this sacred cycle of blessing. How do you receive what God offers—not just in dramatic moments but in daily provisions, relationships, and opportunities? How do you express blessing back to God through thanksgiving, obedience, and worship? How does that blessing then flow through you to others? Remember that this cycle doesn't end with this devotional journey or even with this earthly life. The exchange of blessing between God and His people continues into eternity, growing ever deeper and fuller. As you prepare to conclude this forty-day pilgrimage, recognize that the sacred pattern of reciprocal blessing will continue, drawing you ever closer to the God who both receives and gives blessing in perfect love.

REFLECTION QUESTIONS

1. The psalm presents a cycle where people bless God and God blesses people. In your own spiritual journey, how have you experienced this reciprocal pattern of blessing? When has your worship of God opened you to receive His blessing more fully?

_____

_____

2. The blessing comes specifically "from Zion"—the place of God's presence. Where and how do you most consistently experience God's presence in your life? What practices or environments help you position yourself to receive blessing "from Zion"?

_____

_____

3. God is identified as "he who made heaven and earth," connecting blessing to creation. How does understanding God as Creator affect your concept of blessing? In what specific areas of your created existence (physical, relational, vocational, etc.) are you seeking God's blessing?

_____

_____

4. Israel was blessed to be a blessing to others (Genesis 12:2-3). How are you currently extending the blessing you've received to those around you? Is there anyone in particular to whom God might be calling you to be a conduit of blessing?

_____

_____

5. This verse served as a benediction for pilgrims returning to everyday life after their Jerusalem journey. As you prepare to conclude this forty-day devotional pilgrimage, what blessing are you carrying back into your regular routines and relationships?

_____

_____

6. If you're journeying through this devotional with others, discuss how your community might more intentionally participate in this cycle of blessing—both collectively blessing God and becoming conduits of His blessing to your broader community. What might this look like practically?

PRAYER FOR TODAY

Blessing God,

Today I marvel at the cycle of blessing You have established—how You invite me to bless You and then respond by blessing me in return. Thank You for initiating this sacred exchange, for loving me first so that I might love You back, for blessing me so that I might bless You in response.

I acknowledge that as Creator of heaven and earth, Your capacity to bless infinitely exceeds my own. Everything I have to offer You was first Your gift to me. Yet I'm humbled and amazed that You genuinely receive and value the blessing I offer—my praise, gratitude, obedience, and love. Thank You for blessing me from Your presence—for the tangible ways You provide, protect, guide, and sustain me. Thank You especially for the blessing of relationship with You, made possible through Christ. Help me to recognize Your blessing in all its forms, not just in dramatic moments but in daily provisions, relationships, and opportunities.

Forgive me for the times I've reduced our relationship to transactions—serving You mainly to get things from You or offering worship without truly opening myself to receive what You give in return. Restore the genuine reciprocity of blessing that reflects covenant love rather than mere exchange.

As I prepare to conclude this forty-day pilgrimage, help me carry Your blessing into my everyday life. Make me increasingly aware of Your presence throughout my daily activities. And make me a conduit of Your blessing to others—family, friends, colleagues, neighbors, and especially those who cannot repay.

May the sacred cycle continue—Your blessing generating my praise, my praise opening me to receive more fully, Your blessing flowing through me to others, their flourishing producing more praise. Draw me ever deeper into this beautiful pattern that reflects Your perfect love.

I pray this in the name of Jesus Christ, the ultimate blessing from Zion to all creation, Amen.

Day 35

The Journey Reviewed

"In my distress I called to the LORD, and he answered me..." (Psalm 120:1) "May the LORD bless you from Zion, he who made heaven and earth." (Psalm 134:3)

HISTORICAL CONTEXT

As our forty-day pilgrimage nears its conclusion, we pause today to look back over the path we've traveled through the Songs of Ascent. These fifteen psalms (120-134) formed a cohesive collection that guided ancient Israelite pilgrims on their journey to Jerusalem for the major festivals. Their placement together in the Psalter was intentional, creating a spiritual roadmap for both physical and interior pilgrimages.

For the ancient worshippers, these songs accompanied actual geographical movement—the ascent from various starting points throughout Israel up to Jerusalem, which sat on higher elevation. As pilgrims climbed toward the holy city, these psalms provided language for their experience, helping them process both the physical journey and its spiritual significance.

The collection demonstrates remarkable intentionality in its arrangement. It begins with distress in "foreign lands" (Psalm 120:5) and concludes with blessing in God's presence (Psalm 134:3). Between these endpoints, the psalms address various aspects of the spiritual journey—protection, providence, perseverance, community, and hope. Together, they chart not just a geographical path but a spiritual progression from alienation to intimacy, from anxiety to trust, from isolation to community.

For Jewish pilgrims, these songs would have carried collective memory as well as present experience. As they sang about God's protection, they remembered His faithfulness to previous generations. As they celebrated Zion, they connected to their covenant identity. As they described unity, they experienced it with fellow travelers. The Songs of Ascent thus linked past, present, and future—rooting current pilgrimage in historical faith while anticipating future fulfillment.

MEDITATION: THE SPIRITUAL JOURNEY MAPPED

Looking back across these fifteen psalms, we can trace a meaningful progression that maps not only the ancient pilgrimage but our own spiritual journeys:

The Call to Journey (Psalm 120) "In my distress I called to the LORD, and he answered me."

Our journey began where the ancient pilgrims began—with the recognition of distress and disorientation. Psalm 120 located the psalmist in "Meshech" and "Kedar"—places far from God's presence, surrounded by deceit and conflict. This starting point reminds us that spiritual journeys typically begin not with arrival but with departure—not with answers but with questions, not with comfort but with holy discontent.

How many of us began our own faith journeys from similar places of distress? Perhaps through disappointment with false sources of meaning, through recognition of our own brokenness, or through circumstances that revealed our need for something beyond ourselves. Distress creates the sacred discomfort that motivates movement toward God.

Divine Protection on the Journey (Psalms 121-124) "My help comes from the LORD, the Maker of heaven and earth."

As the pilgrimage began, attention turned to the challenges of the journey—physical dangers on ancient roads and spiritual threats to faith. These psalms acknowledged vulnerability while affirming God's comprehensive protection. The God who "neither slumbers nor sleeps" (121:4) watches over every step. The Creator who made "heaven and earth" (121:2) possesses all resources needed for the journey.

These psalms taught us that spiritual growth requires both human effort and divine protection. We make the journey—taking actual steps, making real choices—but we do so empowered and guarded by God's presence. Without this protection, the smallest obstacle could derail us. With it, even substantial challenges become navigable.

Jerusalem as Destination (Psalms 125-128) "Those who trust in the LORD are like Mount Zion, which cannot be shaken but endures forever."

As the physical city came into view for ancient pilgrims, these psalms celebrated Jerusalem both as geographical location and spiritual symbol. Jerusalem represented God's presence, covenant faithfulness, and promised blessing. These psalms connected obedience with flourishing and trust with stability.

For us, these psalms illuminated the goal of our spiritual journey—not merely improved behavior or religious knowledge but intimate presence with God. They reminded us that spiritual maturity doesn't mean freedom from challenges but rootedness that remains stable amid them. Like Jerusalem surrounded by mountains, the soul anchored in God stands secure.

Perseverance Through Difficulty (Psalms 129-131) "Out of the depths I cry to you, LORD; Lord, hear my voice."

Even as the destination came into view, these psalms acknowledged the ongoing struggles of faith. They expressed lament over persecution (Psalm 129), penitence for sin (Psalm 130), and the humility required for authentic relationship with God (Psalm 131). They reminded pilgrims that arrival at the physical destination didn't automatically resolve interior struggles.

These psalms taught us that spiritual journeys include valleys even after significant progress. Growth isn't linear but cyclical—requiring ongoing repentance, repeated surrender, and renewed humility. The mature soul doesn't claim to have moved beyond struggle but knows how to struggle well—with hope, honesty, and proper perspective.

The Community of Faith (Psalms 132-134) "How good and pleasant it is when God's people live together in unity!"

The final psalms shifted focus from individual experience to collective identity. They celebrated God's covenant with David, His choice of Zion as dwelling place, the beauty of community, and the reciprocal blessing between God and His people. As pilgrims reached Jerusalem and joined the worshipping community, their individual journeys merged into corporate expression.

These psalms reminded us that spiritual growth, while deeply personal, is never purely individual. Authentic faith joins us to others on the same journey—creating bonds of shared experience, mutual support, and collective witness. The culmination of pilgrimage isn't solitary enlightenment but participation in sacred community.

APPLICATION: MARKERS OF GROWTH

As we review our journey through the Songs of Ascent, several markers of spiritual growth emerge that help us evaluate our progress:

From Alienation to Belonging The journey began with the psalmist dwelling in foreign lands (Psalm 120:5) and concluded in the house of the LORD (Psalm 134:1). This movement from alienation to belonging represents a fundamental trajectory of spiritual growth. As we mature, we increasingly recognize our place in God's story and community.

Reflect on your own journey: How has your sense of spiritual belonging developed through this pilgrimage? Where do you experience authentic connection with God and His people? What remaining areas of alienation might God be inviting you to address?

From Anxiety to Trust The early psalms expressed considerable anxiety about threats and dangers. By the journey's end, the tone shifted to confident rest in God's protection and provision. This movement from anxiety to trust marks significant spiritual development—not the absence of challenges but a transformed relationship to them.

Consider your own growth in trust: What concerns do you hold differently now than when you began this journey? How has your understanding of God's character deepened? What practices have helped you move from anxiety toward trust?

From Self-Reliance to Dependence Throughout the collection, the psalms systematically dismantled self-sufficiency. Psalm 127 explicitly stated that human effort without divine blessing proves futile. Psalm 131 described the soul resting like a weaned child, no longer frantically seeking to meet its own needs. This movement from self-reliance to peaceful dependence reflects spiritual maturation.

Assess your own journey toward healthy dependence: Where do you still struggle with the illusion of self-sufficiency? How have you experienced the freedom that comes with surrendering control? What helps you maintain awareness of your dependence on God?

From Isolation to Community The collection's movement culminated in the celebration of unity and shared blessing. The individual distress that began the journey resolved not in private enlightenment but in corporate worship. This trajectory from isolation to community represents essential spiritual development.

Examine your own community connections: How has your appreciation for spiritual community grown during this journey? Where do you contribute to "how good and pleasant it is when God's people live together in unity"? What barriers to deeper community might God be inviting you to address?

As you reflect on your journey through these psalms, remember that spiritual growth rarely follows a perfectly linear path. We often revisit earlier stages, face new versions of old challenges, and discover fresh dimensions of familiar truths. The value lies not in achieving some final destination but in continuing the journey with growing awareness, deepening trust, and expanding love.

Today, give thanks for how far you've come since beginning this pilgrimage. Acknowledge the growth you've experienced, the companions who've walked alongside you, and the God who has both guided and sustained every step. Then look forward with hope, knowing that the journey continues beyond these forty days into the lifelong pilgrimage of faith.

REFLECTION QUESTIONS

1. Looking back across the Songs of Ascent, which psalm or specific verse resonated most deeply with your current spiritual journey? What about that psalm or verse particularly connected with your experience?

_____

_____

2. The collection begins with "distress" (Psalm 120:1) and ends with "blessing" (Psalm 134:3). Reflect on times in your life when distress became the catalyst for spiritual growth that ultimately led to blessing. How has this pattern manifested in your experience?

_____

_____

3. Throughout the Songs of Ascent, the psalmists demonstrate remarkable honesty about struggles, doubts, and failures. How has this devotional journey affected your comfort with expressing your own spiritual struggles honestly? What have you learned about the role of lament and confession in healthy spirituality?

_____

_____

4. The final psalms emphasize the importance of community in spiritual journey. How has your connection with others (either those joining you in this devotional or your broader faith community) contributed to your growth during this pilgrimage? What have you learned about the relationship between individual and communal spirituality?

_____

_____

5. The Songs of Ascent include recurring themes of protection, providence, perseverance, and presence. Which of these aspects of God's character has become more real or meaningful to you through this devotional journey? How has your understanding of God developed or deepened?

_____

_____

6. If you're journeying through this devotional with others, share the most significant insight or change you've experienced during these weeks. What practice or perspective from this journey do you most want to carry forward into your ongoing spiritual life?

_____

_____

PRAYER FOR TODAY

Faithful Guide,

As I look back across the path we've traveled together through these Songs of Ascent, my heart overflows with gratitude. Thank You for meeting me in my initial distress and drawing me toward Your presence. Thank You for protecting every step, providing what I needed, teaching me perseverance, and surrounding me with community along the way.

I recognize now how You've been working even when I couldn't perceive it—transforming anxiety into trust, self-reliance into dependence, isolation into connection. Thank You for Your patient persistence in leading me forward even when I resisted or wandered from the path.

I acknowledge that this journey hasn't been perfectly linear. I've circled back to familiar struggles, faced unexpected detours, and sometimes felt I was making little progress. Yet looking back, I can see the distance traveled—not by my own strength but by Your faithful guidance and sustaining grace.

Forgive me for the times I've questioned Your leadership, preferred my own direction, or failed to trust Your protection. Forgive me for moments of complaining about the journey's challenges rather than recognizing their role in my growth. Create in me a more grateful and trusting heart as I continue walking with You.

As this devotional pilgrimage nears its conclusion, help me integrate what I've learned into my ongoing spiritual journey. Show me how to maintain the perspectives and practices that have fostered growth. Connect me more deeply with fellow pilgrims so we might encourage each other as we continue climbing toward Your presence.

Most of all, keep my heart ever oriented toward Jerusalem—toward the place of Your presence, promise, and blessing. May my soul continually ascend toward deeper communion with You, regardless of external circumstances or internal feelings.

I pray this in the name of Jesus Christ, the perfect pilgrim who journeyed from heaven to earth and back again to prepare our eternal dwelling with You, Amen.

Day 36

New Horizons

Application of the Ascent Journey "I lift up my eyes to the mountains—where does my help come from? My help comes from the LORD, the Maker of heaven and earth." — Psalm 121:1-2

THE CONTINUING JOURNEY

As our forty-day pilgrimage through the Songs of Ascent nears its conclusion, we stand at a significant transition point. Yesterday, we looked back across the path we've traveled through these fifteen psalms. Today, we lift our eyes to the horizon ahead, considering how to carry the wisdom of these ancient songs into our ongoing spiritual journey.

For the ancient Israelite pilgrims, the return home after a festival in Jerusalem marked not the end of their spiritual experience but its integration into everyday life. The insights, encounters, and community connections formed during pilgrimage weren't meant to remain in Jerusalem but to transform their existence back in villages and towns throughout Israel. Similarly, our journey through these psalms isn't meant to conclude with the final page of this devotional but to shape our continued ascent in faith.

The Songs of Ascent themselves hint at this ongoing nature of spiritual pilgrimage. While they culminate in temple worship, they never suggest that arrival at the destination completes the journey. Rather, they describe patterns of relationship with God that continue through all seasons and circumstances. The blessing that concludes the collection in Psalm 134:3 sends pilgrims outward with divine favor, not to conclude their spiritual journey but to continue it in new contexts.

This continuity aligns with the broader biblical understanding of spiritual formation as lifelong process rather than momentary achievement. As Paul writes in Philippians 3:12-14, "Not that I have already obtained all this, or have already arrived at my goal, but I press on to take hold of that for which Christ Jesus took hold of me... Forgetting what is behind and straining toward what is ahead, I press on toward the goal to win the prize for which God has called me heavenward in Christ Jesus."

PRINCIPLES FOR CONTINUED ASCENT

As we consider how to move forward from this devotional journey, several key principles emerge from the Songs of Ascent that can guide our continued growth:

1. Remember the Starting Point

The collection began with honest acknowledgment of distress and disorientation: "In my distress I called to the LORD" (Psalm 120:1). This recognition of need initiated the journey toward God's presence. Similarly, ongoing spiritual growth requires maintained awareness of our continued need for God—not just in obvious crises but in everyday insufficiency.

Spiritual maturity doesn't mean outgrowing our need for God but recognizing it more deeply. As we continue beyond this devotional, we cultivate this awareness not through self-condemnation but through honest assessment of our limitations and genuine receptivity to divine provision. Regular practices of confession, thanksgiving, and intercession help maintain this productive awareness of dependence.

2. Trust Divine Protection

Throughout the collection, the psalms emphasized God's comprehensive protection: "The LORD watches over you—the LORD is your shade at your right hand" (Psalm 121:5). This assurance freed pilgrims to journey forward despite legitimate risks and challenges. Similarly, our continued spiritual ascent requires trust that empowers movement despite uncertainty.

As we venture into new territories of faith, relationships, and service, we will inevitably encounter situations that stretch our capabilities and comfort. Remembering God's protective presence allows us to step forward with appropriate boldness rather than retreating into false security. Practices of remembrance—recalling specific instances of God's faithfulness—help sustain this trust through challenging circumstances.

3. Embrace Both Effort and Grace

The Songs of Ascent balanced human responsibility with divine enabling: "Unless the LORD builds the house, the builders labor in vain" (Psalm 127:1). The pilgrims actively journeyed toward Jerusalem while depending on God's protection and provision. Similarly, our continued growth involves both disciplined effort and receptivity to grace.

As we move forward, we avoid both passive spirituality that expects transformation without participation and self-sufficient striving that attempts growth through willpower alone. Instead, we "work out [our] salvation with fear and trembling, for it is God who works in [us] to will and to act in order to fulfill his good purpose" (Philippians 2:12-13). Practices of both active obedience and contemplative receptivity maintain this balance.

4. Value Sacred Community

The final psalms emphasized the beauty and importance of community: "How good and pleasant it is when God's people live together in unity!" (Psalm 133:1). The pilgrimage journey was inherently communal, with individual paths merging into collective worship. Similarly, our continued spiritual growth flourishes within intentional community.

As we conclude this shared devotional experience, we seek ways to maintain meaningful spiritual connection with others. Whether through small groups, mentoring relationships, service partnerships, or regular worship gatherings, we recognize that isolation threatens sustained growth while community nourishes it. Practices of hospitality, vulnerability, and mutual accountability support this communal dimension of continued ascent.

5. Maintain Upward Focus

Throughout the collection, the psalms directed attention upward: "I lift up my eyes to the mountains—where does my help come from?" (Psalm 121:1). This vertical orientation prevented pilgrims from becoming fixated on obstacles or distractions. Similarly, our continued growth requires maintained focus on God rather than circumstances, challenges, or even spiritual experiences themselves.

As we move forward, we regularly redirect our attention from legitimate but secondary concerns toward the character, promises, and presence of God. This doesn't mean ignoring practical realities but viewing them within the larger context of divine purpose and provision. Practices of worship, Scripture meditation, and breath prayer help maintain this upward orientation amidst daily demands.

PRACTICAL APPLICATIONS

Moving from principles to practice, consider these specific applications for continuing your ascent beyond this devotional:

Establish Sustainable Rhythms

The pilgrimage festivals occurred at regular intervals in Israel's calendar, creating recurring opportunities for intentional spiritual focus. Similarly, establishing sustainable spiritual rhythms helps maintain momentum between intensive growth experiences. Consider which daily, weekly, and seasonal practices will support your continued ascent, being realistic about your current life stage and responsibilities.

This might include brief morning meditation on Scripture, weekly Sabbath practices, monthly reflection on growth areas, or seasonal retreats for extended spiritual focus. The specific practices matter less than their regularity and sustainability—creating patterns that can flex with life's demands while maintaining consistent connection with God.

Identify Next Growth Areas

The Songs of Ascent addressed various aspects of relationship with God—trust, obedience, repentance, worship, community. As this devotional concludes, prayerfully identify specific growth areas God is highlighting for your continued journey. Rather than attempting comprehensive transformation, focus on one or two areas where deeper work seems most timely.

This focused attention doesn't narrow your relationship with God but creates depth that eventually expands to other areas. Like intensive gardening in one plot rather than surface-level care across an entire field, concentrated spiritual attention in specific areas often yields more substantial growth than diffused efforts across many fronts.

Find Traveling Companions

The Israelite pilgrims journeyed together for practical support and shared experience. Similarly, identifying specific companions for your continued spiritual journey provides accountability, encouragement, and perspective. This might involve maintaining connection with others who shared this devotional experience or finding new relationships focused on mutual growth.

The most effective spiritual friendships combine affirmation with challenge, celebrating progress while encouraging continued development. Consider who might serve as both mirror and window in your ongoing journey—reflecting your true condition while opening vistas to new possibilities in Christ

.

Schedule Regular Reviews

The pilgrimage festivals provided regular opportunities to assess Israel's covenant relationship with God. Similarly, scheduling intentional review points helps maintain awareness of your spiritual trajectory. Mark your calendar now for specific dates to evaluate your continued journey—perhaps quarterly or around significant church calendar moments like Advent or Easter.

During these reviews, return to insights recorded during this devotional, evaluate progress in identified growth areas, celebrate evidence of transformation, and adjust practices as needed. These intentional pauses prevent drift while providing opportunities to recognize God's often-subtle work over time.

As you conclude this forty-day pilgrimage through the Songs of Ascent, remember that you've not reached a final destination but a significant waypoint in your lifelong journey with God. The path continues upward, with new vistas of divine truth and love awaiting discovery. May the wisdom gathered from these ancient songs illuminate your path as you continue ascending toward deeper communion with the God who called you to journey with Him.

REFLECTION QUESTIONS

1. Looking back over this forty-day devotional journey, what specific insights or practices have been most transformative for you? How might you intentionally carry these forward into your continuing spiritual journey?

_____

_____

2. The Songs of Ascent present spiritual growth as a continuing ascent rather than arrival at a final destination. What "new horizons" do you sense God inviting you to explore in the next season of your spiritual journey? What specific areas of growth seem most timely?

_____

_____

3. Sustainable spiritual rhythms support continued growth after intensive experiences. What daily, weekly, or seasonal practices would help maintain your momentum while being realistic about your current life circumstances? What might need to be adjusted or pruned to make these rhythms sustainable?

_____

_____

4. The pilgrimage journey was inherently communal for ancient Israelites. Who might serve as traveling companions for your continued spiritual journey? What qualities would you look for in relationships that support authentic growth?

_____

_____

5. The Songs of Ascent balanced human effort with divine enabling in spiritual growth. Where do you tend to fall out of balance—leaning either toward passive waiting or self-sufficient striving? What practices might help you maintain both active participation and receptivity to grace?

---

6. If you're journeying through this devotional with others, discuss how you might continue supporting each other's spiritual growth after completing these forty days. What specific commitments could you make to maintain meaningful connection focused on continued ascent?

PRAYER FOR TODAY

Faithful Guide,

As I near the conclusion of this forty-day journey through the Songs of Ascent, I'm deeply grateful for all You've revealed, healed, and transformed along the way. Thank You for ancient words that have become fresh bread for my soul. Thank You for meeting me in these pages and making this more than an intellectual exercise but a genuine encounter with Your presence.

As I look toward horizons beyond this devotional experience, I ask for wisdom to carry forward what You've begun. Show me which insights and practices are most important to maintain. Help me establish sustainable rhythms that keep me connected to You amid everyday demands and distractions.

I acknowledge that spiritual growth isn't a straight line upward but a continuing journey with valleys, plateaus, and unexpected turns. Give me patience with this process and persistence when progress seems slow. When I can't feel movement, help me trust that roots are deepening even when visible growth isn't apparent.

Thank You for fellow travelers who have shared this journey. For those who have discussed these devotions with me, prayed alongside me, or simply walked parallel paths—I'm grateful for their companionship. Show me how to maintain meaningful spiritual connections that provide both challenge and encouragement for continued growth.

Lord Jesus, You told Your disciples, "I am the vine; you are the branches. If you remain in me and I in you, you will bear much fruit; apart from me you can do nothing." As I continue beyond these forty days, help me remain deeply connected to You as the source of all spiritual vitality and growth.

Holy Spirit, continue the work You've begun in me. Keep drawing my attention upward, expanding my capacity for love, deepening my trust in divine provision, and integrating my faith into every dimension of daily life. May my ongoing journey glorify the Father, embody the Son, and manifest Your transforming presence.

I pray this in the name of Jesus Christ, who pioneered the path of perfect communion with You, Amen.

Day 37

Ascending Together

Community Reflections "I rejoiced with those who said to me, 'Let us go to the house of the LORD.'" — Psalm 122:1

THE SHARED JOURNEY

As our forty-day pilgrimage through the Songs of Ascent approaches its conclusion, we turn our attention explicitly to what has been implicit throughout—the communal nature of spiritual ascent. While personal growth remains essential, the Songs of Ascent consistently present pilgrimage as a shared experience, with individual journeys merging into collective worship and mutual support.

For ancient Israelite pilgrims, the journey to Jerusalem was inherently communal. Families and neighbors traveled together in caravans for practical safety and shared celebration. The roads to Jerusalem filled with diverse pilgrims from various tribes and towns, creating temporary communities united by common destination and purpose. Upon arrival, these groups joined the larger assembly of worshippers, experiencing belonging within the covenant community of Israel.

This communal dimension appears throughout the Songs of Ascent. Psalm 122 expresses joy in the invitation to worship together: "I rejoiced with those who said to me, 'Let us go to the house of the LORD.'" Psalm 125 uses plural language to describe trust in God: "Those who trust in the LORD are like Mount Zion." Psalm 133 explicitly celebrates unity among God's people as precious and life-giving. Even psalms that begin with individual concerns typically broaden to include communal perspectives by their conclusion.

This pattern reflects the fundamental biblical understanding that faith flourishes in community. From God's declaration that "it is not good for the man to be alone" (Genesis 2:18) to Jesus' formation of a community of disciples to Paul's extended metaphor of the church as a body with interdependent parts (1 Corinthians 12), Scripture consistently presents spiritual life as relational rather than solitary. We grow not in isolation but in connection.

THE NECESSITY OF SHARING

Why does spiritual growth require articulation and celebration in community? Several reasons emerge from the Songs of Ascent and broader biblical wisdom:

Shared Language Deepens Experience

The Songs of Ascent provided pilgrims with shared vocabulary for their journey—words to express fears, hopes, struggles, and joys. This common language transformed private experiences into communal understanding. When pilgrims sang, "I lift my eyes to the mountains—where does my help come from?" (Psalm 121:1), individual anxiety found expression in collective acknowledgment, creating both validation and perspective.

Similarly, when we articulate our spiritual journey with others, previously internal experiences gain clarity and depth. Naming what God is doing in our lives—whether breakthrough, struggle, confusion, or insight—helps us recognize patterns we might otherwise miss. The very act of finding words for spiritual experience often reveals its meaning more fully.

Community Provides Essential Perspective

The Songs of Ascent frequently shift perspectives—moving between personal testimony, communal affirmation, and prophetic declaration. This multifaceted viewpoint protects against the distortions that occur when we rely solely on our own perception. Individual spiritual experience, while genuine, remains limited by personal history, temperament, and blind spots.

When we share our journey with others, we gain crucial perspective that either confirms authentic growth or gently corrects misinterpretation. Sometimes others recognize God's work in us before we see it ourselves. Other times, trusted companions help us distinguish between genuine divine guidance and our own preferences or fears. As Proverbs 27:17 observes, "As iron sharpens iron, so one person sharpens another."

Celebration Reinforces Transformation

Throughout Scripture, significant spiritual developments were marked by communal celebration. From Passover commemorating deliverance from Egypt to the early church breaking bread together in remembrance of Christ, shared celebration inscribes spiritual reality more deeply into both individual and collective identity.

When we celebrate growth together—acknowledging steps of faith, breakthrough insights, or evidence of transformation—we reinforce these developments in ourselves and others. Public commitment and affirmation strengthen private conviction. Corporate recognition of God's faithfulness builds collective memory that sustains community through future challenges. Celebration isn't merely the optional afterparty of spiritual growth but an essential component of its integration and continuation.

CREATING SPACES FOR SHARED ASCENT

How do we move from theoretical appreciation of community to practical experience of ascending together? The Songs of Ascent suggest several approaches:

Structured Sharing
The Songs of Ascent provided structured opportunities for pilgrims to share their experiences. The psalms themselves offered frameworks for expressing fear, gratitude, repentance, and hope. Their familiar patterns helped pilgrims articulate experiences that might otherwise have remained formless or unexpressed.

Similarly, we benefit from intentional structures for spiritual sharing. These might include guided group discussions, regular check-ins around specific growth areas, spiritual direction relationships, or journaling exchanges. Such structures create safety through clear expectations while providing helpful prompts for reflection and articulation.

Authentic Vulnerability
Throughout the collection, the psalm writers model remarkable honesty. They acknowledge distress (Psalm 120), confess sin (Psalm 130), and express struggles with pride (Psalm 131). This authenticity creates space for genuine rather than performative community—connection based on shared humanity rather than projected perfection.

Creating communities where spiritual ascent can be truly shared requires cultivation of appropriate vulnerability. This doesn't mean sharing everything with everyone but developing relationships where both struggles and victories can be honestly acknowledged. As James 5:16 instructs, "Therefore confess your sins to each other and pray for each other so that you may be healed."

Celebratory Rituals
The pilgrim festivals themselves provided ritualized celebration of God's character and action. Through prescribed offerings, readings, prayers, and shared meals, Israel regularly commemorated divine faithfulness and recommitted to covenant relationship. These rituals transformed individual experiences into collective testimony.

Similarly, we benefit from intentional celebration of spiritual milestones and divine faithfulness. These celebrations might include communion services, testimony sharing, creative expressions of growth, or simple meals where God's work is acknowledged and praised. Such rituals help us recognize significant developments that might otherwise pass unnoticed in the flow of daily experience.

PRACTICAL APPLICATIONS

As you near the conclusion of this devotional journey, consider these practical ways to strengthen the communal dimension of your spiritual ascent:

Schedule a Sharing Gathering

If you've been journeying through this devotional with others, schedule a specific time to share your experiences. Create a simple format where each person can identify significant insights, challenges, or growth points from the journey. Consider questions like: What psalm resonated most deeply with your current experience? What new understanding of God emerged during this devotional? What practice would you like to continue beyond these forty days?

If you've been journeying alone, identify someone—a friend, family member, pastor, or spiritual director—with whom you might share key takeaways from this experience. The act of articulating what you've learned to someone else helps solidify insights and opens opportunity for additional perspective.

Create Tangible Remembrances

The ancient pilgrims often brought home small tokens from Jerusalem to remember their pilgrimage experience. Similarly, consider creating tangible reminders of this devotional journey—perhaps journaling your key insights, selecting a verse for display in your home, or creating a simple artistic expression of what you've learned.

If sharing with others, these remembrances might become communal projects—perhaps a collection of testimonies, a shared meal incorporating symbolic elements from the psalms, or a creative collaboration that expresses collective learning. Such tangible expressions help transfer insights from the devotional period into ongoing life.

Establish Continuing Connections

For ancient pilgrims, the journey to Jerusalem strengthened bonds that continued after returning home. Shared experiences created lasting connections that supported ongoing spiritual growth between festival gatherings. Similarly, consider how connections formed or deepened during this devotional might continue supporting your spiritual journey.

This might involve establishing regular check-ins with fellow journeyers, forming a spiritual friendship focused on continued growth, or joining an existing community committed to authentic spiritual sharing. The specific structure matters less than the continued opportunity to articulate and celebrate your ongoing ascent in the company of others who understand both the challenges and joys of the journey.

As you implement these practices, remember that authentic community develops gradually through consistent investment rather than instant formation. The vulnerabilities, perspectives, and celebrations that characterize mature spiritual community emerge through patient commitment to shared journey. Like the ancient pilgrims who returned to Jerusalem year after year, building communal identity through repeated shared experience, we develop meaningful spiritual community through regular practices of presence, attentiveness, and mutual support.

Today, give thanks for those who have shared any portion of this devotional journey with you—whether through direct discussion, parallel experience, or even historic connection through these ancient psalms. Recognize that your individual ascent toward God has always been part of a larger communal pilgrimage stretching across time and geography. Commit to nurturing connections that support your continued climb toward deeper communion with God and authentic community with fellow pilgrims.

REFLECTION QUESTIONS

1. If you've been journeying through this devotional with others, what has been most valuable about the shared experience? How has community enriched your understanding or application of the Songs of Ascent? If you've been journeying alone, with whom might you share key insights from this experience?

_____

_____

2. The Songs of Ascent provided ancient pilgrims with common language for spiritual journey. What words, phrases, or images from these psalms have helped you articulate your own spiritual experience more clearly? How might these become ongoing vocabulary for your continued ascent?

_____

_____

3. Throughout the collection, psalm writers model authenticity about struggles, questions, and failures. What makes vulnerability in spiritual community difficult for you? What helps you share honestly about your journey with trusted others?

_____

_____

4. Psalm 133 describes unity among believers as precious oil and life-giving dew. Where have you experienced this kind of life-giving spiritual community? What qualities made that experience particularly meaningful or growth-producing?

_____

_____

5. The pilgrimage festivals provided regular opportunities for Israel to celebrate God's faithfulness together. What spiritual milestones or evidences of divine faithfulness from this devotional journey would you like to celebrate with others? How might you mark these developments in tangible ways?

_____

_____

6. As this devotional journey concludes, what specific commitments might help you maintain meaningful spiritual community beyond these forty days? Consider both structures (regular gatherings, intentional conversations) and qualities (vulnerability, attentiveness, celebration) that support shared spiritual ascent.

_____

_____

PRAYER FOR TODAY

Community-creating God,

From the beginning, You declared it "not good" for us to be alone, creating us for relationship with You and each other. Thank You for the gift of community along this devotional journey—for those who have shared insights, asked questions, offered perspectives, and provided support. Thank You especially for the ancient community of faith that preserved these psalms, creating connection across millennia through shared spiritual language.

Forgive me for the times I've attempted to journey alone, relying solely on my own understanding or keeping growth experiences private out of fear, pride, or simple neglect. Forgive me for missing opportunities to support others through attentive presence and authentic sharing. Create in me both courage to be known and patience to truly know others.

Lord Jesus, You modeled spiritual community by gathering disciples who journeyed with You through teaching, questions, misunderstandings, failures, and ultimately transformation. Help me follow Your example in both offering and receiving the gift of spiritual companionship. Show me what healthy vulnerability looks like in my current relationships and circumstances.

Holy Spirit, You create genuine community by breaking down barriers and uniting diverse people in common purpose. Continue this work among those who have shared this devotional journey, deepening connections begun during these forty days. Guide us in establishing ongoing practices that support our continued ascent together.

As I prepare to conclude this devotional experience, show me specific ways to articulate and celebrate what You've revealed. Give me wisdom to identify trusted others with whom to share significant insights, courage to express both struggles and victories, and creativity to mark important developments in tangible ways.

Thank You for the assurance that I am never truly alone on this journey—that my individual ascent joins a great company of pilgrims climbing toward deeper communion with You. Unite my heart with others who seek Your face, creating community that nourishes faith, hope, and love for the journey ahead.

I pray this in the name of Jesus Christ, who makes us one body through His Spirit, Amen.

Day 38

Daily Ascents

Incorporating the Pilgrim Spirit "Blessed are those whose strength is in you, whose hearts are set on pilgrimage." — Psalm 84:5

THE EVERYDAY JOURNEY

As our forty-day pilgrimage through the Songs of Ascent nears completion, we consider how to incorporate the pilgrim spirit into our everyday lives. For ancient Israelites, physical pilgrimages to Jerusalem marked special occasions—three times yearly at most. The rest of their lives unfolded in fields and villages, amid ordinary responsibilities and routines. Yet the pilgrim spirit wasn't meant to be confined to these special journeys but to infuse their entire approach to life.

Scripture affirms this broader understanding of pilgrimage. Psalm 84:5 declares, "Blessed are those whose strength is in you, whose hearts are set on pilgrimage." This suggests a continuous orientation rather than occasional experience. Similarly, Hebrews 11:13 describes people of faith as "foreigners and strangers on earth," indicating an ongoing pilgrim identity rather than temporary pilgrim activities.

For Christians, this pilgrim spirit finds explicit expression in Peter's exhortation to live as "foreigners and exiles" (1 Peter 2:11) and Paul's reminder that "our citizenship is in heaven" (Philippians 3:20). These passages suggest that authentic spiritual life maintains a pilgrim perspective not just during devoted religious seasons but amid everyday activities and responsibilities.

The challenge we face is avoiding two opposite errors: either compartmentalizing our spiritual journey to designated times and activities, or abstracting it so completely that it loses concrete expression in daily life. The wisdom of the Songs of Ascent helps us navigate between these extremes, showing how ordinary experiences can become sacred journeys when approached with pilgrim hearts.

LESSONS FROM THE PILGRIM PSALMS

What aspects of the pilgrim spirit might we incorporate into everyday life? The Songs of Ascent suggest several transferable pilgrim qualities:

Intentional Direction

The pilgrim journey had clear direction—upward toward Jerusalem, God's dwelling place. Pilgrims didn't wander aimlessly but moved purposefully toward a specific destination. Similarly, incorporating the pilgrim spirit means maintaining directional clarity in daily life—orienting small decisions and routine activities toward deeper communion with God and greater alignment with His purposes.

This intentionality transforms mundane routines from circular patterns that merely maintain existence into linear journeys that build toward meaning. The question shifts from "How do I get through this day?" to "How does this day move me closer to God?" When we maintain this directional awareness, even ordinary responsibilities become meaningful steps on sacred journey.

Present Attentiveness

While pilgrims maintained awareness of their destination, they simultaneously remained attentive to present experience—noting dangers, appreciating beauty, and recognizing divine provision along the way. Psalms 121, 123, and 124 particularly emphasize this attentiveness, describing pilgrims who notice both threats and help, both challenges and deliverances.

Similarly, incorporating the pilgrim spirit means cultivating awareness of God's presence and activity in current circumstances rather than postponing spiritual alertness to designated "religious" moments. This attentiveness transforms ordinary encounters into sacred opportunities, routine activities into worship, and daily provisions into evidence of divine care.

Communal Support

The pilgrim journey was inherently communal, with travelers supporting each other through shared resources, encouragement, and protection. Psalms 122 and 133 especially celebrate the beauty of journeying together toward God's presence. This mutual support wasn't just practical assistance but spiritual reinforcement that helped pilgrims persevere despite difficulties.

Similarly, incorporating the pilgrim spirit means recognizing our need for others on the spiritual journey—not just during intensive experiences but in daily life. We weren't designed to climb alone. The small, consistent ways we offer and receive support—through conversation, prayer, practical help, and simple presence—become sacred exchanges that sustain our daily ascent.

Adaptive Perseverance

The pilgrim journey required continuing forward despite changing conditions—whether scorching sun, unexpected threats, or personal weariness. Psalm 121's assurance that "the sun will not harm you by day, nor the moon by night" acknowledges these challenges while affirming divine protection that enables ongoing progress.

Similarly, incorporating the pilgrim spirit means maintaining spiritual momentum through changing circumstances and internal states. Some days the journey feels inspired and energizing; other days it feels mechanical or difficult. The pilgrim continues climbing regardless, adapting pace and expectations to current conditions while maintaining forward movement.

TRANSFORMING DAILY ROUTINES

How might these pilgrim qualities transform specific aspects of everyday life? Consider these practical applications:

Sacred Commutes

For many people, daily commutes represent significant time commitments that often generate frustration. Yet viewed through pilgrim perspective, these regular journeys can become meaningful ascents. The intentional direction of the pilgrim transforms routine travel into symbolic movement toward God. Present attentiveness turns annoying delays into opportunities for prayer, reflection, or simply noticing beauty amid hurry. Even traffic congestion becomes opportunity for practicing patience and surrender.

Try designating your daily commute as pilgrim space—perhaps by beginning with brief prayer that consecrates the journey, using travel time for Scripture meditation or spiritual reflection, practicing gratitude for specific aspects of the day, or simply remaining attentive to God's presence in surrounding details. These small adjustments transform frustrating necessity into sacred journey.

Meaningful Work

Daily work occupies substantial portions of most people's lives yet often feels disconnected from spiritual journey. The pilgrim spirit transforms work by reconceiving it as meaningful participation in God's ongoing creativity and provision rather than mere economic necessity. Intentional direction means viewing work tasks as opportunities to express faithfulness, develop character, or serve others rather than simply completing requirements. Present attentiveness transforms routine activities into opportunities for practicing presence, offering excellence, and noticing God's enabling grace in ordinary accomplishments.

Try identifying specific aspects of your work that connect to larger purpose—ways your tasks serve others, develop your character, or express creativity. Consider how each responsibility might become opportunity for practicing pilgrim qualities like perseverance, attentiveness, or community. Even work that feels meaningless in itself can become meaningful when approached as territory for spiritual formation.

Household Responsibilities

Daily household tasks—cooking, cleaning, maintenance, administration—easily become burdensome routines that feel separate from spiritual life. Yet viewed through pilgrim perspective, these activities become tangible expressions of love, stewardship, and participation in God's ordering work. Intentional direction means approaching these tasks as meaningful contributions to household flourishing rather than annoying interruptions. Present attentiveness transforms routine chores into opportunities for gratitude, prayer, or simply practicing faithful presence in small things.

Try designating certain household tasks as explicit opportunities for spiritual practice—perhaps using dishwashing time for confession, laundry folding for intercessory prayer, or yard work for practicing attentiveness to creation. These connections transform necessary maintenance into meaningful pilgrimage.

Relational Encounters

Daily interactions with family members, colleagues, neighbors, and strangers often occur on automatic pilot, governed by habit rather than intentionality. The pilgrim spirit transforms these encounters by approaching each person as fellow traveler made in God's image. Intentional direction means viewing relationships as opportunities for mutual encouragement and growth rather than mere social convention. Present attentiveness transforms routine conversations into opportunities for genuine connection, compassionate listening, and authentic presence.

Try approaching one conversation each day with explicit pilgrim awareness—perhaps beginning with brief internal prayer, listening with heightened attention, looking for evidence of God's work in the other person, or simply practicing genuine interest rather than task-focused interaction. These small adjustments transform casual encounters into sacred connections.

As you incorporate these pilgrim practices into daily life, remember that transformation happens gradually through consistent small adjustments rather than dramatic overhauls. Don't attempt to revolutionize every aspect of life simultaneously. Instead, identify one or two daily activities that seem particularly ripe for pilgrim perspective, and practice viewing these through the lens of sacred journey. As these practices become habitual, gradually expand the pilgrim perspective to additional areas.

Remember too that the pilgrim spirit embraces both extraordinary and ordinary aspects of spiritual journey. Just as ancient Israelites valued both special pilgrimages to Jerusalem and faithful daily life in their hometowns, we need both intensive spiritual experiences and everyday faithfulness. The wisdom lies not in choosing between them but in allowing each to inform and enrich the other—intensive experiences providing direction and inspiration for daily ascents, and daily ascents preparing us for deeper engagement with intensive experiences.

Today, as you continue your pilgrimage, look for opportunities to transform one ordinary routine into sacred journey. Notice how pilgrim perspective changes both the experience itself and your relationship to it. Then consider how this perspective might gradually infuse additional aspects of daily life, until your entire existence becomes continuous ascent toward deeper communion with the God who invites you to journey with Him.

REFLECTION QUESTIONS

1. Looking at your typical daily routines, which activities seem most disconnected from your spiritual journey? Choose one of these activities and consider how pilgrim qualities (intentional direction, present attentiveness, communal support, adaptive perseverance) might transform it into sacred journey.

_____

_____

2. The concept of "intentional direction" suggests that even small decisions and routine activities can move us toward deeper communion with God. What daily decision points might become opportunities for more conscious spiritual direction in your life? How might awareness of spiritual destination influence these choices?

_____

_____

3. Present attentiveness transforms ordinary moments into sacred encounters. When during your typical day do you find it most difficult to maintain awareness of God's presence? What specific practice might help you cultivate greater attentiveness during these times?

_____

_____

4. The pilgrim journey was inherently communal, with travelers supporting each other along the way. Who currently provides support for your everyday spiritual journey? What small, consistent ways might you offer and receive pilgrim encouragement in daily life?

_____

_____

5. Adaptive perseverance means continuing forward despite changing conditions and internal states. What particular challenges tend to interrupt your spiritual momentum in everyday life? How might pilgrim perspective help you adapt to these challenges while maintaining forward movement?

_____

_____

6. If you're journeying through this devotional with others, discuss how you might support each other in maintaining pilgrim perspective beyond these forty days. What specific commitments or practices might help you encourage each other's daily ascents?

_____

_____

PRAYER FOR TODAY

Ever-present God,

As I near the conclusion of this forty-day pilgrimage through the Songs of Ascent, I'm grateful for extraordinary insights and experiences. Yet I recognize that most of my spiritual journey unfolds not in dramatic moments but in ordinary days filled with routine activities and familiar responsibilities. Help me transform these everyday realities into sacred journey by incorporating the pilgrim spirit into all dimensions of my life.

Give me intentional direction that orients even small decisions and mundane tasks toward deeper communion with You. When I'm tempted to compartmentalize my spiritual life or postpone faithfulness to designated religious times, remind me that every moment offers opportunity to move closer to Your presence.

Develop in me present attentiveness that recognizes Your activity in current circumstances rather than rushing past signs of Your grace. Help me notice beauty amid hurry, discover meaning in routine tasks, and recognize divine provisions in daily bread. Transform my ordinary encounters into sacred opportunities through the simple practice of paying attention.

Connect me with fellow pilgrims who provide support for everyday journey. Show me both how to offer and how to receive the small, consistent encouragements that sustain spiritual momentum. Replace my tendencies toward independence with genuine appreciation for how much I need others to climb well.

Grant me adaptive perseverance that continues forward despite changing conditions and internal states. When enthusiasm wanes or difficulties arise, help me adjust expectations and methods while maintaining movement toward Your presence. Remind me that faithful plodding counts as much as passionate sprinting in the journey toward heaven.

Today, I specifically offer You [name a routine activity] as sacred journey. Transform this ordinary activity through pilgrim perspective, helping me discover its spiritual significance and practice Your presence within it. Then gradually extend this perspective to additional areas until my entire existence becomes continuous ascent toward deeper communion with You.

Thank You for inviting me into relationship that encompasses both mountain-top experiences and valley routines, both extraordinary encounters and everyday faithfulness. May my life increasingly reflect the blessed reality of "those whose strength is in you, whose hearts are set on pilgrimage."

I pray this in the name of Jesus Christ, who transformed ordinary bread and wine into sacred communion, ordinary relationships into divine encounters, and ordinary existence into extraordinary purpose, Amen.

Day 39

The Ultimate Jerusalem - Heavenly Hope

"But you have come to Mount Zion, to the city of the living God, the heavenly Jerusalem. You have come to thousands upon thousands of angels in joyful assembly, to the church of the firstborn, whose names are written in heaven. You have come to God, the Judge of all, to the spirits of the righteous made perfect, to Jesus the mediator of a new covenant, and to the sprinkled blood that speaks a better word than the blood of Abel." — Hebrews 12:22-24

HISTORICAL CONTEXT

As our forty-day journey through the Songs of Ascent draws near its conclusion, we turn our gaze toward the ultimate destination that these psalms foreshadowed. For the ancient Hebrew pilgrims, Jerusalem represented the pinnacle of their spiritual journey—the place where heaven and earth intersected, where God's presence dwelled in the temple. Their ascent to the physical city was a profound spiritual experience, but it pointed to something even greater.

Throughout Israel's history, particularly after periods of exile and displacement, Jerusalem took on increasingly eschatological dimensions. The prophets spoke of a "new Jerusalem" (Isaiah 65:17-19, 66:22) that would transcend the limitations of the earthly city. By the New Testament era, this hope had crystallized into the expectation of a heavenly Jerusalem—the true home that all earthly pilgrimages ultimately seek.

The Songs of Ascent that guided pilgrims on their journey to the earthly Jerusalem were always whispering of another city—one "whose architect and builder is God" (Hebrews 11:10). As we complete our devotional pilgrimage, we recognize that our spiritual practices aren't merely about enriching our present experience but about preparing us for our ultimate destination in God's presence.

MEDITATION: THE CITY THAT AWAITS US

"But you have come to Mount Zion, to the city of the living God, the heavenly Jerusalem."

Notice the present tense in this passage from Hebrews—"you have come." While the fullness of the heavenly Jerusalem awaits the return of Christ and the new creation, Scripture insists that believers already participate in its reality through faith. Our citizenship in the heavenly city isn't merely future but present, though partially veiled.

The earthly Jerusalem that pilgrims sought with such devotion was always intended to be a shadow, a signpost pointing toward this greater reality. When Jesus told the Samaritan woman that a time was coming "when you will worship the Father neither on this mountain nor in Jerusalem" (John 4:21), He wasn't diminishing the significance of sacred space but expanding it. The worship that was concentrated in Jerusalem would become accessible wherever people worship "in spirit and in truth."

Yet this expansion doesn't eliminate our need for destination. We still journey toward something—not merely away from sin and brokenness, but toward the fullness of God's presence. The heavenly Jerusalem represents this destination, the consummation of all our spiritual longings.

As you near the end of this devotional journey, consider how the practices and insights of these forty days have been preparing you not just for a deeper life now, but for your ultimate home. The disciplines of prayer, community, worship, and ethical living practiced by pilgrims weren't merely about making the journey meaningful; they were rehearsals for life in the heavenly city.

THE COMMUNITY THAT AWAITS US

"You have come to thousands upon thousands of angels in joyful assembly, to the church of the firstborn, whose names are written in heaven."

The physical Jerusalem that ancient pilgrims sought was powerful not just because of its location but because of the community gathered there. Three times a year, scattered Israelites from across the known world would converge on the holy city, renewing bonds of kinship and covenant identity. The journey was profoundly communal.

Similarly, the heavenly Jerusalem is described primarily in terms of its inhabitants. It is a city teeming with life—angels in "joyful assembly" and the church of the firstborn. The Greek word for "assembly" (panēgyrei) suggests a festive gathering, a celebration. The heavenly city isn't a place of solemn isolation but of joyful communion.

This has profound implications for how we understand our spiritual practices. The disciplines we cultivate—prayer, scripture reading, worship, service—aren't preparing us for a disembodied spiritual existence but for perfect community. Every act of forgiveness, every moment of shared worship, every experience of genuine fellowship is a foretaste of the heavenly city's life.

If you've been journeying through this devotional with others, you've already experienced something of this reality. The connections formed through shared spiritual practice aren't incidental to the journey but central to it. In reflecting together, praying together, and supporting one another's growth, you've been rehearsing for the perfect communion of the heavenly Jerusalem.

THE PRESENCE THAT AWAITS US

"You have come to God, the Judge of all, to the spirits of the righteous made perfect, to Jesus the mediator of a new covenant..."

At the heart of the heavenly Jerusalem is not a temple but a Person. The goal of all spiritual journeying is direct communion with God Himself. The earthly Jerusalem housed the temple, where God's presence was veiled behind layers of restricted access. Only the high priest could enter the Holy of Holies, and only once a year. The journey to Jerusalem brought pilgrims near to God's presence, but barriers remained.

The heavenly Jerusalem removes these barriers. Through Christ, we gain direct access to God—not just to His benefits or blessings, but to relationship with Him. The writer of Hebrews emphasizes this by placing "God, the Judge of all" and "Jesus the mediator" at the center of his description of the heavenly city.

This tells us something crucial about the purpose of our spiritual practices. Bible study, prayer, worship, and service aren't ends in themselves but means of deepening our communion with God. They prepare us for the direct presence that awaits us. Every moment of genuine connection with God in prayer, every insight gained through Scripture, every experience of His presence in worship is a foretaste of what awaits in fullness.

APPLICATION: LIVING TOWARD OUR DESTINATION

How do we live in light of our heavenly destination? The New Testament suggests several responses:

First, we cultivate heavenly citizenship while remaining engaged with earthly responsibilities. Paul writes that "our citizenship is in heaven" (Philippians 3:20), yet this heavenly orientation doesn't lead to disengagement but to more faithful presence in the world. Like the exiles in Babylon who were called to "seek the peace and prosperity of the city" (Jeremiah 29:7), we work for flourishing in our earthly contexts precisely because we know they aren't ultimate.

Second, we recognize that our spiritual practices aren't merely about personal development but about preparation for eternal reality. When we worship, we join a chorus that began before creation and will continue into eternity. When we serve others, we practice the selfless love that will characterize life in the heavenly city. When we study Scripture, we're not just acquiring information but learning the language of our true home.

Finally, we hold the tension between "already" and "not yet." The writer of Hebrews insists that we "have come" to the heavenly Jerusalem—it's a present reality accessed by faith. Yet we also join creation in "groaning" for the full revelation of this reality (Romans 8:22-23). Our spiritual practices help us live in this tension, experiencing foretastes of heaven's joy while acknowledging that the fullness awaits Christ's return.

As your forty-day journey concludes, carry these insights forward. The practices you've developed aren't meant to end with this devotional but to continue shaping you for your ultimate destination—the heavenly Jerusalem where God dwells in unhindered communion with His people.

REFLECTION QUESTIONS

1. How has your understanding of spiritual "destination" changed through this forty-day journey? In what ways do you now see your spiritual practices as preparation for heavenly reality?

_____

_____

2. The heavenly Jerusalem is described primarily as a community. How does this shape your understanding of the purpose of spiritual growth? How might it change your approach to church and other forms of Christian fellowship?

_____

_____

3. What aspects of the heavenly city described in Hebrews 12:22-24 most capture your imagination or longing? What does this reveal about your spiritual journey?

_____

_____

4. How do you experience the tension between the "already" (ways you already participate in heavenly realities) and "not yet" (aspects that await Christ's return) in your spiritual life?

_____

_____

5. As this devotional journey concludes, which spiritual practices have become most meaningful to you? How will you continue to cultivate them as preparation for your ultimate destination?

_____

_____

6. If you've been journeying through this devotional with others, how has your shared experience provided a foretaste of the heavenly community? What commitments might you make to continue growing together?

_____

_____

PRAYER FOR TODAY

Eternal God,

As I near the end of this forty-day journey, I lift my eyes beyond the horizons of this world to the heavenly Jerusalem—the city You have prepared for those who love You. Thank You that through Christ, I have already come to Mount Zion, the city of the living God, even as I await its full revelation.

Forgive me for the times I've treated spiritual practices as ends in themselves rather than preparation for eternal communion with You. Help me see each moment of prayer, each insight from Scripture, each act of worship and service as rehearsal for life in Your presence.

Thank You for the community You've provided along this journey—both the visible fellowship of fellow pilgrims and the invisible communion of saints and angels with whom I already join in worship. Deepen my appreciation for the corporate nature of faith, knowing that the heavenly city is filled not with isolated individuals but with a joyful assembly.

As this devotional journey concludes, help me maintain the practices and perspectives it has cultivated. May I live as a citizen of heaven even as I engage faithfully with earthly responsibilities. May I hold the tension between the "already" of faith's present experience and the "not yet" of future glory.

And finally, Lord, increase my longing for that day when faith becomes sight, when the heavenly Jerusalem descends as a bride adorned for her husband, when You will dwell with Your people in unhindered communion. Until that day, may every step of my continued pilgrimage draw me closer to this ultimate destination—not just a place, but a Person—You, revealed in perfect glory.

In the name of Jesus Christ, the mediator of the new covenant, Amen.

Day 40

Arriving to Begin Again - The Cyclical Journey

"Praise the LORD, all you servants of the LORD who minister by night in the house of the LORD. Lift up your hands in the sanctuary and praise the LORD. May the LORD bless you from Zion, he who is the Maker of heaven and earth." — *Psalm 134:1-3*

HISTORICAL CONTEXT

We arrive today at Psalm 134, the final Song of Ascent. Fittingly, this brief psalm captures both the culmination of the pilgrimage journey and the transition to what comes next. For ancient Hebrew pilgrims, arriving in Jerusalem wasn't the end of their spiritual experience but a new beginning.

After the long journey up to Jerusalem, pilgrims would participate in festival celebrations, worship at the temple, and then eventually make their way back home. The conclusion of one pilgrimage naturally set the stage for the next. The Jewish calendar established this rhythm with three annual pilgrimage festivals—Passover, Pentecost, and Tabernacles—creating a cyclical pattern of spiritual journey, arrival, celebration, and return.

This psalm likely represents a liturgical exchange between arriving pilgrims and the temple servants (Levites) who maintained continuous worship. The first two verses contain the pilgrims' call to the temple servants to praise the Lord, while the final verse represents the servants' blessing upon the pilgrims as they prepare to depart. In this exchange, we see the beautiful recognition that arriving at one destination becomes the departure point for the next phase of the journey.

As we complete our forty-day devotional journey, this final psalm teaches us that spiritual growth isn't linear but cyclical—a series of arrivals that become new beginnings, a spiral of ascending ever higher through repeated patterns of seeking, finding, and seeking again.

MEDITATION: THE NATURE OF ARRIVAL

"Praise the LORD, all you servants of the LORD who minister by night in the house of the LORD."

There's a profound insight embedded in the opening of this psalm. The pilgrims have completed their journey—they've arrived at the destination they sought for so long. Yet their first act isn't to celebrate their accomplishment but to acknowledge those who maintain continuous worship. The "servants of the LORD who minister by night" are the Levites who keep the temple worship ongoing, even when pilgrims aren't present.

True spiritual arrival is marked not by self-congratulation but by recognition of the larger worship context we enter. Our individual journeys participate in something much more extensive—the continuous worship of God that precedes us and will continue long after we're gone. Spiritual maturity brings the humbling awareness that we join a story already in progress.

Consider how this applies to your completion of this forty-day devotional journey. Whatever insights, growth, or transformation you've experienced hasn't brought you to the end but to a new beginning. You haven't "arrived" in the sense of finishing but in the sense of joining—entering more deeply into the ongoing worship of God that has continued uninterrupted throughout history.

THE POSTURE OF TRANSITION

"Lift up your hands in the sanctuary and praise the LORD."

The lifted hands mentioned in verse 2 represent both surrender and receptivity—a physical expression of spiritual readiness for what comes next. This posture acknowledges that what we've received through our journey now prepares us for a new phase of discipleship.

For the ancient pilgrims, the experience of Jerusalem wasn't meant to be hoarded or merely remembered but to transform how they lived when they returned home. The insights, renewal, and community experienced during festival time were meant to reshape their ordinary days. Similarly, what you've gained through these forty days isn't meant merely to be a pleasant spiritual memory but a foundation for continued growth.

Notice that this verse directs praise toward the Lord, not toward the journey itself or the pilgrim's accomplishment. The goal of spiritual journey is never self-improvement for its own sake but deeper communion with God. As you complete this devotional, the appropriate response isn't pride in having "finished" but praise to the One who has sustained you through it.

THE BLESSING THAT SENDS

"May the LORD bless you from Zion, he who is the Maker of heaven and earth."

The final verse shifts from the pilgrims' address to the temple servants to the servants' blessing upon the pilgrims. This blessing contains both intimacy and vastness—it comes from "Zion" (the specific, localized presence of God) yet flows from "the Maker of heaven and earth" (the universal, cosmic Creator).

This blessing wasn't meant merely to make the pilgrims feel good but to empower them for the journey ahead. It reminded them that they carried something back from Jerusalem—not just memories or souvenirs, but the blessing of God's presence that would accompany them wherever they went.

As you complete these forty days, receive this same blessing. Whatever growth, insight, or renewal you've experienced isn't meant to be confined to this devotional period but to accompany you into whatever comes next. The God who has sustained your attention through these reflections— the intimate God of Zion who is also the cosmic Creator—sends you forward with blessing.

APPLICATION: EMBRACING SPIRITUAL RHYTHMS

The cyclical nature of the pilgrimage calendar offers a profound model for sustainable spiritual growth. It suggests that maturity comes not through constant novelty or linear progression but through deepening engagement with foundational rhythms and practices.

First, recognize that spiritual plateaus aren't necessarily failures. The ancient pilgrims experienced the intensity of Jerusalem's festivals and then returned to ordinary life—not as a letdown but as the necessary counterbalance that made the next pilgrimage meaningful. If you feel a natural ebb after the focused intensity of these forty days, understand this as part of the rhythm rather than a regression.

Second, anticipate and plan for your next "ascent." The Jewish calendar built in multiple pilgrimage festivals each year, creating a natural pattern of spiritual focus. What will be your next intentional season of heightened spiritual attention? Perhaps it's another devotional journey, a retreat, or a focused season of serving others. Don't wait for inspiration—schedule your next ascent as an act of intention.

Third, identify what you'll carry forward from this journey. The pilgrims took specific practices and insights from Jerusalem back into their daily lives. What practices from these forty days have become most life-giving for you? Which insights continue to resonate? Commit to integrating these into your ongoing spiritual rhythm.

Finally, embrace the communal dimension of cyclical journey. The pilgrims never ascended alone—they journeyed in community and were blessed by those who maintained worship in their absence. How might you stay connected to those who've shared this journey with you? How might you bless and be blessed by the wider community of faith that continues worship when your attention necessarily turns elsewhere?

As our forty days together conclude, remember that we don't arrive at spiritual maturity through a single journey but through faithfully embracing the cycle of ascent, again and again, each time spiraling higher in our knowledge of God and ourselves.

REFLECTION QUESTIONS

1. Looking back over the forty-day journey, what has been your most significant insight or transformation? How do you sense this preparing you for what comes next in your spiritual life?

_____

_____

2. The psalm depicts an exchange between arriving pilgrims and temple servants who maintain continuous worship. Who are the "temple servants" in your life—those who have maintained faithful spiritual practices and helped create space for your growth? How might you acknowledge them?

_____

_____

3. The lifted hands in verse 2 represent both surrender and receptivity. What do you need to surrender as this devotional journey ends? What are you ready to receive for the next phase of your journey?

_____

_____

4. How has your understanding of spiritual "arrival" changed through this devotional? In what ways do you see spiritual growth as cyclical rather than purely linear?

_____

_____

5. What practices from these forty days do you want to carry forward? How might you integrate them into your ongoing rhythms of life and faith?

_____

_____

6. If you've been journeying through this devotional with others, how has shared experience enriched your journey? What commitments might you make to continue supporting one another's spiritual growth beyond these forty days?

_____

_____

PRAYER FOR TODAY

Faithful God,

As I reach the end of these forty days, I recognize that I haven't simply arrived at a destination but at a new beginning. Thank You for sustaining my attention, challenging my assumptions, and deepening my faith throughout this journey. Thank You for the companions You've provided along the way, both those journeying beside me and those who've maintained faithful worship across generations.

Like the ancient pilgrims, I lift my hands in a posture of both surrender and receptivity. I surrender the need to see spiritual growth as a task to complete rather than a relationship to nurture. I open myself to receive Your blessing for whatever comes next in my journey with You.

Help me integrate what I've learned into the rhythm of my daily life. Show me how to carry the insights of these forty days forward, not as a memory of a special time but as a foundation for continued growth. Give me wisdom to recognize the natural ebb and flow of spiritual intensity, neither becoming complacent in ordinary seasons nor burning out in seasons of heightened focus.

As I join the generations of pilgrims who have completed their ascent only to begin again, I praise You as both the God of Zion—present in specific moments and places—and the Maker of heaven and earth—transcending all time and space. May the blessing that sends me forth from this devotional journey empower me for faithful presence in every context to which You call me.

Thank You that arriving with You always means beginning again—not in futile repetition but in ever-deepening spirals of knowledge, love, and service. I recommit my journey to You, trusting that each arrival becomes a new departure into greater understanding of Your heart.
In the name of Jesus Christ, who makes our journey possible, Amen.

A Final Word from the Author

Dear Fellow Pilgrim,

If you're reading these words, you've completed a forty-day journey through the Songs of Ascent. Together, we've traveled from the psalmist's initial cry of distress in a foreign land to the final benediction in the sanctuary. We've explored valleys of shadow and heights of celebration, moments of individual wrestling and experiences of corporate worship. Like the ancient pilgrims who sang these songs on their way to Jerusalem, you've completed an ascent—not of physical elevation but of spiritual attention.

First, I want to acknowledge this accomplishment. In our distracted age, sustaining spiritual focus for forty days represents a genuine achievement. You've given these ancient songs the gift of your attention, allowing their wisdom to speak into your life. You've created space for reflection, prayer, and perhaps conversation with fellow travelers. This intentional practice of presence deserves recognition.

Yet as we explored in our final reflection, arrival is always also a new beginning. The ancient pilgrims who reached Jerusalem didn't remain there indefinitely—they celebrated, worshipped, and then returned to their homes, carrying something of the sanctuary with them into everyday life. Similarly, completing this devotional isn't meant to be an ending but a transition into what comes next in your spiritual journey.

So what does come next? Allow me to offer a few thoughts as you consider the path forward:

First, take time to integrate. Before rushing to the next spiritual program or book, create space to reflect on what these forty days have meant for you. Perhaps journal about the insights that most deeply resonated, the questions that remain unresolved, or the practices that have become most life-giving. Consider revisiting your notes or highlights from particularly meaningful days. Integration isn't an additional task but a necessary space for allowing your experience to take root.

Second, identify the practices you'll carry forward. Throughout our journey, we've engaged with various spiritual disciplines—prayer, meditation on Scripture, communal worship, ethical reflection, and more. Which of these have you found most life-giving? Rather than trying to maintain everything, consider selecting one or two practices to incorporate more intentionally into your ongoing rhythms. Sustainable growth comes not through sporadic intensity but through consistent, modest commitments over time.

Third, honor the communal dimension of spirituality. If you've journeyed through this devotional with others, consider how you might maintain those connections. Perhaps a monthly gathering to discuss your ongoing spiritual journeys, a weekly check-in about a shared practice, or simply an openness to reaching out when you need support. If you've journeyed alone, might this be a moment to invite others into your spiritual path? The Songs of Ascent remind us repeatedly that we were never meant to walk in isolation.

Fourth, embrace the cyclical nature of spiritual growth. You may find yourself drawn back to these psalms in different seasons, discovering that they speak in new ways as your life context changes. Don't hesitate to revisit this devotional in the future—not as a repetition but as a spiral that takes you deeper with each cycle. The ancient Hebrews returned to Jerusalem three times annually, finding fresh meaning in familiar practices. We too can discover new depths by returning to well-trodden paths.

Finally, remember that the ultimate goal was never to finish a devotional but to deepen your relationship with the living God. The Songs of Ascent themselves were not the destination for ancient pilgrims but the companions for a journey whose true purpose was encounter. Similarly, whatever insights or practices you've gained through these forty days are valuable not in themselves but in how they facilitate ongoing communion with God and authentic connection with others.

As we part ways, I'm reminded of the beautiful exchange in Psalm 134, where the arriving pilgrims call the temple servants to praise, and the servants respond with blessing. Let me offer that same blessing to you as you continue your journey:

"May the LORD bless you from Zion, he who is the Maker of heaven and earth."

This blessing contains both intimacy and vastness—the specific presence of God in your particular life circumstances and the cosmic power of the Creator who holds all things. My prayer is that you continue to experience both dimensions of God's reality: the personal God who knows your name and the transcendent God who numbers the stars.

The Songs of Ascent begin with a cry of distress and end with a blessing of peace. My hope is that whatever distress first set you on this forty-day journey has found, if not complete resolution, at least the perspective that comes from placing it within the larger context of God's faithfulness. And I pray that the peace which passes understanding would accompany you as you continue to ascend—not always in straight lines or constant progress, but in the beautiful, spiraling pattern of a life oriented toward the presence of God.

The journey continues. The path stretches before you. And the One who began a good work in you will be faithful to complete it.

With gratitude for our shared journey,

Dr. John R. Sconiers II

"Peace be on Israel."

— Psalm 128:6

About the Author

Dr. John R. Sconiers, II, DMin, is a senior pastor, preacher, mentor, board certified chaplain and evangelism coordinator. Dr. Sconiers' education includes DMin in evangelism and church planting, DIT in Security, MAPM (MDIV Equivalent), MIS Security, BSIT as well as postgraduate work in counseling and theology. He also holds several certifications and has hosted numerous training sessions in the area of evangelism, small groups, and other topics. Dr. Sconiers has lived and preached in various parts of the world and has a passion for seeing lives transformed by the power of the Holy Spirit and seeks to point others to the good news of Jesus Christ. Dr. Sconiers currently serves as a senior pastor in the North Georgia area. He is married to one wife, Nicole, and they share five amazing children.

You can connect with Dr. John R Sconiers II via:

Instagram: @johnsconiers
Twitter: @johnsconiers
YouTube: @JohnSconiers
Email: John@johnsconiersministries.com
Website: https://www.johnsconiersministries.com